The Book

An Old Guy Guide to How and Why We Do This

Foreword

Here we go on the latest iteration of the book I started lo, these fifteen odd years ago.

The previous editions were all based on words hand-printed in a coil-bound notebook and sketches done in pencil and pen on tracing paper in the early 'nineties. For this I make no apology, but it's time to make a new beginning in hopes of getting my ideas out there in a form that is more in keeping with the modern world. I'm still espousing a fairly primitive form of goldsmithing, granted, but that's because I consider the old techniques important enough to put down on paper. Or to stick on-line, god help me.

The people I hope to affect with these words would be the more idealistic sorts that see the creation of fine jewellery as something more than simply a way to make a living, or, worse yet, a profit. That being said, the preponderance of ring-based techniques laid out here present a bit of a barrier to the artistically minded. I have come to love the challenge of editing the pictures in my head, whittling the initial concept down to the absolute essentials to create a wearable and durable, but always beautiful piece of art. Learning to think in the round, as it were, opens up the possibilities, but it's still a small and static medium. Painters are still doing some fairly interesting work confined to the rectangle, so there's that to consider.

To me, the whole thing is about longevity. I want the stuff I put together to last a long time and I want some way for the techniques I've come up with, and absorbed from others, to live on. Too many goldsmiths have come to the ends of their careers with nothing to show for it but a box of tools that nobody wants. Granted, that's where I got a lot of my favourite tools, so I guess I shouldn't complain.

In that light, I should thank some of those who've helped me along the way: Roy Beach, my watch repair instructor, for instilling in me a love of precision and the beauty to be found in the guts of a watch; Jack Dunn for giving me the chance to be an actual professional goldsmith; Clarence Marcotte, who talked my ear off for an afternoon, but left me with some good ideas; Jack White, whom I never met, but whose love of life came through in the stories I heard (his was the best box of tools I was privileged to root through); and all the people I've trained, from whom I've learned so much.

I should give special mention to two of my own special old guys. I worked next to Bert Cruse for my entire time at Dunn's and, aside from a tendency to gleefully emit foul-smelling farts in my general direction, he was always helpful and supportive. There's a whole book in Bert stories, but this ain't it. Bert never did much manufacturing, being a master at the repair end of the trade, but the technical tips he gave me always saved time and headaches. Joe Parnoutsoukian was the manufacturing genius at Dunn's, and he showed me how it was done in Lebanon. It's partly from him that I picked up my low-tech methods, some of which I improved and others that are timeless. His idiosyncratic approach to the English language has left a legacy of phrases I use almost every day.

I guess what I'm saying is that old guys are important to any trade. Let me be your old guy.

Warning: There will be some cussin'. Live with it, it's part of my charm.

Contents

So You Want to be a Goldsmith

It's only the greatest job in the world and I can't imagine why more people aren't getting into it. (Perhaps it's because it's a hell of a lot of work and a lousy way to get rich.)

As with many artistic pursuits, the passion usually comes first, but my job is to help with some of the technical aspects that will ease the transition from idealistic upstart to functioning member of society. "An expert is a person who has made all the mistakes that can be made in a very narrow field," said Niels Bohr. When once you can get past the technical difficulties, then you can apply yourself to the art.

If you've never gotten your hands dirty in a goldsmith shop, then a lot of this will be Greek to you. It's not a lesson in goldsmithery as much as me trying to pass on some hard-won knowledge to people who already have some.

It's also a small shop book, a sort of 'Goldsmithing for Dummies' book, based on my belief that one should learn simple techniques before moving on to the more advanced ones. A lot of my techniques are quite primitive, based on very simple tools and a ton of experience. I'm starting to become acquainted with some of the more modern tools, and can see their value in the world of goldsmithing, but I still believe that there is a lot to be said for a good solid base of getting one's hands dirty with the old methods. Besides, getting into the business this way is far cheaper: no need to spend huge sums of cash on before figuring out how to do the job. I set up my business using a small loan from the First National Bank of Mom, so the initial budget was limited. I was able to get down to work and accumulate the more complex tools over time, but the most important thing was to be able to get going.

For example, you should know, at least in a rudimentary way, how to make a band out of a piece of gold. Or how to carve something vaguely ring-like out of a piece of wax. What I will try to convey is how, through my experiences, I manage to save myself a lot of headaches. Most of what you'll see here is the result of years of taking on more than I had time to accomplish, making mistakes and doing my best to save my ass. I read somewhere that there's not much difference between a good surgeon and a bad one, unless something goes wrong. That's when the skills really come out. Experience is simply the result of accumulated errors, fixed and recalled.

One of the recurring themes in this little endeavour is that it's easier to keep than it is to get back. Everything: money; fitness; reputation; the love of a good woman; a kite. Each step of an operation should be completed to perfection (or as closely as practical) before moving on to the next. In this business, as in many others, things proceed in an orderly manner, one step at a time. Make each step perfect and the next will follow smoothly. If you rush one step or just plain get it rong, you can't go back. You will try. You'll chase your tail and you might even make it a couple steps down the line before you find that the little error has grown very large indeed. It's getting more and more complicated and you're out of your depth and you're fiddling about....shit. There is no BackSpace key. You've just wasted several steps and you haven't got time to start over. At this point, reflection is difficult if not impossible as panic has set in, but you can sometimes look back over the previous steps and determine exactly where you went *w*rong and perhaps fix it. Or perhaps not.

This brings us to the second important theme: you have to know when it's fucked. It was fucked several steps back and you simply missed it -- or ignored it, more like. It will often save time in the long run to start over on a job that has been rendered hopeless, because you already know how to do the preceding steps, right? Extra time spent in planning the job will be more than repaid by avoiding false starts and costly errors.

One thing I will not attempt here is to tell you how to do anything that I'm not very good at or don't believe in. Certain things in this life still baffle the hell out me: channel-setting (to an extent); "invisible" diamond-setting; thong underwear. You know, it kinda looks intriguing, attractive even, but what if something goes wrong? How practical is it? Would you want your wife wearing it?

Another Way to Look at Things

One of the problems that I run into when trying to teach people how to do this is that I have a different way of looking at things. Apparently I was genetically predisposed to be a goldsmith. I was born extremely nearsighted in my left eye, to the extent that I never developed binocular vision. As a little kid, this didn't bother me overly, as my world was fairly intimate. If I wanted to look at something closely, I looked at it very closely with my left eye. The right eye was fine for distant objects, but they didn't tend to be as important to me. I didn't much care for sports, for example, based on the combination of complete incompetence and a tendency to lead with my face. Not getting picked for the team left me with more time to devote to my hobbies, as well as decreasing my chance of getting clonked on the noggin. It's a win-win situation.

Add to this the fact that I am right-handed and you've got the makings of a perfect setup for a goldsmith. When I'm working up close, my knuckles are not in the way, as they would be were I to be looking with my right eye. Try it yourself and you'll see what I mean. I've modified the standard spectacle-mounted dual-lens jeweller's loupe to suit my peculiarities and it has worked out for a great many years. It's comfortable and easy to fold out of the way when it's not in use. It also doesn't muss up my hair the way a headband-style magnifier would. I'm vain that way.

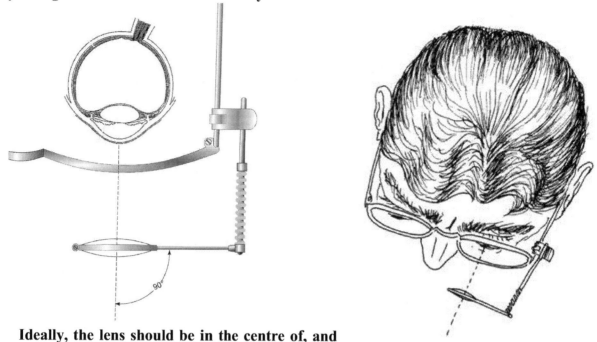

Ideally, the lens should be in the centre of, and perpendicular to your line of sight. In addition, it should be positioned so that it is looking sort of across your nose a bit, so that you are comfortable working up close.

One little exercise worth trying is to take a close look at a perfect square or right-angle grid under magnification. If the loupe isn't perpendicular to your line of sight, the square will be skewed one way or another. This will play havoc with your judgment of symmetry and such, and if you find that you're getting diamond-splinter headaches, it may be that your loupe needs a tweak.

Having said all this, find the magnification system that works best for you, and don't be afraid to experiment. I tried out a half dozen spectacle prescriptions before I settled on one that works well under the conditions I encounter day-to-day. Find yourself a good optometrist and make sure that she understands your very special needs.

So, how to look at stuff is thus:

-Relax.

-Swing the loupe into position in the centre of your field of vision. Somewhat in front of your nose as opposed to directly in front of your eye.

-With your eyes nice and relaxed, as if you're looking into the middle distance, bring the work into the center of your field of vision. Adjust your loupe and seating position until you're comfortable and relaxed. Don't be trying to swing your head around and squint things into focus, you'll just tire yourself out and, trust me, you're going to be in this position for a long time. I've watched a lot of people setting and, either because they're right-eye dominant or, perish forfend, binocular, they've got to crank their heads way over or swing back, chin to chest, just to see what they're doing. This can't be comfortable.

It looks like we're drifting over into the subject of basic working position so let's review: You should be relaxed, not using eye muscles to focus, just adjusting focal distances 'til everything is comfy.

Where are your arms?

Chiropractors go nuts when I describe my working position because it just seems so abnatural. Well, mostly it is, but with planning this can be fixed.

Ideally, the bench is designed for you. If it isn't, it should at least be designed correctly. Chairs are adjustable in my world and if the bench is properly constructed, height is the only major variable.

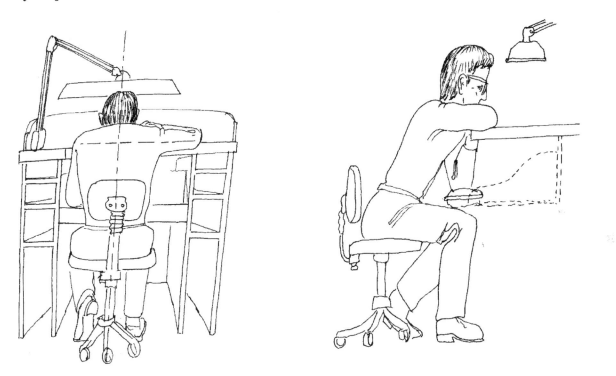

While working (setting, specifically) your back should be straight; not vertical, by any means, but neither slouched nor rigid.

Relaxation is the thing. Remember, we're going to be doing this all day so we shouldn't be fighting every step of the way.

The left arm, holding the work, should be supported at the elbow by a pad of some sort. Nothing too mooshy, though, just enough so that the elbow pressure is nicely distributed. I use a leather pad that is frankly, much too firm, but I'm trapped by traditions of my own making. Maybe something in a nice baby-butt suede. The height of the pad, or perhaps the whole drawer, should be adjusted so that it allows the work to be presented conveniently against the bench pin. Your right arm should be at a comfortable height, so that your shoulders are horizontal. Once again, this is to avoid fatigue. It's a weird position, granted, but once it's set up properly you should be able to sleep there. Some do.

Your back is straight, but not rigid. One arm up, one down, and you're neither leaning on them, nor holding them up with your shoulder muscles. I don't care what you do with your feet, just so long as you're comfortable and relaxed.

Of course, most of what I'm talking about here is the position I use while doing setting work. The manufacturing process demands a different sort of focus, but the best rule to remember is don't slouch. My personal old guy, Bert was a repair goldsmith for fifty years and always had excellent posture and no back problems.

The advent of the bench-mounted microscope has improved the working position for setting and certain manufacturing processes, but the bench goldsmith will still spend a fair amount of time holding little things in her fingers, filing and bending, hammering and soldering, and good posture will always be in style.

Tool Time

I still use a lot of pointy sticks and bludgeoning instruments to work my magic, and am convinced that anything fancier just gets in the way. While I may well be incorrect in this, I do have to get into the subject somehow, and this is how I'm going to do it for now.

The traditions of goldsmithing go back to the earliest times of humankind and have evolved with advances in technology, but the basic principles remain the same; creating items of personal decoration using materials of little intrinsic value that, through their use in such items, have achieved great huge importance in the economies of the world. The evolution of the tools has certainly affected the nature of the pieces produced but the principles remain.

I suppose that I'm setting this down for the upstart goldsmiths like the long-ago me. There was never quite enough money for the fancy tools, and then I realized that I could get along very well without them. This attitude sort of got out of control in my later career and has turned me into bit of a Luddite, but I can't help feeling that learning to use the simple tools is crucial before stepping up to the fancy gizmos. When you're just starting up, it's important to focus on honing the skills rather than amassing tools. That being said, I will put together a list of the tools used in this book that I consider indispensable when setting up your first shop. It'll be somewhere in the back of the book.

Gravers

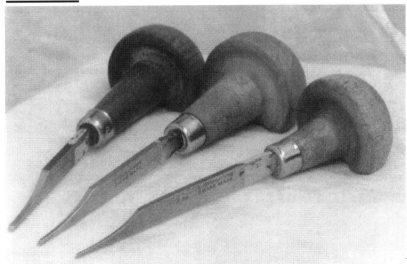

Gravers are your friends, cherish them.

This would be the most notable of the pointy stick category of tools, the care and maintenance of which is, in my opinion, the very foundation of the trade, most especially in stone setting. Decorative hand-engraving is something I won't get into because, frankly, there are better books out there to study and I consider myself a journeyman engraver at best.

By the way, this chapter will be devoted to the traditional, so-called palm-push graver. The more advanced GraverMeister and GraverMax systems are lovely and everything, but have no place in this low-tech venue. The air-powered gravers can do amazing things, but they're quite costly and starting to use one of them without knowing how to use and maintain the standard tools is folly.

The main shapes that we'll concern ourselves with here are, in order of importance, flat, round, triangular, and square. The flat and round are commercial gravers shown above, Glardon-Vallorbe; in my experience, the finest quality available. They are fine grained high-speed steel that combines toughness and a superior edge-holding ability that works for me. I continue to try new alloys whenever they become available, but these little yellow-tanged beauties have become my favourites. If you find better ones, let me know. The triangular and square I like to make out of old needle files, which are also made of fine quality Swiss steel, so are very suitable to our needs. Cheap, too.

At this point I should mention that I am very wary of false economies and they are a subject that will come up often. Using quality, old steel to make cheap gravers is never to be confused with using cheap gravers. Cheap gravers don't last as long and are more time-consuming to maintain so, in the long run, cost more. Add to this the fact that you will tend to do bad work with shabby tools and it just doesn't seem worth it. The temper of the steel, the combination of hardness and toughness, is the culmination of millennia of metallurgy and is not something to be messed with lightly. We'll get into just that subject a little later in this section of the book.

The basis of pointy-stick technology is to make the tool an extension of the body, so that we can accomplish a job that is impossible to do using mere flesh and bone. Because pointy sticks tend to be more or less pointy on both ends, a well-designed handle makes it easier to meld the muscle and steel.

Graver handles come in several lengths so that, as the steel is used up, the longer handles can be substituted for the shorter, thereby extending the working life of the valuable steel. By setting up several handles in various lengths, there's always one available when needed. The handles can be used for the flats and the rounds interchangeably, as well, so there's a whole world of possibilities.

Half-round mushroom handles are my preferred shape, but as usual, we have to dick with them a little to make them perfect for our needs. The flat bit, for example, needs to be absolutely flat. The reason for this will become apparent later, but for now we'll deal with a standard, high-quality wood handle with a lovely flat surface.

In this case, we'll deal with a 1m/m wide flat graver, my personal favourite, just to have an actual thing to work with.

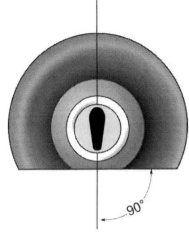

First take a 3mm drill and run it into the handle, all the while ensuring that it's going in straight in relation to the axis of the handle. This can be checked by letting go of the handle while drilling and letting it spin free. If it seems to be running true, you're good to carry on. It's hard to miss, really. Go in an inch, or 3cm or so, then expand the hole up and down by wiggling the drill to cut a rectangular channel to accept the tang of the graver. If you're careful (and you are careful, aren't you?) then the hole is perpendicular to the flat bottom of the handle.

Grind the tang of the graver to a shape that will fit into the handle tightly, keeping a bit

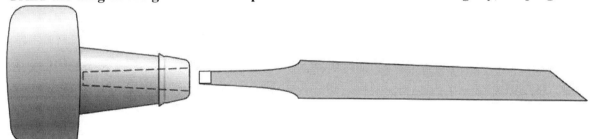

of taper to ensure a proper fit. You'll be forming a tapered tang about 30 m/m long, sharpened at the end like a nail. There should be a distinctly shaped shoulder that will butt up against the handle once it's been seated. For now, though, the tang should fit into the handle with the shoulder about 7-10mm from the handle. It takes a bit of practice to perfect the shape of the tang, but time spent now will be well-rewarded later.

Grasping the handle lightly in your left hand with the graver pointing away from you, smack it sharply with a light hammer. This will force the graver into the handle using inertia rather than brute force. (The same thing could be accomplished, more or less, by standing the graver on end and pounding it into the handle, but this is messes up the tip,

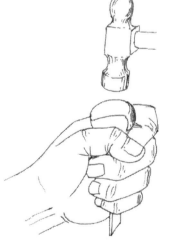

Be very careful that you don't whack the webby bit between your thumb and forefinger. It hurts.

and could result in the graver shattering into sharp, dangerous shards. Don't do it.)

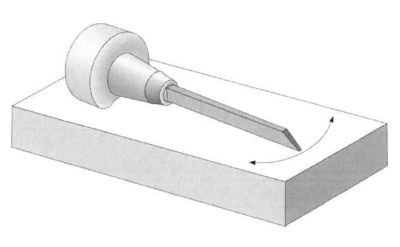

Before the tang is all the way in, though, you should check to see that it is going in straight. To do so, lay the base of the handle on your oilstone and slide the tip back and forth to form a shallow-angled flat on the bottom of the tip. The flat so formed should make a nice perpendicular line. If it doesn't, which it won't, twist the graver and check it again.

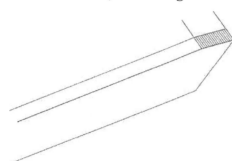

It's important to try not to fudge this step, as it will definitely come back to haunt you.

Check, whack, twist. Repeat as necessary.

Sharpening a long, flat surface such as that on the business end of the graver now is basically impossible, so we won't try. We'll be grinding away all but a small face, which is efficient and easy to work with. It goes without saying that you're using plenty of water on your grinding wheel so's to avoid buggering up the temper of your fine Swiss steel. Trust me, you can't duplicate the temper of a quality graver using shop techniques. Don't fuck with a good thing.

The shape that we're grinding the end to is based on a perfectly formed balance-wheel

pivot, by the way; a short parallel section and then a smooth curve based on a parabola. This is the perfect compromise between strength and delicacy and will be renewed as the graver is used up.

Looking at the graver tip head-on, the top of the face should be absolutely parallel to the bottom. If you compromise on this point, it will continue to give you no end of trouble later on.

So, what you have is a trapezoidal face, top and bottom perfectly parallel, and perpendicular to the axis of the graver.

At this point, though, it's not all that sharp. In the interests of efficiency, it's important to be able to sharpen quickly, accurately, and often. Speed will develop over time, but it's best if we get set up properly first.

The angle ground into the face of the graver at the factory is about 45°, and that's as good a place as any to start. We'll be dicking about a little with the angles as we go along, but for now place the existing face flat against the oilstone. Handle cupped in your hand and index finger extended along the graver, feel the way it makes contact with the oilstone. Take your time and feel the feeling of perfect. This is concept that will come up repeatedly in this book; the ability to feel whether something is right without having to look at it. It's a form of proprioception that will develop over time.

Keeping the angle the same, slide the face back and forth on the stone a few times and check it. The face should still be a nice, flat trapezoid with no extra facets. Flatitude: Get used to it and enjoy it while you can, because you're about to modify it and it may be a while before you can get it back.

The actual process of sharpening is very straightforward and simple and will become easy after about thirty years, or at least I hope it will. I'll keep you up to date.

Once you've got it nice and sharp, it's time to fix up the underbelly so that bright-cutting will be possible. This is the easiest thing in the whole process.

I have made a little block that sits behind the stone, raising the handle of the graver about 5mm above the surface of the hard Arkansas stone. The same thing can be accomplished by cutting a small rectangle of wood or plastic of the appropriate thickness and setting it on the stone. The style used mostly depends on the size of your Hard Arkansas stone.

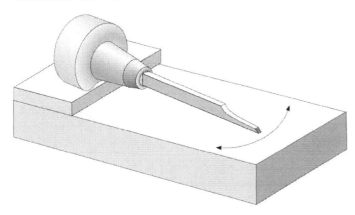

Simply place the flat of the handle on the little, raised block and slide the face of the graver back and forth a few times. This will not only remove the burr that was formed in sharpening the face, but will remove any scratches that are on the underside. Scratches on the belly will be transferred to the metal surface and will look awful.

This is a concept that comes up with most gravers; that the final finishing should be done parallel to the cutting edge. The burnishing effect smooths out the cut as the cut is made. (Some books advocate a sort of figure-eight sharpening process for the face of the graver to achieve the same result, but I find that getting a perfectly flat face is more difficult. Sometimes I do it because it's sort of fun, but that's just me.)

Once again, wipe off the goop and check your edge. Looking at the graver end on, you should see a sharp transition from top to bottom face. No extra facets or little bright flashes, just two perfect planes meeting at an angle. This is your cutting edge. Cherish it.

The edge can be further checked by touching it to your thumbnail. It should immediately grab without skidding at all. It's not necessary to actually gouge the nail at all. In fact, if you have to use any pressure at all to get it to bite, it's not sharp. Make it so.

One final point about the fine art of graver sharpening: since it's usually the tip of the graver that snaps off, or wears off against diamonds and such, it's a common mistake to cheat the sharpening process towards the tip, thereby increasing the angle at the tip. With repeated sharpening, the angle increases. This means that it takes more pressure to force the graver through the material, thereby increasing the risk of taking off the tip.

For this reason, it's important to take the time to maintain the angle each time it's sharpened, or even cheat it backwards a little. This makes sense on another level since the initial stages of, for example, trimming up a bead-setting involve heaving out a fair bit of material. For this process a shorter angle reduces tip breakage. As the process continues toward finishing, less pressure is applied and more of a slicing motion is used. The final cuts are done with a very acute angle and polishing the graver more frequently to leave the smooth and pristine surface we so desire.

Mounting the other commercial gravers is done using more or less the same techniques. They are a bit less fussy, as the bottom facet of the cutting edge is not as critical, but any extra time spent getting all the angles right will more than repay you later, when you're trying to concentrate on simply getting some work done. Also, if you drill the hole for the handle accurately, the handle from a round graver can be used for a flat graver, and vice versa, when it comes time to change handles.

The triangular and square gravers are neat, in that they are free. Well, free in that they are recycled from old needle files. This is why I'm rendered speechless with rage when I see that some mindless mutt has fried his old file by using it as a solder pick. It isn't nice to waste a good piece of steel.

To make a file into a graver, we first have to break it off to the correct length. The remaining steel, the file's handle, makes an excellent punch once the end is ground off to the appropriate shape. (More about punches, later.) The handle is simply drilled with a round hole, and the proto-graver inserted

It's important, with the triangular graver in particular, to finish off two sides very accurately so that it will present a consistent angle as it is ground down. Personally, I think it looks kind of cool to leave the top face of the file intact. Maybe it provides a better grip.

At the same time, take the upper corners off a bit as they will definitely shred your fingers as you work.

In any case, grind a tang on the handle end, and relieve the business end to present a smaller face. The square graver is muy simple, now that we've set up the others. Tang, face, corners, Voila.

Inside Graver

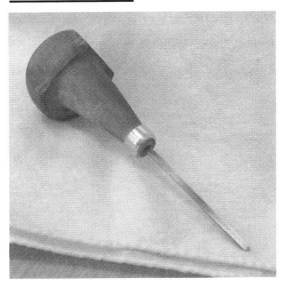

One of the primary engraving jobs encountered day to day, is that of engraving inscriptions inside rings. In my case, the trademark and karat stamp are hand-engraved into each finished ring, so I'm in there a lot. I have modified a square graver, made from an old needle file, of course. In order to cut accurately, this graver needs a bit of a belly to provide clearance when cutting. The way I've achieved this is to cut the handle so that it forms a right angle instead of a single flat surface. This is easily done with a saw of some sort. Just make sure that the two flats are equal and accurate. The exact angle at which they meet is not that important, just so long as it's 90° or less. An oblique angle makes for an unmanageable cutting edge. This allows you to use your handle as a guide for forming the undercut.

The cutting edge thus formed is very suitable in that it is already provides a bit of relief behind the tip to lift the handle end up for clearance. It's very easy to keep this one in order as each time you clean up the bottom of the face, you're extending the flat.

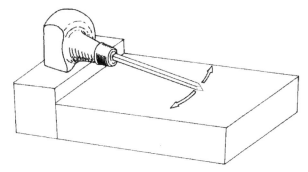

By grinding the sides of the square smooth, we protect the edges of the ring from damage, as the graver rubs against it often in the process of cutting inside the ring. Do the top, as well, and you'll protect your finger from abuse.

If you don't know how to hand-engrave inside rings, you probably won't need one of these, but they do come in handy.

Truth be told, it's probably a handy way to build a standard graver, as it is so easy to refinish the underside, but I personally don't like the shape of the handle. That's just me.

Offset Gravers

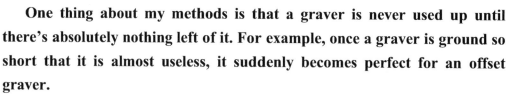

One thing about my methods is that a graver is never used up until there's absolutely nothing left of it. For example, once a graver is ground so short that it is almost useless, it suddenly becomes perfect for an offset graver.

These little fellas work if best they're short, as they need to be very controllable. They're used to cut bearings in collets, flush settings and the like, and are very double-plus handy things.

All you need to do is grind off your stubby old flat graver at an angle as shown in the picture. The belly remains the same as a standard graver. If you have one of each, or even a couple different sizes of each, you will undoubtedly find many other uses for them besides cutting bearings, which we will delve into in the setting section.

Pushers

There are basically only two kinds of pushers that we need to concern ourselves with here; flat and round.

Both are, in effect, a piece of square steel stock set into a handle with the end ground to shape. I suppose that you could use the same pusher all the time, modifying it as needed, but you'd end up spending an inordinate amount of time doing so. Better you should have a few. They are cheap and easy to put together from old burs and file handles and the like.

The flat pusher is your production pusher because it's used for basic claw setting and for light collet work. I find that grinding a bit of "tooth" into the business end of your pusher will give you a great deal of control over the force that you can apply to a given bit of metal. If you know that the pusher isn't going to slip forward or back, then you can concentrate on making it work in the correct direction. Jack, for whom I used to work, used a pusher with a polished end for setting, but he had enormous shoulders and tremendous control over everything except his life. More about that at another time. (The flat pusher in the picture is one I "inherited" from Jack White. It was old when I got it.)

With the round pusher, you have to be prepared to grind the business-end to the appropriate radius for any given job. This causes it to wear out rather quickly, so it's lucky that it is made from "scrap" steel. You'll work it out as you go. The one in the photo is a big, heavy duty one that sees the most use.

It's important that the pusher be made of good-quality steel because, while it isn't a cutting tool, it needs to hold the "tooth" to keep it from slipping. Commercial pushers are, in my experience, crap. Make your own out of old files, and you'll be fine.

I always check the end to see that I've got the striations going perpendicular to the direction of the force. This doesn't make a lot of sense until the first time you go skidding off a claw and remove the side of a diamond. That'll make your stomach hurt.

We'll go into some more specialized pushers in the setting section, so stay tuned.

Tool Manufacture and Maintenance

Back when I was taking a watch repair course, I found in the library at the school a very interesting old book on jewellery repair. Upon further reflection, I should have yielded to temptation and stolen it, as it turns out that the philosophy expressed therein was right in line with what I have come to believe about the trade. The book was published in the very early nineteen-hundreds and made no assumptions concerning the availability of tools and equipment necessary to the repair and manufactured of jewellery, so a lot of attention was paid to the making and maintenance of tools. One of my basic philosophies is that if other people can do the job, let them, particularly if they can do it better or more efficiently. A good piece of steel is the culmination of thousands of years of accumulated knowledge all packed into a very tight crystal structure, and you're very mistaken if you think that I'm going to get into that whole thing. It is for that reason that I don't recommend trying to re-establish the temper of a commercial graver or file: they're pretty much perfect as is. What I will try to do is tell you what you need to know in order to get on with your job. That is, to anneal, harden, and temper your own steel so you don't inadvertently waste a lot of your time. Or mine if you happen to be working for me.

The most commonly created tools are the pushers, punches, and burnishers. The faces of both pushers and punches should be hardened, but tempered only slightly to avoid chipping either the stone or the face of the pusher. The main difference between a pusher and a punch lies in the treatment of the handle end; a pusher is like a punch with a handle. A punch should be hardened at the working end, but annealed at the hitting end so that the hammer-face is not marred. Some of this will be covered later, but for now, some of the basics can be covered by looking at beaders.

Maintaining Your Beaders

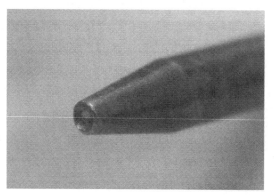

A beader is a steel rod, tapered at one end, with a cup-shaped depression in the end. It is used for shaping beads. Hence the name. They are available from tool suppliers in a variety of qualities, but as usual I am going to insist that you buy only the best. These are of Swiss steel and come in about thirty different sizes. In general, this is an embarrassment of riches, as I usually only use about seven different sizes on a day-to-day basis. The others are for very select jobs, and as spares. A good piece of steel is a wonderful thing and should be cherished. However, we do have to maintain our beaders. Otherwise the title of the section will have to be changed.

From time to time the business end of the beader becomes all mooshy and indistinct (like my prose) and needs to be reshaped. The big question in my life was always, "How does one shape hardened steel?" with the answer, of course, being, "One doesn't; one shapes annealed steel." One needs one's head read, one suspects.

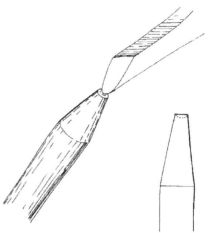

Annealing is simply heating the steel to a dull red and allowing it to cool slowly. This softens it so that we can do stuff to it. I usually end up doing a bunch of beaders at a time because it's a pain in the ass and I'm like that. I put it off, you know. Besides, while one is cooling down, you can work on one of the others. So there is method.

Once it's cool, the end can be filed flat, ensuring that the filed end remains perpendicular to the shaft. The end presents a perfect circle, maybe with the remainder of the former cup showing in the middle. This is good. Using your round graver, open up the cup a little at a time until it's nice and round and deep. You know, cup-shaped. Check the pristine, unused beaders in the set to get an idea of how they should look. There will always be several unused as they are simply the wrong size.

Sometimes, in order to maintain the size of the cup, you have to reduce the end of the beader. This is no problem, as long as you file the taper accurately making sure that the end remains centered. Round, too. It's gotta be round. I used to do this with a watchmaker's lathe, when I had access to such, but now I just chuck it into a pin-vise and roll-file it, trying to be as lathe-like as I can. Get the end down to the correct size and cut the cup into the end. No problem. Well, perhaps the first couple of dozen times you'll have a few difficulties but, if you persevere, things will go well for you. The thing to remember is to keep the taper quite long, sort of as illustrated. The tendency is to save time by shortening up the taper but too stubby a taper makes for an indistinct cup in the end and, not incidentally, interferes with your view of the working area.

Now we get into the tool-maker's conundrum. To make a tool, sometimes it's necessary to first make a tool. To properly shape the inside of a beader, you need something the shape of a bead. This is where all the spare beaders come in so very handy. Take a couple of these, anneal them, and cut each into two or three pieces. Don't cry, the reason for this sacrilege will become apparent. Actually, any good piece of good quality, round bar-stock will do. Drill-rod if you have any, old file handles if you don't. In any case, file a taper on the end and round it off into the shape of a perfect bead. What you are making, more or less, is a rod the same shape as a beader, except convex. It's not necessary to undercut it at all, just make it nice and round. Make several sizes, 'cause you only want to do this once. Seven or eight should do. Check the picture and all will become clear.

Now it's time to harden them. This is done by heating each one up to a nice cheery, cherry red and cooling it by dumping it unceremoniously into water. This hardens the bejeezus out of it, a condition known as glass-hard. It is now extremely hard, but brittle. This isn't a concern, though, as maximum hardness is what we're looking for here. Now fine sand and polish the tip of what has now become a burnisher. What we're doing here is making tools to make tools. Actually, you've made a bunch of new tools, in several sizes that you will use for the rest of your natural life. Store these little beauties in a wood block and you're ready to roll.

The annealed beader is forced onto the end of the appropriately sized burnisher and rolled around to shape and burnish the inner surface of the beader.

Now it's time to harden and temper the beader. This is a two part process that I have reduced to one, with some success. Hardening the "official" way is done the same way as with the burnisher; red heat and quench. Then the piece, which is now hard and very brittle, is polished and reheated very carefully 'til the end oxidizes to a light straw color, then quenched. Properly done, this yields a hard, but tough crystal structure that will last a long time without needing further conditioning.

My method is not foolproof, but then again, I've not had much success with the "official" method. What I do is heat the piece up to a dull red, wait a second for it to cool just a touch; then quench it. This hardens it, but not as much as quenching it at a bright red. It works pretty well nine times out of ten, which isn't bad, considering the time you can save. Test the temper with a file. Run a medium file along the end of the beader. If it drags or cuts at all, then it's not hard enough, so you'll have to heat it up a little harder and quench it a little sooner.

Now you can polish the cup again. This is done with the same burnisher as before, but first you smear a little bit of the black goop from your oilstone on the end of the beader.

This is hopelessly low-tech, but works quite well. Give the beader a bit of a spin and really moosh it around. Clean it up and it's ready to use.

You'll find that the first few times you redo the ends of your beaders you end up shortening them as you try to get them perfect. This is a normal part of the learning process and is another reason for having a lot of beaders that you don't use much.

Sharpening Drills

In the course of developing our setting skills, I will occasionally nag about keeping drills sharp. That's all well and good but it does raise the question, "What is the best way to sharpen a drill?"

As usual, I'm not going to just up and answer the question. Rather I'm going to kind of slide into it sideways by approaching it from a more theoretical standpoint.

A handy little tool that I ran into in an ancient watch repair manual was a doodle called a pivot drill. This is a single-use, custom-made drill, usually exceedingly tiny, that you make when absolutely nothing else will do. My most common impetus for whipping up a pivot drill is when the teensy drill I'm using, through no fault of my own of course, takes it into its tiny brain to snap off at or near the end of the flutes. Those are the twisty bits which carry out the removed material and keep them from clogging the process.

If you start off with a broken drill, it's basically just a steel rod. If you grind away all but a narrow strip down the middle then, presto-change-o, you've invented the world's tiniest screwdriver. In a larger size this is the basis for a half-pearl drill, but that's for another day.

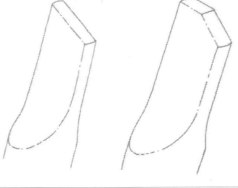

If you were to then grind it off to a bit of a point it would be useless as a screwdriver, but unfortunately also as a drill, as it lacks a cutting edge. By simply changing the angle a bit we create more of a chisel end. Make sure that the angle will cut when the drill is rotated clockwise or it will just be embarrassing.

This little gem works adequately for panic situations but it is necessary to pull it out from time to time to clear the chips since it lacks the aforementioned flutes. What I want to note, however is the angle that is formed by the two cutting edges. If we've done our jobs correctly we will find that they meet at a forty-five degree angle. Keep that angle clear in your head because it is the same one you will find on a properly sharpened twist drill.

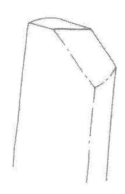

There are machinist's guides that go into incredible detail on the perfect angles of attack for the leading edge as well as a bunch of other stuff that really doesn't concern us and our meatball approach to metal work. One point worth considering here, however, is the trailing edge.

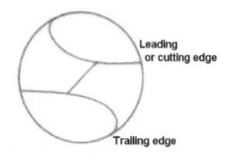

Leading
or cutting edge

Trailing edge

If you look at the way that the cutting edge meets the surface to be drilled, you will see that the trailing edge will ride on the material already cut and prevent the drill from advancing. For this reason it is important to remove a tiny bit of the trailing edge by sort of rolling it off the grinding surface. In the official machinist's method, as shown in the photo at the top of the section, the trailing edge is ground off in a series of facets which constitute a curved surface and work quite well. For our purposes, being as how we're using such tiny drills, it is best to make a single facet and simply soften the trailing edge a bit. This is accomplished best by sharpening the drill as you would a graver, then on the last stroke twisting the drill and decreasing the angle in a way that's impossible to describe. It's also best done under magnification, which would make any demonstration photos problematic.

If you start to notice that your drill is requiring too much pressure to work, it's probably best to stop and resharpen it, as it only takes a moment. It will most likely save you from snapping the drill off in the work (see the Addendum).

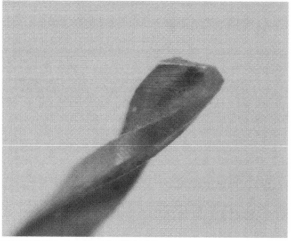

Another situation that arises all too frequently is that a twist drill shows up from the factory looking like this. Such a drill may cut into the metal after a fashion, but will certainly cause problems.

Y'see, I'm kind of a pain in the ass about doing stuff as opposed to talking about it, so try sharpening a few drills and find out what works. As well, don't always trust the factory-made drills, as they are not always perfect. If the drill ain't drilling, it ain't a drill. It's a stick.

Addendum:

For whatever reason, drills break. Thanks to Murphy's Law, they will invariably do so at the most inconvenient time. Should a drill break off in the metal and prove to be impossible to dig out without destroying the piece, acid is the answer. This will take some time, so you'll have to plan ahead.

Let's say that it snapped off in the process of drilling the third of twenty holes for a pavé setting. This is typical. Rather than interrupting the job right then, it makes sense to drill the rest of the holes, as bad things happen in groups of three, and you might as well get them over with.

Fill a small plastic container, like a 35mm film canister, if such things still exist, about half-way with water and add about a teaspoon of Sparex or the equivalent. What you want is a saturated solution, so a few of the crystals remain undissolved. This is the strongest solution possible. Drop in the offending piece, with its stupid broken drill still in it, and put it in the ultrasonic. Make sure that the lid fits tightly and, just for extra security, rig a wire hanger of some sort to keep the container vertical in the ultrasonic. You do not want this stuff getting into your cleaning solution, trust me on this.

A small drill will take a couple of hours, at least, to dissolve away completely. Don't rush it. The drill will theoretically dissolve without putting it in the ultrasonic, but it will take a lot longer. The way I figure it, the acid dissolves a little of the drill, but is then rendered pretty much neutral. What the ultrasonic does is sort of circulate the acid into and out of the hole so that new acid is introduced to the job to speed it up. The piece may develop a copper flash-plating during the process. Don't freak out, it will go away.

Scraper

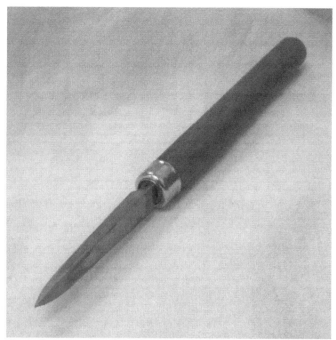

Yet another fabulous tool reclaimable from old steel, the scraper is the exact opposite of a gizmo. It is so useful on so many levels that I just can't believe it.

A scraper is basically just a triangular length of steel; say an old triangular file, mounted in a handle. By careful shaping and grinding, it presents three lovely sixty-degree cutting edges. These edges are easy to maintain by honing flat on an oilstone. The honing process is made even simpler if each face has been slightly hollow-ground, thereby presenting less material to remove in the honing process. It's important to keep each face flat; otherwise the cutting edge becomes inconsistent and inefficient. A cutting edge of sixty degrees is close to perfect for scraper-type applications, so why dick with it?

The scraper is largely an emergency tool; when you need it, you really need it. Spending some time now on preparations means that later, when you really need it, it will be ready.

Used originally to repair engraving errors, it soon becomes indispensable for myriad little jobs. It's perfect, for example for taking the sharp edge off the inner corner of a ring; kind of a quick, low-tech comfort fit. Used in conjunction with a burnisher, it saves a lot of pointless trips to the polishing room.

There are commercial scrapers available, but they suffer the usual problem with mass-produced tools; crummy steel. As is so often the case with my favorite tools, my scraper was made by Jack White, the old engraver from whom I inherited some of my best stuff. Kinda gives you a clue as to the longevity of a well-made tool.

Burnishers

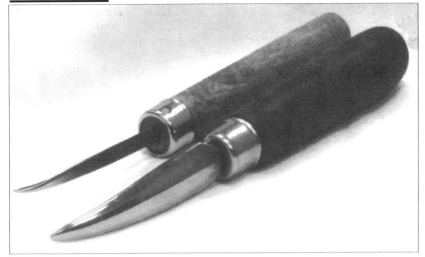

A burnisher is a polished piece of hardened steel used to smooth and polish the surface of a softer metal.

The commercial variety is uniformly (in my learned opinion) useless, as somebody evidently forgot about the "hardened" part. However, being as how we have a bunch of old files sitting about, (we never throw away a piece of steel, remember?) we can make a wonderful burnisher ourselves.

Start off with a half-round file that is no longer any use as such and anneal it. This will allow us to have our way with it. Just heat it up to a dull, cherry red and let it cool slowly. Now you can file and grind it with alacrity, without worrying about drawing the temper.

The shape of the normal half-round is not quite suitable for a good, general purpose burnisher, so grind it down to a rounder, blunter shape. Once it's more or less the correct shape, give it a bit of a curve, so's to present a longer working surface. Do this by bracing the tip of the rough burnisher against a hard steel surface and heating it up red-hot again. As you heat it, bear down on it 'til it bends. The exact amount of bend is a matter of personal preference, so as you use the tool, you will be in a good position to decide. Pretty wishy-washy advice, huh?

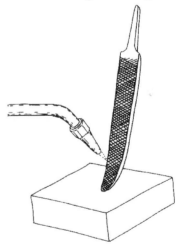

(Actually, in this example, we have the raw materials for two, count'em two, lovely burnishers. Cut the file in half, grind a tang on the narrow end to make a small one, and you're left with a big stubby on the old tang. Shape it as you please.)

Once again, let it cool down slowly because we still have to shape it to fit a handle. Y'see it's way too long as it is, and the tang of the original file is not a shape conducive to proper gripping. There are two ways to go from here: one is to round off the base of the file to make a comfortable handle, the other is to cut it off and fashion a new tang. Either way is good, although the handle idea will ultimately yield a more controllable tool.

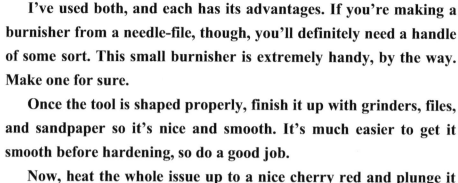

I've used both, and each has its advantages. If you're making a burnisher from a needle-file, though, you'll definitely need a handle of some sort. This small burnisher is extremely handy, by the way. Make one for sure.

Once the tool is shaped properly, finish it up with grinders, files, and sandpaper so it's nice and smooth. It's much easier to get it smooth before hardening, so do a good job.

Now, heat the whole issue up to a nice cherry red and plunge it into cold water. Keep it moving, in effect stirring the water with it. This prevents a bubble of steam from forming around the heated tool, which would slow the cooling process and result in a softer crystal structure. Not good.

The burnisher is now what's known as "glass hard". If you run a file against it, it dances off with the high-pitched ringing tone of something that's way too hard to file.

Now use fine sandpaper to finish the working surface of your new burnisher and get ready to polish it. This is done with a hard compound such as Fabulustre or tin oxide. Pretty much any compound suitable for polishing platinum or stainless steel will work. Bring it to a high lustre, with no scratches or pits and presto! You got yourself a burnisher. The finish will need to be renewed from time to time, but you already know how to do it. Luckily, it's not necessary to anneal and reharden each time.

Some books I've read advise an agate burnisher, but these seem to be somewhat fragile and hard to maintain, so I don't like 'em. Well-hardened steel is as hard as agate, anyway, so why bother? Carbide burnishers seem like a good idea, but once again, maintenance would be an issue. You'd have to use diamond compound every time you wanted to touch it up. Granted, it wouldn't need much touching up, but I like to be realistic. I like to play with toys that I can fix if the need arises. And the need always arises.

The small burnisher has myriad uses, primarily in polishing in places where normal polishing is impossible. However, the usual polishing caveats apply; don't try to polish anything that isn't already fairly smooth, and don't try to polish out fireskin. It won't work.

Over the years, you will come upon numerous situations where only a burnisher will do, and a specially shaped one at that. So by all means, make several. The situation may arise again, and a well-made tool is a thing of beauty and a joy forever. Plus you'll probably find other uses for it.

A handy addition to my finishing repertoire is a product called MicroMesh. It is an ultrafine abrasive cloth which replaces a lot of other products in the quest to avoid the polishing room at all costs. As an encore, it is exceedingly convenient for refinishing burnishers at the bench. I find the 6000 grit to do an excellent job, although the 12,000 is lovely for the truly anal, providing a mirror-bright finish.

A Gizmo

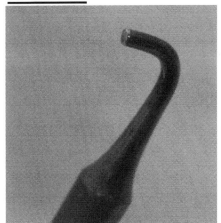

This little doodle is a handy tool for poking stones out of a ring without having to remove it from the clamp. It's a goofy thing, but Jeez, it comes in handy.

It's up made from scrap steel and it's a little fussy to get the correct combination of strength and delicacy but, since it's scrap, a couple of unsuccessful attempts are not just a waste of time.

Don't make the end too skinny or too long as it will lack the strength and simply snap off every time you try to use it. Once again, the shape of a balance pivot comes into play; a short straight section and a smooth curving taper so that the stresses are evenly distributed through the working end.

Once the taper is established, the end is bent in much the same way as the burnisher. Hold the end against your steel block and heat it with a fairly tight flame 'til it bends to the desired right angle. Make sure that you don't overheat it as this makes for a weak and useless implement. It should start to bend at a dull red.

Once it is the desired shape, let it air cool. The annealed steel will be strong enough to do the job. Hardened steel will have a tendency to snap as it is too brittle or, worse yet, it will be hard enough to take the bottom off your stone. This would be bad. If you're trying to lever a stone out of a setting and the tool bends, you're trying too hard and something bad is going to happen. Trust me on this.

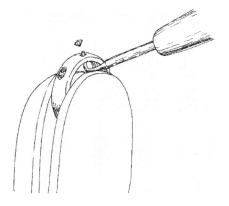

Cheater File

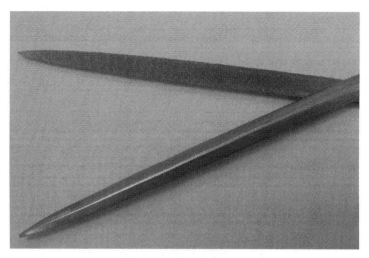

The cheater file is a medium-cut barrette file ground down to a knife-edge, thereby presenting a file that can fit into tight spaces and only cut on one side.

The reason for the appellation is that, when used in setting, it can relieve the claws where they bend and protect fragile stones. Actually, that is a perfectly reasonable use for it. It only becomes a cheater file when it is used as a matter of course to protect a mutt from having to learn to set properly.

When grinding the file down, it is exceedingly important to keep from over-heating it as there is no practical way to retrieve the perfect temper that the original makers achieved. Keep in mind that this is probably a twenty buck file. Don't fuck it up.

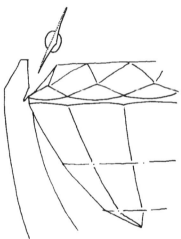

Once you have one of these, you will find new uses for it almost daily. Just remember that it's sharp and fairly fragile. (Actually, it's nice to have a coarse and fine version for finishing purposes. Look after them.)

Tungsten Pick

If you ever do platinum work, and you intend to be poking around at it while hot, it is absolutely essential to use tungsten as just about anything else is sure to contaminate your platinum. Trust me, the first time you melt the end of a regular poker into a mass of platinum that you can ill afford to replace, you'll know what I mean.

Once again, there are commercial picks available from tool suppliers, but they tend to be a bit flimsy. Best you should get in touch with an industrial welding tool supplier (that would be Acklands/Grainger around here) and find something a little more robust. In my case, the piece of tungsten is simply a rod about 1.5mm in diameter set into an old pin-vise.

It provides a nicely balanced, delicate feel for poking parts while doing regular gold soldering as well. Just be careful not to contaminate the end of it with gold or solder, as this will bugger up your platinum just as sure as anything less noble. The advantage to having a cheap source of tungsten is that you don't feel bad about grinding the end off if you have the slightest suspicion that it may be contaminated. Do so often, just in case.

Just because I'm who I am, I'm experimenting with mounting the rod into a tube of platinum that I had just sort of laying around. Platinum itself has a very low rate of heat transfer, so it should protect the handle from overheating. Probably not strictly necessary, but I like it.

In a pinch, it can also be used as an all-purpose, slim pointy thing, but why not just make up your own?

Slim Pointy Thing

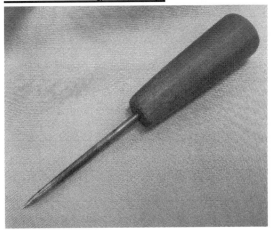

This is one of those simple, all-purpose tools that come in handy on so many levels. It's just a tapered piece of steel, possibly an old round needle file, fitted into a handle and ground down to a fine, tapered point. It's handy for poking stones out of drilled holes when you're not overly concerned about either the stone or the tool, mixing glue, and for making sandpaper sticks-- anywhere that you need a pointy thing where there's a good chance that it will get worn down or broken in use. It'll be ground down as it is used, so it's semi-disposable.

Having one of these around will hopefully stop you from grabbing something else that's close at hand and doing something stupid with it. I've broken the tips off files and gravers by using them as rudimentary prying implements because I'm stupid, and I'm trying to prevent you, Grasshopper, from falling into the same lazy trap.

Rodico One-Touch

I ran into this stuff while taking a watch-repair course. Its primary use was as a remover of dust, oil, and fingerprints from the pristine inner areas of a watch, but I saw its potential as a multi-purpose substitute for plasticine. It resembles plasticine but is a little more rubbery. This presents some "springiness" problems, but it is not grease, or oil-based which more than makes up for that.

Poking it into the holes prior to setting stones removes the oil and cuttings which could cause problems. See the Pavé Setting section for another use. Jamming burs into it cleans away debris. Oh heck, there are lots of places it comes in handy.

Problem is that, as a watchmaker's "tool", it is vastly overpriced. Fortunately, a cheaper and all but identical substance is easily available from stationery stores. Called Plasti-tac or Fun-tac, it has the added bonus of being available in white. This makes it perfect for showing stones arranged for pavé setting jobs. It stands to reason that the stones always look better face-up on a white background than other alternatives. The white stuff, however, seems to dry out much sooner than the blue stuff, which is problematic, but since it usually gets so dirty as to be useless at about the same time as it dries out, you can simply throw it away and buy some new. It's cheap.

Eventually, however, the ball of plasti-tac gets so gunked up with oil and crap that it loses all its elasticity and becomes useless. Before throwing it out, let's reflect on the fact that this shit is probably about 5% gold by weight. Chuck it in with the sweeps, rather than the scrap gold, as the refiners never know what to do with it. Just don't throw it in the garbage.

Sandpaper Sticks

One thing that you'll develop a need for early on is a nice sandpaper stick. I'm probably overly proud of my ability to make perfect sticks because of the time Bert, my particular old guy, asked me to make him one 'cause mine were so good. On reflection, though, he may have been Sawyering me. "Gee, your sticks are so much nicer than mine, (and if I play my cards right, I'll never have to make another one myself again)."

In any case, here's how I make a sandpaper stick.

First of all, I believe that you can make a purse out of a sow's ear, but it won't be a very good purse. You can make a sandpaper stick out of a paint stick that you cadged from a paint store, if you get a bunch of them and pick out the straightest one and hope that it doesn't warp over time. I've seen sticks made from paint sticks, with the paper stapled, or worse yet taped down, and while I'm sure they work adequately, they look like crap and we're better than all that. The other problem is that the last inch or so of the sandpaper is rendered useless. Unnecessary waste, don't you know.

Contrariwise, you can just act like a pro and use a piece of good wood that will last for generations. Take, for example, a piece of quality oak moulding about a quarter inch thick by one inch wide. You could put your hands on four feet of this shit for about a buck and a half and have enough for four top quality sticks. The wood is cured and hard, the corners sharp, and it's straight. Whaddya think? Avoid false economies.

Lay a piece of sandpaper, rough side down, on a clean, flat surface. Place your stick flat on the back of the paper, a bit less than the thickness of the stick from the end. You want the stick perfectly parallel to the edge of the paper. There should be about a centimeter of stick hanging out at either end. I suppose I could actually measure one of these things, but I'm very busy right now, doing things. Busy, important things..

Now, with your handy slim, pointy thing, lightly scribe the paper so that it will fold accurately and fold it up against the stick. Make sure it's nice and snug against the stick, all nestled in, and scribe a line on the other side of the stick. Now roll the stick up on its edge and scribe the line where the next fold will be. Do the same thing again, ensuring that everything stays nice and snug. We've come to the most important part of the trip now, so pay attention.

You want the folds of sandpaper to be extremely tight against the stick, so when you scribe this next line, let the previous fold go, without moving the stick, so that you're scribing against stick, not sandpaper. This will allow you to cheat a bit on this first round so that the paper is really tight. This is important. Now fold the paper, tucking the first edge of the paper tightly into the fold. This is important. Did I mention that this is important? Well, it is. If you've done a real good job on the first turn, the rest is smooth sailing. Simply scribe and fold repeatedly until you reach the end of the paper. You want to end on a short side, and then scribe it twice, not enough to cut through, but enough so that you will be able to tear it off cleanly. Don't tear it off yet. Hold it tightly so it won't unravel, and poke a hole through all the layers of paper, on the short edge, about a centimeter from the edge of the paper, and poke a little brad or cigar-box nail into the hole. You can pick up about a million of these at a hardware store. They come in very handy for a lot of stuff. Whack the nail into place, but not so deeply that it cuts into the paper, 'cause then it won't hold anything. At this point, thinking about the future, you use your dividers to measure the distance from the nail to end of the stick, and mark this distance on the other end. Poke a guide hole, whack another nail in, and the paper is secured.

You're not done with the nailing part yet, though. Measure, counter-punch and nail the two edges on the opposite side of the stick as well. This way, as the paper wears out, you can peel off a half-turn of the worn stuff, exposing a nice new layer. In this way, as you remove layers, you'll always have a brand new coarse layer as well as a smoother, half-worn layer. This is very handy.

Tear off the excess paper and wonder at the glory of it all. Well, actually, you will notice a fairly floppy sort of consistency to the whole thing because all the layers are not quite parallel, or are not folded quite tightly enough, or what have you. Don't worry; the next one will be better. Experience, you know. The reason I keep going on about the tight thing will become clear as you use the stick. If it's not nice and snug, it has a greater tendency to tear during hard use.

When once you have worn out the last layer and it comes time to apply a new sheet of sandpaper, pull all the nails and measure the location of the holes with your dividers. Lay out the paper and wrap it in the usual way. The nails will go in much easier this time, and on all future occasions, because the holes are already there waiting, which means that you won't have to pound a whole bunch of new holes in your stick. That would make it weak and lumpy, which would be bad.

I usually have three grades of sandpaper stick, but two are often adequate for day-to-day use. Mostly I get away with 360 grit and 600, but 1200 is very nice, and more or less mandatory for platinum work. Oh, yeah. Use good quality Wet-or-Dry silicon carbide grit with a sturdy backing. Beware of false economies.

The Torch

The day I first walked into Dunn's I saw the torches happily burning away and thought, "This is where I belong."

Most of the shops I see these days are equipped with those teeny little mini-torches. Perfect for very fine work, they are pretty much useless for anything else. And anything else is exactly what I do.

Versatility is what I think this is all about. I know there are a great many better setters out there, and better manufacturers and engravers and designers, but jeez, there's just me around here and it's kind of up to me to be all those things and a goddamn business-guy on top of it all.

Sorry, just lost my head for a moment, I'm all right now.

Anyway, with this superannuated torch of mine, I can do great things. Originally designated a Purox lead-burning torch, it's a solid brass bit of magic that can perform single link solders on the tiniest chains, and still melt fifty grams of platinum with just a switch of tips. Oh, and some practice.

Somewhere in my deep, dark memory I recall having five separate tips for it, ranging from an orifice of about .5mm to some sort of cavernous three millimeter behemoth. At this point in my life, however, I manage with three: small, medium and large, I call them.

The reasoning behind using such a primitive instrument goes way back to my own particular old guy, Bert. He trained me to make parts fit perfectly, so that any inherent tensions were removed as heat was applied. Heat the whole piece to near soldering temp and there will be no nasty surprises in the future. Your present will generally be a little more exciting than the norm, but the upside is a bit more control of the situation in the long run.

Manufacturing is a somewhat different animal from repair work, so it stands to reason that the tools will have to differ somewhat. In order to avoid a lot of nasty surprises while doing repair work, it is often necessary to confine the heat to the immediate vicinity of the repair. This is where mini-torches shine.

If, however, you need to solder a white gold plate to a gent's ring, you want the entire assembly to reach soldering temperature so that the solder has a chance to flow naturally, by capillary action. This sort of heat distribution is impossible with the little laser-beam flame put out by a mini. Matter of fact, you're far more likely to laser out the side of a ring than not.

So get a big torch, already.

The Bench

Having amassed all these tools, I suppose we need somewhere to keep them all. A bench, for instance. Granted, some of the tools will be scattered about the shop in spaces of their own, but it is muy importante to have your day-to-day favorites close to hand.

My bench evolved from the one I worked at Dunn's during my formative years. This old fossil had been thrown together after the war by Jack's grandfather. It was constructed of some primitive precursor to plywood which had deteriorated over time to something resembling petrified books, all crumbly and dog-eared at the edges. The top had crevices that you could lose a quarter in. It shook like the palsied when I did any serious filing, and hammering anything would cause everything else on the top to rattle off onto the floor. Setting stones at a bench that sort of skitters away from one is an experience best left in the past as well. Bert worked at that bench for years, though, so it can't have been all that bad.

Bert's newer bench was constructed of nice hardwood with drawers and everything. Drawers upon which he would constantly bark his knees, as he left them open all the time.

I liked the concept of hardwood, but the drawers had to go. Shelves are far more accessible, if not as neat-looking, and, while pretty is nice, practicality is what we should be shooting for. Think of the bench as a tool and good design becomes beauty.

The top of the bench takes the most abuse, most particularly the front portions, so it makes sense to construct this of the hardest material practical. Granite? I don't think so, but hard rock maple comes close, and should last out the millennium. A raised rail around the back and sides is indispensable, of course, to keep shit from rolling off into the unknown.

The only parts of the bench that should be subject to major wear in the course of normal work are the bench pin (or file peg), and the saw peg. These should be attached by screws or bolts for easy replacement. Actually, the right-hand front of the top takes a hell of a beating on a setter's bench as the ring clamp is tightened by whacking it sharply against this area. It would be great to have this portion of the top reinforced, maybe with a replaceable piece of vulcanite or something. That's hard rubber, by the way, bowling ball material.

As far as basic construction is concerned, that pretty much sums it up. It's a dead-simple piece of furniture, practical in design and solid in construction. Size is more or less dependent upon the goldsmith. Height is, of course, the main variable. Mine is forty-two inches tall, but I'm tall. According to my extensive research into the subject, the top of the

BENCH
Constructed of 3/4 inch plywood unless otherwise noted.

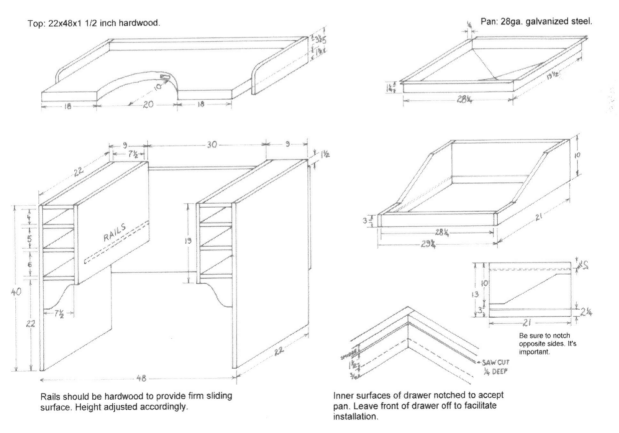

Rails should be hardwood to provide firm sliding surface. Height adjusted accordingly.

Inner surfaces of drawer notched to accept pan. Leave front of drawer off to facilitate installation.

bench should come up to your hip while standing, and the middle of your sternum while seated. I asked around.

This is the bench, more or less, that I spend a good deal of my life at. It's loosely based on the ancient piece of crap I worked at in my first paying job. Previous to that, I had worked at a door balanced on cinder blocks, so the old bench didn't seem so bad at the time. It was kind of short, way too narrow, and none too solid, but it was home.

When it came time to build my own, I tried to correct those difficulties and, since I was in the process of starting a business, do so cheaply. I'm not a woodworker and power tools scare me, so I tried to keep the construction simple. Another concern was my gypsy existence to this point in my life, so I also made it portable. It breaks down to five manageable chunks; top, sides, back and pan. With the removal of a few screws it will fit into a small-car trunk.

It's an adaptable design, as well, in that the sides can be cut off to shorten it and the rails that hold the pan are easily moved. I'm six feet tall, so the dimensions as given work for me, but this is a recipe, not a blueprint.

The top was the only wildcard at the time. I couldn't afford the two-inch laminated rock maple top that I so desired and had to settle for a slab of one and a half inch pine shelving. It suited my purposes, though, and the original bench is still in regular use after thirty years and counting, so it can't have been all that bad.

The slot for the bench peg is a bit fussy, as there are at least two "standard" sizes available, and I picked the wrong one for my first bench. Of course it had to be the largest one so I am compelled for all eternity to shim the smaller pegs to fit. Properly done, though, a single screw put in from underneath is all that is necessary to lock the peg into place.

One design flaw that shows up at the most inopportune moments is the fact that the bottom of the shelves, and that little decorative brace, are situated at perfect knee level. What this means is that, should you wheel your chair into place with a bit too much abandon, the bottom corner whacks into the point of your patella with a pain that is just exquisite. Maybe round off those edges a little, in anticipation of the inevitable.

The most complicated part of the bench is the drawer. I like to have a metal pan, somewhat deeper in the middle than at the edges. It is mounted without a wooden base as it makes it easier to find stuff by tapping on the bottom. The pan itself does need to be an integral part of the drawer, however, for strength. For this reason, the sides of the drawer have been notched to accept the lip of the pan. During assembly, the slight gap should be filled with some sort of silicone caulking; both to hold it solidly, and to ensure that tiny objects don't end up stuck in the crack. Nothing worse than tiny objects stuck in your crack.

The height of the drawer rails should be established once the overall height of the bench is deemed to be correct. The peg should be situated at sternum level. Then, while resting an imaginary ring clamp against the peg, the pan height can be determined. I rest my elbow on a leather pad placed in the front, left corner of the pan, so the pan is lowered accordingly. Trust me, you're going to want to use a pad.

Pretty much everything else is a matter of preference. As I said, it's a recipe, feel free to adapt it to your needs.

Construction

This is where the old guys hang out.

The way jewellery was made a long time ago was to start out with a lump of gold and, using all the standard bludgeoning instruments and pointy sticks, whip it into some kind of shape. The Etruscans were able to create masterpieces using the most primitive techniques, yet I hear people saying that it's impossible to get anything done without a Cad-Cam system and a laser-welder.

I grant you that the more modern tools make the job a lot easier and sometimes faster but jeez, you're a goldsmith. You're supposed to be able to work miracles with a hammer. Smite something for Christ's sake. It's great experience, for example, to make a bead of gold (a smartie) into a length of wire, using nothing but a hammer. Okay, maybe not on my time.

The hardest part of construction work should be done before you even get your hands dirty. Since you're working with precious metals, you want to minimize waste of materials without wasting a lot of time. You keep banging your head against the point of diminishing returns and, trust me, it'll start to hurt. So what I'm trying to say is, plan ahead.

Mental imaging is important so that the picture in your head will match the eventual product. This image will become clearer with experience, so my best advice is to keep it simple at first. There's no point in designing grandiose master works that you can't possibly execute. Trust me, this I know. I started out in this industry using only the most primitive of tools and believe that a good grounding in the basics is important.

This is probably as good a place as any to get into some basic design concepts. Engineering is important if we are to be making jewellery to last. If, for example, the ring is going to have a stone star-set into the top, this has to be taken into account in the design of the band. The star-setting weakens the top of the ring, so we need to make the top thicker so as to maintain its strength. If it's a solitaire shank which will have a setting spudded on top, the top should be thinner or opened up somehow, to keep the overall height down, while the bottom of the shank should be heavier, and quite possibly squared to provide a counterweight which will keep the top on top. It's important to think these things through.

What I'm trying to convey here is not so much some dopey project to make boring old bands or settings that could be ordered at a fraction of the cost of making one. These things are the starting point for myriad interesting pieces, limited only by your imagination. The skills will develop with time and, by occasionally overextending yourself technically, you'll advance all the more quickly. The rules are simple; the results don't have to be.

What I'll try to do for you is give you some basic construction techniques that may also make the imaging thing a bit easier.

What I've found in my own research into the art (if art it be) is that if a book gives me even one useful item of information, then it was worth the trouble of reading it, maybe even paying for it.

I hope this is worth it.

The Bar

When I started this section originally, the first step was to construct a plain band, but that left open the chicken-and-egg question of what comes before. Well, raw materials, I suppose, but we're not going to get into the finer points of alloying gold, refining gold, mining gold, and all that, because that would be dumb. What we will start off with, though, is some sort of gold that we will melt down and cast into a bar.

This gold can be in the form of casting grain, ordered from a refiner, or scrap gold from previous projects. It is important when doing a lot of this sort of thing not to fall victim to the false economy of using just any old sort of scrap. Any scrap gold that may contain appreciable quantities of solder, for example, can cause a multitude of problems further on in the process, and is to be avoided. Gold is eminently reusable, but only within reason. Each time it is melted, it absorbs a tiny amount of oxygen and sulfur from the atmosphere and, over time, this affects the working properties of the material. You can always recognize products made from bad old gold by the spotty finish and cracks in the surface. Sometimes these can be rendered invisible by burnishing and careful polishing, but this beauty is only skin-deep; the ugly goes all the way to the bone.

There's probably a whole nother chapter on the topic, so we'll just assume that we've got a suitable amount of clean scrap gold, maybe with some new casting grain to round things out, so that there will be no excuses should the bar not turn out. It's all down to technique.

A covered crucible is my preferred container for melting gold with a propane-oxygen torch, as it provides the all-important reducing atmosphere that will discourage the absorption of the aforementioned gases. A two-piece ingot mold is the weapon of choice for forming the bar. It can make square or rectangular bar or flat sheets, so comes in handy for all sorts of projects.

The treatment of the crucible is somewhat contentious, but my preferred method, when starting with a brand-new crucible is to heat it up 'til it's glowing a bit, and sprinkling a coating of powdered borax in to form a glassy coating on the bottom surface and the area of the pouring spout. This allows the gold to move freely over the ceramic surface of the crucible and out the spout, which will be important when it comes to the melting and pouring process.

While the inside of the crucible is nice and hot (there is also controversy about pre-heating the crucible before melting), dump in the appropriate amount of gold and pour the heat to it. Never mind what the appropriate amount is, that has presumably already been determined by algebra, physics, experience or, my personal favourite, guesswork. The torch flame that works best is one that is hot enough, but not too hot. I don't even know why I'm trying to describe this in words, because it's so much a matter of feel.

In any case, once the gold starts to melt, carefully shake the crucible to distribute the material and keep it moving. It tends to melt unevenly at first, and you don't want to overheat any particular area. If you see sparks flaring from the surface, maybe it's time to back off a little. Once the gold has taken on a liquid state, like mercury, we're about ready to pour. If it's still kind of lumpy and semi-solid, adjust the torch for a hotter flame. Be patient with this part because we want to get it right the first time.

Now, there are several schools of thought concerning the pre-heating of the ingot mold, whether to soot it up real good, whether to use oil or graphite as a mold-release, and all like that, but I always seem to come back to the simplest method, which is a clean, dry, cold mold. It's my belief that the more quickly the metal cools when it hits the mold, the more successful will be the final product. This is a subject of much semi-religious debate and not something I'm going to get into here. My book, my shop. Sorry.

So, when once the gold is all nice and melty, moving smoothly and fluidly, keep it moving and move the spout to the opening of the ingot mold. Keep the flame concentrated on the spout as you prepare for the big moment. Now is not the moment for self-doubt or hesitation. Pour the metal quickly but smoothly. Hesitation will cause the metal to freeze in several pieces rather than one smooth bar, which is bad. Contrariwise, lunging into the pour, dumping it out in one big lump, may cause it to block the opening of the mold. This, with the rapidly heating air trapped inside, can cause a highly disconcerting pop and spray of molten gold to be emitted from the mold. It's freaky but seldom results in anything worse than some wasted metal or Randy's hair catching on fire. But that's another story. Best you just pour with confidence and hope for the best. Wear old clothes.

When the torch is out and the crucible safely set aside, the ingot mold is opened up to see what we've got. The bar should be smooth and reasonably shiny, with a little bit of flashing where the two sections of the mold come together (with little vent sprues, if the mold is so-equipped) and come out without too much prying. There are myriad problems that can result from bad melting and pouring technique, but I'll go into those some other time.

With a coarse file, remove any flashing or vent sprues to present a bar with nice smooth corners. Don't go nuts on making it all tidy, simply ensure that there are no areas of the bar that will fold over and cause problems later. Start rolling the bar through the rolling mill's square holes, choosing the first one that will accept the bar without creasing it. This will be easy if you've made the bar perfectly square, but if you're starting with a rectangle, be careful.

How aggressively to reduce the size of the bar at this point is largely dependent upon the particular style of rolling mill you're working with. The main thing to avoid is attempting to reduce the size too much all in one bite. This results in a bar with irritating fins which must be removed before proceeding. If ignored, these fins will fold into the body of the bar and become a major problem further into the process.

Other than that caveat, the bar is simply a bar right now and can become virtually anything you want it to be. With the proper convincing, of course.

Plain Band

Perhaps the best place to start is with a plain band. This will give us a place to develop good habits, or not, depending on how it goes.

First, make a picture of the desired band. It can be on paper or in your head, just so long as you're sure. Gent's six-millimeter wide, two millimeter thick low-dome half-round, size nine. Got it?

We'll want a rectangular bar about 2.2mm thick and 6mm wide. It needs to be a little thicker than the final measurement because we're going to be hammering on it. Some extra width will be provided by spreading during the hammering process, so 6.0mm should allow for finishing afterwards.

The big question we have to answer is how long the bar needs to be. I generally eyeball it and get it wrong, so let's try this. Measure the diameter of your mandrel at the size 9 mark, add half the thickness or 1.0mm, and multiply by 3.14. Mark this length on your blank by whatever means you find convenient. Unless you made your blank too short, in which case you're fucked at this all-too-early stage and need to make a new blank. You'll want to have extra length at each end for the process, so don't be stingy.

There are plenty of books on goldsmithing that will give you formulae and graphs to determine exactly how long the bar of gold should be for a band like this, and it's handy to know more than one method. According to one such chart, the blank should measure 66.6mm in length. Armed with this knowledge, I suggest making a blank at least 10mm longer than this for reasons that will soon become evident. Mark your 66.6mm on the

blank, but don't go right to the end of the blank. The main reason for this is that the end of the blank is sometimes compromised after all the abuse it has suffered in the rolling process. The end may have puckered up through compression, or contain oxidation left over from casting. The other reason is that it is all but impossible to bend anything accurately right at the very end of

the bar. The amount of pressure necessary to do so is sure to mangle the end of the bar to such an extent that the two ends will never line up properly when it comes time to join them.

My usual method is to start bending the blank at the ends, gripping it in the area that will be cut off anyway, and then cutting the excess off at the marks. Do the two ends and leave the middle area straight for now. This can be done with pliers and brute strength, or we can use the ring bender. This is a very simple implement that comes in very handy in

construction. It will bend fairly heavy material with very little stress. You need one.

Now it's time to close up the ring the rest of the way.

This is where your visualizing skills come into play. As we file the ends of the blank square and flat, we must do so in such a way that the ends will meet perfectly when we close the ring up. See?

Spend the time necessary to make the ends close up with no light showing through. This will take a lot of backing and forthing as you open and close the ring, but persevere. It usually works best to close the ring to a slight oval with the joint at the shorter end. Then the ring is closed further by squeezing down one long side and then the other. This ensures that the joint is closed under tension. Try to retain the roundness of the piece through this whole ordeal so as to keep stress on the joint to a minimum.

Should the joint not close up perfectly after all this, a saw-blade may be run carefully through the joint. Thanks to the tension in the ring, it will close with a satisfying snap as the saw blade passes through. Actually, if there's enough tension it will snap your saw blade just as it's emerging from the other side, which is annoying.

There are some schools of thought that hold that the joint shouldn't fit tightly, as it is impossible for the solder to flow through. This may be true, but I find it to be an important skill to develop nonetheless. If you've done everything else correctly, the solder will flow, trust me. Besides, a thick solder joint will just look ugly no matter how hard you try.

So close up the joint, ensuring that the ends are aligned perfectly, and solder it, already. Use the hardest solder practicable, as we are going to be whacking away at it quite extensively. This raises the question of "how much solder?"

Good question. "Enough, but not too much," would be the short answer, but let's try this. Try to imagine the amount of surface area there is within the joint. In this case it would be 2x6mm, which are the dimensions of the bar. If the joint is as tightly fitted as we think it is, then a piece of solder 2x6mm, or three pieces at 2x2mm each would be ample lots. And ample lots is what we want, because we're going to be whacking the crap out of this band and we'll want a bit of excess.

Make sure that the solder has indeed flowed through the joint and not simply flooded around the ring by heating from the inside (if the solder's on the outside) until the solder flows, then moving the flame to the outside of the band to draw the solder back through. Many times I have started pounding away on a band and had it crack in the early going. On closer investigation, I could still see the file marks on the inside of the joint; clear evidence that the solder had flowed around and not through. The reason it flows around rather than through is because the flux did not flow through the joint. Heat plus no flux equals fireskin to which solder will not stick.

With high-karat gold, it is possible to weld the joint using an extremely thin foil of the same karat gold inserted in the joint, much as is done with platinum. This foil melts just before the surrounding gold and provides a very strong and invisible join. It is possible to weld 14K, but the results are spotty and often not worth the risks of porosity and cracking.

Once you're satisfied that the solder has flowed properly, and while the ring is still red hot, quench it quickly in your coffee cup full of water. Well, that's what I use. You can adapt.

In any case, once the band's cooled down and pickled, slide it onto the mandrel and whack it down tight to make it round. Knock it off the mandrel, flip it, and round it up the other way as well. You don't want it tapered at this juncture. What you will find is that it is very close to being a size 9, which is too damn bad, because I forgot to allow a size or so for hammering the band to a half-round. Poop. Okay, let's say that, in the course of filing the ends to fit you inadvertently removed a size or so. Now it's a size 8, which is great. Yes, this is indeed the way I work. Sad, really.

Now, nestling the mandrel firmly in the palm of your left hand, and with the ring between your thumb and index finger, commence to pounding it up the mandrel. Not down, as this would tighten it onto the mandrel and make the next trick impossible. As you whack, you rotate the ring so that the impact of the hammer is at a consistent angle. The other advantage to holding the mandrel firmly is that it doesn't make the horrid high-pitched ringing clang of an unclenched mandrel. I generally have the butt of the mandrel jammed in or about my navel during this process to keep it steady. This keeps the operation quieter as well.

Also, as if you don't have enough to think about, it's important to keep the ring perpendicular to the mandrel. This will reduce the risk of introducing a twist into the ring. A twist is a bad thing. It appears without any apparent cause and is nearly impossible to remove without heroic measures. Twists can often be avoided by annealing. If you don't already know, annealing is simply heating the ring up to a dull red heat, then quenching it. This realigns the crystal structure of the metal, in effect relaxing it so that it's not fighting you every step of the way. Annealing white gold is especially important due to its crystal structure. It should be heated to a bright, cherry red and quenched while it is still very hot.

Another point about annealing concerns the almost inevitable cracking that occurs thanks to the tremendous stresses that the solder joint is undergoing. What I have found to work is to do the initial soldering with more solder than would usually be considered prudent. Don't flood on enough to create a big lump, but make sure there's some extra for later. When it comes time to anneal, apply some borax to the joint and anneal the ring slowly. If you heat near the joint first, the stress causes the joint to pop open, necessitating a messy bit of refitting and re-soldering,

Instead, start heating the ring at the point opposite the joint and relieve the stresses first. Then, when you get to the joint, make sure that you reflow the solder, and quench the ring immediately. This has been working for me lately and, until I come up with something better, it's gospel.

If the shaping process has been extensive, or if the ring has been pounded up several sizes, there will have been a bunch of stretching around the solder joint. While finishing, this joint will show up much wider than necessary, so it sometimes makes sense, just before the final round of shaping, to cut through the joint and re-solder it. This leaves a nice tight joint with not a lot of solder in it. Solder being softer than the gold itself, it sometimes shows itself by a slight depression in the surface. Keeping this to a minimum would seem to be important in the pursuit of style points.

From time to time during the shaping process, place the ring on a steel block and smack it flat. This is not meant to remove twists or inconsistencies, but rather to alleviate the mushroom effect of hammering. This is the inevitable folding-over of the metal as the corners are pounded down, and needn't become a problem if attended to frequently.

Right now you're just taking off the corners of the bar all the way around the ring. Flip the ring and do the other side, so that what you've got is a flat band with beveled edges. Anneal the ring to remove the stresses within the metal, and repeat the process, this time hammering out the sharp angle that you made in the first course of pounding. Hopefully, I didn't screw up too badly on how much allowance to make for one size of hammering, because we should be getting close to the planishing stage.

These are the finishing strokes with a hammer, not necessarily increasing the size of the ring, but removing the facet effect of the previous blows. What you're shooting for is a process that shapes the ring without any filing. Oh, you'll file, don't worry, but if everything else is done right, it'll be minimal.

Another thing that you're doing in the planishing stage is hardening the gold. The pounding that you are doling out here is tightening the crystal structure and rendering the metal stiffer and more resistant to scratches. Pretty cool, huh?

Metal is just like clay, only slower, and can be moved in remarkable ways if its properties are kept in mind.

Now it's time to remove some metal.

The only truly immutable dimension we have to deal with is the size. Everything else is more or less a matter of taste. So clean up the inside first.

If I've had the sense to use a reasonably smooth mandrel during the planishing stage, then the inside of the ring will be quite smooth, so I like to use a medium file initially, just to get through the fireskin. At this point I'll usually take the sharp edge off the inside of the band, forming a bit of a comfort fit. I used to pride myself on how crisp the inner edge rings were, until I realized that putting the ring on and taking it off was removing a layer of skin each time. Ouch.

I then finish the inside up with a nice 6-cut half-round. The fine file marks run perpendicular to the direction of polishing, thereby making things a bit easier, in that this is fine enough that it can usually be tripolied without any sanding.

Usually, I flatten the sides of the band next, so's to have a good reference as to the shape of things. Ensure that the sides are nice and parallel and consistent. The woofer is usually necessary for this step due to the mushroom effect, and the band having spread a bit. Check the width before moving on with fine filing and sandpapering the sides.

Now the outside of the band is attended to. Since we did such an admirable job of planishing, there's not a lot of actual shaping to be done, so we'll concentrate on a nice, consistent surface, free of lumps and bumps.

In order to file consistently, you've got to imagine that you're a lathe. Rotate the ring towards yourself as you stroke the file forward. Don't use too much pressure and keep the ring moving. This will ensure that you are removing the high spots and not creating new flat spots that will have to be removed later. The greater the number of strokes, the more consistent the final result, so don't rush this step.

Once you've removed all evidence of hammering, it's time to check your work. Look the ring over and measure it. Run it around between your fingers to feel for lumps and flats. Make sure it's right because the woofer is the file you need if you must modify the shape of the ring in any way, all other files being, in effect, part of the finishing process.

This is one of those rules of life that I try to live by. The purpose of a given file is to remove the effects of the previous tool. If the ring is twisted, this is not a problem to be solved with a file. Twists must be corrected by hammering them out, not removing a bunch of metal. If there are flat spots, they should be gone before you set aside your woofer. If you notice deep file marks while you are sanding, then you missed a spot with your fine file. This goes back to my basic tenet that you have to complete each step to perfection before moving on to the next. Otherwise, you're just wasting time and subjecting your tools to premature wear.

The rest of the process is simply making the scratches in the surface smaller and smaller 'til it's perfectly smooth and ready to polish.

You may have noticed that there was no final annealing after planishing. This is a good thing on account of the fact that hammering compresses the crystal structure of the metal, rendering it a lot harder and more resistant to scratching and denting. I've made bands in 24K that were quite wearable. To be sure, they scratch up pretty easily, but if custy wants, custy gets. Keep in mind, however, that if such a ring is ever put through the fire, it is, in effect, useless. It can now be twisted into a pretzel with no more that finger pressure. The only solution would be to compress the ring to a smaller size, then hammer it back up to the proper size.

Tapered Band

Using the rolls as a shaping tool is a little trick that was developed in the late seventies and early eighties, apparently by me. I say this simply because I've never run into anyone else who does much of it. Of course, this makes it problematic trying to teach the method to anyone as an established technique, being as how I largely make it up as I go.

The first time I used the rolling mill, I started to see its potential as more than just a tool to make thin stuff out of thick stuff. I'd done some rudimentary forging work and found all the usual things going wrong; square bars coming out diamond-shaped; bars bending and twisting where they shouldn't. You know, the usual crap. Maybe the rolls, because of their apparently unlimited compressive strength, combined with great precision, would help to solve some of the difficulties associated with forming metal in an organized manner.

Up until this point (starting at Dunn's), I was constructing rings much like any other basement jeweller; purchasing sheets of gold and piercing out whatever pattern my fertile imagination was able to devise. The problem with this method is that it's so confining.

You're stuck with a single thickness, unless you order extremely thick plate. It's also rather inefficient, in that the leftover sheet has to be recast and, if you haven't got rolls, you're at the mercy of your supplier. Not an enviable position in which to find yourself in, which.

The basic function of a standard rolling mill is, as mentioned above, that of making thick stuff thinner. It does this by duplicating the effect of a hammer, but in a very controlled manner. This allows it to move a whole bunch of material without introducing any of those nasty inconsistencies to which our foolish flesh is prone.

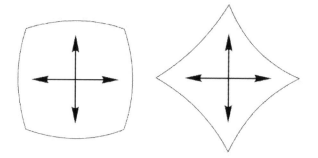

Here's a simple example. Say we have a square of material three millimeters thick and ten millimeters on a side. If we roll it one direction, we could end up with a one m/m thick plate, ten m/m by thirty. If we roll it alternately, each pass at a right angle to the last, the result will be a one m/m plate about 17m/m on a side. Rolling diagonally, corner to corner, in one direction, will yield a long one m/m thick parallelogram square root twenty wide and Pythagoras only knows how long. The math gets way out of hand at that point.

Y'see, we can't change the volume of the piece, we can only convert thickness to length, but we get to decide whether that is length as length or width.

All this having been said, what actually happens in the above scenarios is not quite as expected. Rolling the piece straight through squeezes the bar marginally wider as it lengthens, so this must be allowed for.

Rolling the piece side to side, each run at right angles eventually yields a cushion-shaped plate, while the diagonal method will give you a pointy kind of star-shaped doodle.

What you need to pay attention to is the direction in which the piece is entering the rolls, keeping in mind the fact that it is getting longer in the direction of travel. Based on that simple concept, there are manifold amazing tricks that can be played with as simple a tool as this.

For now, though let's get back to the tapered band. Let's call it a tapered version of the plain band we made before: size nine; half-round; six millimeter wide; but tapered down to 3mm at the back.

Start off with a regular bar, let's say 6mm square, and about 20mm long. I'm vague as hell, as usual, because it really doesn't matter right now in that this is primarily an exercise in roll control, but that's as good a place to start as any. The emphasis here is on ensuring that symmetry is preserved at each step. If you don't pay attention to each step, distortions will creep in and most assuredly lead to a lot of pointless filing later. (Actually, it makes sense now to mark a nice center line or punch a center hole to make the symmetry more visible during the rest of the process. I always forget to do this and generally regret it later.) The whole point of making rings this way is to save time when it isn't practical to carve a wax, and if you do a bad job, then you're simply wasting time and gold.

After squaring up the bar nicely at 6mm, anneal it and crank down the setting on the rolls about a half-turn. The amount that you reduce the size will vary according to the style of rolling-mill, but suffice it to say that you want to reduce the size by a sufficient amount so that a distinct step can be seen. Roll it in to not-quite-half-way, rotate it 90° and square it up. Then swap ends and do precisely the same thing to the other end. Get a feel for how far you are advancing the handle of the rolls so that you can roll the bar the identical amount without having to measure.

Crank the rolls down again by the same amount as before and repeat the process. This time you'll stop a little way further along the bar so that you have two distinct steps. Repeat the process, remembering to square up the bar each time, and keeping the steps uniform and symmetrical. You may have to adjust the steps as you go so as to ensure a smooth taper.

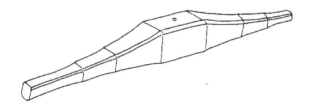

This is strange work, in that you must visualize the finished bar and how it will look when it's rolled down flat and formed into a ring. This is one of the skills that we are trying to develop, so keep your mind open and follow the pictures in your head. Actually, if you've made detailed sketches of your proposed ring, with all the pertinent measurements worked out, you should have a fairly good vision of the product as you go.

By now, you will probably find that your bar is looking quite a bit too long, or leastways we hope so. This is good, judging by the number of times I've had to start over at this point because of my being just a little bit stingy on the length of the original bar.

Now it's a simple matter to roll the tapered bar down to a hair over 2mm and make it into a nice tapered band. Just remember to leave your excess material on the ends to ease the bending process. Soldering and finishing from this point is fairly

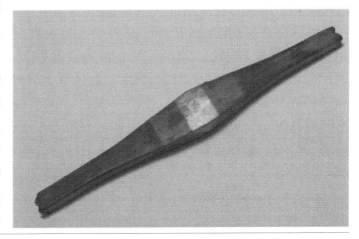

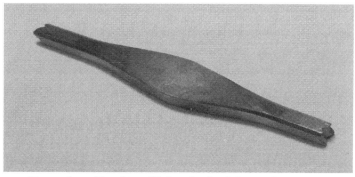

straightforward, but with the added complication of keeping the band symmetrical. Use all the tricks at your disposal to keep it so. (Notice that, in this example, I have neglected to establish a center point. Story of my life.)

Occasionally, it will be desirable to have the top of a tapered band thicker as well as wider say, for example, if there is a stone to be set in the ring.

This is done by planning the rolling process a bit more carefully. The bar, having been 6mm square, is now nicely tapered and quite hard on the areas that have been compressed. (This photo actually illustrates the relative hardnesses of the various steps, from softest to hardest. The center is still annealed, and we can use this to our advantage. It will naturally be more likely to bend at the annealed area than the hardened areas, despite their being thinner. Using the ring-bender, heave away at the middle of the bar. This can also be done using a swage block or some other smithing equipment, but the ring-bender is one of those perfectly simple implements that come in so handy as to be indispensable.

Now bend the ends of the bar, using the same logic as in the plain band example; bend the ends, cut them off at the correct angle, then finish closing the band up. Once again, if you can keep the ring reasonably round during this part of the process, then the rest of the operation will go better for you. The remainder of the operation is straightforward finishing, once again with the added dimension of symmetry. Enjoy.

White Gold Plates

Soldering a white gold plate onto a plain band is one of the first projects that will be presented to a manufacturing goldsmith, and from the very outset we have a problem.

The reasoning behind this is a bit hard to conceptualize, as it seems so simple to just make the band, curve the plate to fit, and solder the sucker on. Couldn't be simpler.

Well, it seems simple until you've tried it a few times. What happens is that you find you've spent an inordinate amount of time trying to eliminate those last little gaps between the band and the plate, so you try to fill in the spaces with solder. Now you've flooded the whole vicinity with solder, reflowed it a couple of times in a vain attempt to make it look like something, and then tried to file out all the lumps and pits. Then you finally come to the conclusion that this just ain't working and there must be a better way.

Part of the problem has to do with the concept of differing coefficients of expansion: when heated, yellow gold and white gold expand at different rates. The same is true of gold and platinum, but more so. If you were to solder a yellow gold strip to a white gold strip and smack the resulting piece flat, you would find that, upon heating it up even slightly, it would bend. (It's something I've always wanted to do so that I could state with authority exactly which way it will bend, but I haven't. Trust me, it bends.)

So, not only are you starting out with the hoary little problem of fitting two curved surfaces, the curves change upon heating.

Luckily, there is a solution, but you can't go on thinking about "soldering on" and start thinking about "fitting in". At first, this method seems to take way too long to be practical, but we've already determined that the easy way just ain't so easy.

Let's say we're inlaying a plate that will be set with diamonds, which is the most common situation where a plate is required. I would start out with a plate the correct width for the stones and slightly thicker than the band. The extra thickness is so that the edges of the plate will end up slightly above the level of the surface of the band, and flush on the inside. The plate should be longer than necessary for now, so that we have some extra material to make an accurate bend without buggering up the ends too much. (I covered this in more detail in the section about plain bands and will continue to nag about it for the foreseeable future.)

Bend the white gold plate to the same radius as that of the band using the excess material as a handle. The best way to ensure an accurate curve is to bend the plate a bit too far, ie: a smaller size, and then tap it round to the correct size on your mandrel. Now cut it off to the correct length and tidy up the edges nicely. Filing just the slightest top-to-bottom taper on the plate will ease fitting somewhat as well. Just make sure it's accurate and consistent. Make sure that all fireskin is removed from the inside of the plate, as this will cause problems later. Now mark the band where you want the plate situated, using a sharp scriber or X-acto blade. Just hold the plate in the proper position and trace around it. This line will probably disappear in the final stages of fitting, but it's important to start out accurately. Best mark one end of the plate now, because, even if it's cut perfectly, there will be slight differences between the ends that will cause headaches later.

Drill a hole in the band, thread a sawblade into it, and saw inside the line to open up the area into which the plate will fit. By paying attention to the angle of the sawblade and staying inside the guidelines, you will ensure that you don't cut out too much material. Tidy up the edges of the hole and start opening it up until the plate starts to drop in. Take your time and try the fit often. When the plate begins to go into the hole, force it slightly then pull it out. You will see, inside the hole, little bright spots where the plate is hung up on the inner surface. This is where we'll concentrate our filing. Between this technique and the simple expedient of holding the ring up to the light and seeing where the light shines through the joint, we will eliminate all gaps. By repeatedly fitting and filing, the plate will gradually drop further into the band. Just make sure to only remove material from the contact points and slightly below because we already know that the plate will fit that far, and if we remove material above that, it will just result in unsightly gaps when it comes time to solder it in.

Keep this up until the plate is at the proper depth and you may find that the plate actually gets stuck in the hole. This is good. What you want is for the plate to be in contact all the way around the hole, with no light showing through. At this point it will be ready for soldering.

If the band is mostly finished, clean it well and apply three or four thin layers of boric acid to the band, fusing them to a nice glassy surface. Scrape away the boric from the area inside the hole where we want the solder to flow, as well as the inside of the band where we will be applying solder.

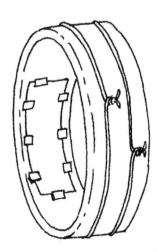

Now, all we have to do is make certain that the plate is going to stay in place during soldering. The problem here is that we want the solder inside, but we want to heat the ring from the outside. This means that the plate is going to fall out, or the solder is going to fall off. By wrapping the ring in iron binding wire, we eliminate the problem. In addition, despite all our finicky fitting, there is always the chance that the plate will shift during heating. It's that old devil coefficient of expansion.

Apply a solution of borax, or the flux of your choice, to the joint, ensuring that it flows through the entire joint. You don't want fireskin getting in there. Warm the ring up a bit and apply small snippets of solder across the joint on the inside of the ring, spacing them evenly. The correct amount of solder is always a tricky subject, which I went into somewhat back in the plain band section, so try to imagine the amount of surface area within the joint and use enough to cover it. Too much at this point would be worse than not enough, as it could flow all over the outer surface, creating a clean-up nightmare.

Heat the ring up from the outside, with a flame that's not too intense as we don't want to nuke through our binding wire. Heat it until the solder flows and observe the joint carefully. The solder flows towards the source of heat, so it is possible to pull the solder along the joint. A bit more solder may be added, but if you're pretty sure that there is ample and it still won't flow properly, it may be time to introduce the subject of the reflow.

I have developed an almost religious belief in the reflow and am not willing to dick with what works. Basically, if the solder won't flow, something in the joint is preventing it from properly filling the joint, be it dirt, oxides, or magic. Either way, anything that you do to try to convince it to flow will simply make it worse, so don't try. Put the whole piece in the pickle and just leave it alone. (Make sure that you've removed the binding wire as it causes the weirdest copper plating to be deposited on the ring, as well as anything else in the pickle pot.) I'm sure you have other things to work on. In fact, I find it best to have two or three pieces on the go so as to make the best use of such down time.

After the piece has soaked overnight (I mean it, don't rush this), it can be well cleaned in the ultrasonic, steamed, boricked up, and the whole shootin' match heated up to soldering temp. Lo and behold, the solder, she flows. I don't know why, exactly, this works, or why it has to be overnight, but I just know that if I try to rush it, it goes wrong. Not every time, mind, but often enough to make me very wary. Like I say, mysterious.

If the gods have been with us, however, the solder joint is a perfect fillet running all the way along the joint, making clean-up a breeze.

As you get into more complex assemblies, the binding wire method becomes a bit cumbersome. Ideally, the pieces that you will be soldering together should be so well fitted that they stay together without any outside help. Tension, dovetail joints, pegs, any number of methods can be used. If the pieces stay together of their own accord then they will be less likely to fall apart the next time the piece is put through the fire.

This, by the way, is the gospel according to Bert. He taught me to prepare the piece, and the pieces to be soldered to it, in such a way that little or no poking would be necessary to keep everything in place under fire. Extra time spent in setup and preparation is more than repaid down the road.

Split Shank

This is basically just a tapered band, split down the middle, but it can go so wrong, so quick, that you just can't believe it. In spite of this, it's an excellent basis for a great variety of rings. As usual, I'm going to be stressing strict anal attention to detail every step of the way to avoid problems later. It's my way, and I'm sorry, but if things go haywire for you, don't come crying to me.

We start off with a tapered band, heavier at the top, though not necessarily wider. Through careful forging, and judicious filing, the ring is brought to a fine state of symmetry, checked and rechecked.

Now, the ring is annealed one final time, both to remove stresses and to leave a nice oxide layer upon which to do our layout work.

A center punch or graver mark to establish the top dead center of the ring, a clear center line, and some perpendicular lines down the sides of the band are a good start. If any discrepancies in the symmetry are noticed, now is the time to fix them.

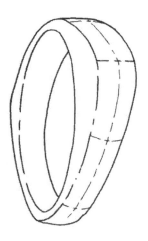

Chuck a brandy-new blade into your saw. Always start with a new blade, so that, when things go awry, you'll know whom to blame.

There are two schools of thought on the subject of what particular breed of saw blade to use. Some folks say an 8/0 blade makes a finer cut, therefore a tidier job. Others, that would be me, say that the 2/0 offers greater control.

In addition to the divergence of opinion on which blade is best, there are also different ways of cutting, either of which is quite effective if done right. Cutting straight down, starting at the top center, switching sides often to maintain symmetry, keeps the cut straight if you're careful, but is often a bitch to clean up later. Going around the whole ring and making the cut gradually deeper all the way along makes for a very tidy cut, if everything goes according to plan. Try both ways and make up a few of your own, but take your time in any case. Any difference in the thickness of the sides will cause major headaches later on in the process.

Once the shank is split and the success of the cutting is assessed, it's time to open 'er up. I generally do this with the ring clamped into my ring clamp. Nice rhythmic sentence, that, if a tad redundant. A bench knife is inserted into the split and the ring gradually opened. The principle of leverage comes into play in a big way here, since moving the fulcrum and using the mechanical advantage allows you to control exactly where the sides of the ring bend. Granted, if the cut isn't symmetrical it'll be damn near impossible to open it up perfectly, but do your best. Once it's open a goodly way, it's time to decide, based on your initial design, how it's going to look. Straight sides are kind of easy, in that you're already there, but introducing a nice curve can give it a sort of antique-style charm. Besides, the easy way leaves the sides flaring out with the skinniest part of the head on the finger. This tends to look kind of unstable and uncomfortable, in my opinion, but is common in more modern designs. Modern designs tend to look unstable and uncomfortable as a general rule anyway, I think that's what makes them modern.

Getting the curve into it in an organized manner requires a little bit of extra infrastructure, in the form of some bending pliers. Use these to gradually bend the sides to a pleasing curve that will properly cradle your head, or bezel, or what have you.

Once you have the curve just about where you want it, you'll be shocked to discover that the ring is no longer round. Nor is it the correct size. This calls for a good deal of control and patience as you carefully coax the ring round while at the same time maintaining the shape and symmetry. It helps to anneal the ring so that it isn't fighting you the whole way. As a matter of fact, it's imperative.

Once it's all tickittyboo, it's time to clean it up.

Here, the usual rules apply. First the size needs to be corrected through careful forging and filing. Then the inside of the split is corrected for symmetry and finished up perfectly, and the seat for the bezel cut or filed. The reason for doing the inside first is that, if there's any problem with the shape, it's a lot better to find out while the maximum amount of gold is still available for leeway. Besides, thanks to our being excellent forgers, we already know that the outside of the ring is perfectly shaped. Right?

The rest of the game is easy. Just poke and file and sand 'til it's all lovely. Polish up the inner area before soldering in the head and for heaven's sake be careful. Chances are, you have the better part of a day invested in this pig and you don't want to blow it now. Most of the problems that arise at this point have to do with badly fitted heads. If it doesn't sit securely in the seat, or if you haven't wired it in place or otherwise planned for its security, it will surely flop around and give you a major headache. Invest a little bit more time to avoid major aggravation later. Now, the ring at the top of this section features a platinum head because it is a sort of copy of an antique ring. The stones are old-cuts, which need to be individually fitted, so I used platinum. This allows the stones to be set very securely with little risk on account of platinum's like that. It also wears like stink so the ring has a chance to become an antique again.

A very adaptable design, it can also be constructed inside-out. That is, by carefully rolling the middle of the shank thinner and soldering it at the top, we can split it and open it up to accept a head. I suppose the same thing could be accomplished the regular way, but that would entail cutting it at the top while the original solder joint is at the bottom. Two solder joints? I don't think so. Style points, don't

you know.

This is an example made up in 18K white that turned out quite well. 18K white is harder than the hubs of hell but polishes up just beautifully. Mixed blessings y'know. It's also great for detailed work like the pierced-out areas of the collet. This would tend to get mushy and indistinct if attempted in platinum, simply because of platinum's idiosyncratic ways. **<u>Passing Shank</u>**

I didn't know what else to call this style of forged shank, but it shows up often enough that I figured I had to call it something.

This is an extension of the inside-out forged wing ring that we discussed earlier, but it's got this kind of weird crossover design that I love so well.

I've always been fascinated by three-dimensional shapes that start out as one shape and flow into another. In this case, it's the flat, wide shank at the back of the ring, under the finger, that gradually morphs as it flows around the finger. At some point, it becomes square, but it's hard to tell exactly where.

Actually, it starts out square. So let's start there.

Using the rolls, we create a reverse tapered square bar. This is accomplished by cranking down the thickness setting of the rolls while at the same time heaving the crank back and forth slightly to spread the effect somewhat. Christ, I have enough trouble illustrating this sort of thing with pictures. Are you telling me I need videos now? Gah.

When once we have a bit of a dog-bone kind of shape, nicely symmetrical, it's time to anneal and prepare for the next step.

Flatten the middle part (which will become the back of the shank) one way, and the ends at a right angle to that. Boy-o-boy do we need pictures for this. In this case, as in almost all the rings I make, there will be a squared shank. It makes the forging a bit more challenging, but hey, nobody said this was going to be easy.

With repeated forging and annealing, the blank will become long enough to bend into a rough ring shape. It should be substantially too long at this point so that we have a lot of extra material for leverage because, by cracky we're going to need it.

Once again, repeated hammering and annealing will bring the blank around to a more ring-like configuration.

Sometimes it is easier to solder the ends together so that the forging process is more straightforward, but it often messes with the finishing process later. It is also easier to

introduce an irritating twist into the ring without noticing. Either way, flattening the ring out from time to time is crucial and will reduce the amount of heavy filing later.

The blank should now be fairly close to the correct size, but the passing section should be way too long. This is good, because we're going to cut it off so that the inner curve is consistent with the rest of the band. As you can see in the photo in the middle, it is impossible to get the very ends down flush with the mandrel.

The ring is indeed square at a point about halfway up the shoulder, but the transition is so smooth as to be magical.

At this point, the rest of the operation is fairly straightforward: The sides can be left straight and pierced as in the example at the beginning of the section, or a subtle curve, or

series of curves, can be introduced into the shape as in the three-stone collet-set ring shown at the end of the section. An important point here is to leave yourself a little bit of extra material at the ends if you intend to introduce any compound curves. Once again, it's necessary to have some mechanical advantage when bending near the end of a piece of material.

In the case of the collet-set ring, the collets themselves become a part of the structure of the ring, whereas the radiant-cut design at the beginning of the section has a reinforcement bar installed under the stone for strength.

This is a very adaptable basis for a great many rings. It can be done in a more asymmetrical style as well, which is easier in some ways, but harder to visualize in the early going.

Truth be told, it's probably easier to carve a wax for these, but it's a good exercise in forging.

Hey, let's do some collets so that we can finish this puppy off.

<u>Collets</u>

Before we get into that, I suppose we should define exactly what a collet is. I go into it in the setting section a bit, but that's way elsewhere in the book, so it bears mentioning here.

The term bezel and collet are often used interchangeably, but not here, by cracky. A bezel is a ribbon of metal that is, in effect, wrapped around a stone and soldered. Then a support of some sort, called a bearing, is added to keep the stone from falling right through. This can be a wire soldered inside the bezel or the entire bezel can be soldered to a flat sheet of metal. A collet, contrariwise, is a thicker band of metal made up with an interior dimension slightly smaller than that of the stone. The bearing is then cut into the inside portion of the collet to support the stone. Each has its advantage in a given situation, but for now we'll stick with the collet.

At its simplest, a collet is a slightly tapered tube into which a gemstone is fitted and the metal compressed over the crown at the girdle, thus securing it for all time. It can be thin, forming a fine ring of material surrounding the stone, or a fat ol' doughnut of gold with the stone nestled within. It can be open on two sides, forming a half-bezel, or open on one side, although I don't have a specific name for such a thing at present. Perhaps a drive bezel, in honour of Circle Drive here in Saskatoon, which doesn't go all the way around the city. Stupid.

All in all, though, it's a very adaptable beast.

Here's how to make one.

This method begins with the premise that the job is much easier if you have a handle on things, so start off with a strip of material the height of the proposed collet plus a half-millimeter or so for finishing. Make the strip at least inch or two long, because the whole point of this exercise is to save time and not worry about a little extra gold. Besides, gold is recyclable in the extreme and, using this method, the scraps are mostly just that, whereas filing down a lumpy, crudely made collet is, indeed, wasteful.

The thickness of the collet will also be a factor, depending upon its function and desired appearance. For example, should it be the central section of a constructed ring, great strength is desirable as it is a structural part of the piece. For 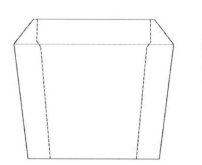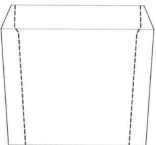 this reason, we would be inclined to make it rather heavy, with a sharply tapering inner core. This keeps it strong, but not too heavy-looking. If it will be soldered into a band, however, this excess weight is unnecessary, and so is the height. Convincing solder to flow all the way down the gap between a deep collet and a deep hole is difficult at best. Not to mention wasteful.

Occasionally, a doughnut effect is desired, such as that in a halo setting, and in this case 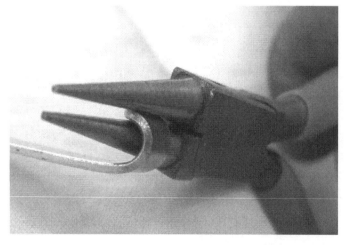 it is especially useful to do most of the shaping before soldering, as the stresses that build up in such a compact ring of material cause it to crack repeatedly. Better it should be more or less the correct shape to start off with. Of course, this isn't the case with oval collets, but them's entirely different critters.

So, all that having been said, take your strip, which is the correct thickness and height according to the aforementioned parameters, and, using round-nosed pliers, bend one end around to the radius of your stone. Keep close to the end, but don't kill yourself. You will see that the pliers have left an ugly dent in the gold. Don't worry about it: just bend it around so the dented end is past parallel to the rest of the strip: we're going to cut it off anyway.

Do so. Saw it off more or less perpendicular to the strip. Now we bend the other end, careful not to crimp the good bit. What we're trying to do is use leverage to bend the material, not brute force. The problem with brute force is that it tends to mar the object of such force, especially if the object is clamped in pliers.) Make this bend quite close to the other curve. A certain amount of brute force does come into it. A lot of problems are caused by making the collet too thick, but I like them hefty, so I'm stuck with it.

What you're shooting for is an open, roughly oval shape, so cut the strip, once again more or less perpendicular to the bar. Actually, the cut is on the radius line, pointing to the center of the curve, but that just seems so technical and approximately impossible to achieve in the real world.

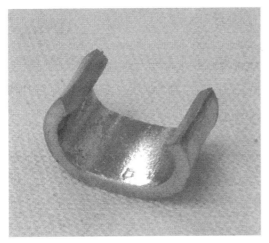

Speaking of technical, we need to do some serious skullwork at this point; actually, just at the point before we cut it off. The final shape should be two curves, with a radius equal to the stone's, and separated by a short, flat section. What we need to do is saw it off leaving a gap equal to the length of the flat bit. This simple equation means that when we close this oval, the ends will meet perfectly. Good luck. Look at the pictures carefully and it may become clearer. They're pretty good pictures.

No guts, no glory, though, and it's time to close the circle. Granted, we aren't going to make it into a circle just yet. The springiness of the metal means that it isn't quite possible to simply squeeze the circle shut. What you have to do is use the qualities of the metal to achieve the result.

I don't know what that means, so let's try this: squeeze the collet shut while holding it with your round-nose pliers opposite the gap to keep it from flying across the room. You'll notice that it won't close completely because of the residual woing in the material. So squeeze it just past round, sort of oval-like, and prepare to do some magic. Moving the round-nose pliers around to one side, gently squeeze one side back to round; then reverse the process.

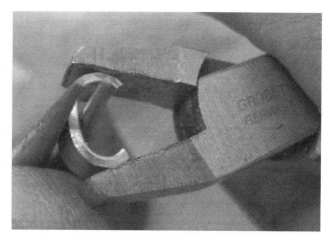

Should the size turn out to be wrong, no surprise. Simply cut out a little material. Just remember that cutting a millimeter out of the circumference only reduces the diameter by about a third of a millimeter. What you're looking for is something that, when it's tapped round after soldering, has an inside diameter just a hair smaller that of the stone so that the process of rounding it up and tapering it will yield the exactly perfect size.

So solder it, already. Use the hardest solder practical so that it's nice and strong and the joint won't show up later.

For rounding it up and introducing the slight taper we so love, I've found that a nail-set is just the ticket. A nail-set is a low-end carpentry tool that can usually be had for a couple of bucks for a set of three. Hell, sometimes they throw in a center-punch to sweeten the deal. I find that the bezel mandrels sold for use in the industry aren't tapered enough for my purposes and besides, I like to hammer the end to stretch it and that's tough to do with a commercial mandrel.

One indispensable item in the collet-making game is a bench block with holes in it. What this little gem is actually called varies from catalogue to catalogue, so I'll just show you a picture. It comes in handy for a million uses, so picking one up is mandatory.

Fit the soldered and pickled collet onto this ersatz mandrel, placed over a hole that allows some clearance (you don't want to get the punch jammed into one of the holes, trust me) and smacked smartly. Turn the mandrel as you do so to equalize the stresses on the collet and ensure that it's going on straight. If you've done the previous fitting accurately, it shouldn't take too much hammering. If it's a bit out of round, then it can be hammered on the block to fit it tightly against the mandrel. Knock it off the punch and check its size against the stone. The stone should just drop into the collet and be supported all the way around.

If you need two matching collets, for a pair of earrings for example, then make the initial bar twice as wide and taper it evenly from both ends. Mark the mandrel with a Sharpie or something to ensure that the holes at each end are exactly equal. Then it can be finished as one piece before separating them. Saves a little time.

File the collet's top and bottom flat and parallel, checking to see that it's straight and even. (Best to make sure early on, as it will cause major headaches later if it isn't) Fit it back onto the punch and secure it with a judicious whack. Now it's a simple matter to roll-file it smooth and, at the same time correct the taper; for example, to make the taper match the bur that will be used to fit the collet into the piece.

All this having been said, the design of the piece will dictate the exact shape of the collet: whether it be a free-standing setting like an earring or pendant; or fitted into a hole in a band; or possibly cut out in some way as with the antique head coming up later in the book. If it is to be an actual structural part of a ring, it will have to be heavy enough so as not to be distorted by normal wear. Keep the process simple and the simple collets will be dead easy, while the more complex ones will be easier than would otherwise be the case.

Antique Head

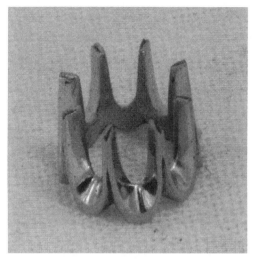

These things are exceedingly cool from a fool-the-eye standpoint, in that it isn't immediately obvious how the hell they are put together. I love that. I originally thought that, perhaps, some bozo built a bunch of perfect scallopy kind of U-shaped thingies, and by some form of magic, got them all to stick together without collapsing.

This, of course, is not the case. In keeping with my basic premise of reducing the number of components in a particular piece, there is an easy way to accomplish an apparent miracle without losing your mind. Skull-work, don't you know.

The tools used in this operation can be as simple or as complex as you like, but, wherever possible, I tend to favour the simple, gizmo-free method. Like, do you have the time to make it in the fussy manner I describe here, or is it necessary to get it done for the end of the working day? I'll try to touch on both as we proceed, but it's generally best to do it the hard way before starting down the slippery slope of technological dependence.

Basically, we're going to start off with a big ol' collet. It's not necessary to taper it too much as this diminishes the effect of the final piece. Make certain that it's perfectly straight and round and everything, even going as far as to fine-sandpaper it, sharpening up the edges and giving us a clear view of the surface.

We'll start off with a 4-claw head, since it's a little more forgiving in the early stages. Mark the upper end of the collet, the bigger end with four scrupulously even lines. Establish them well, once you've ensured that they are indeed well-spaced, as they will provide guidance throughout the operation. (Use the method described in the Wire Head section.) I like to cut them in with an X-acto knife or knife graver to provide a deep, well-defined line. This method also allows you to make the lines straight across, removing further doubt.

Establish some vertical lines from these to the bottom of the collet to make sure that your claws will be just so. A line parallel to the bottom, and about a quarter of the way up will establish the lower limit of your first cuts. Check your work carefully before proceeding; it's best to find out now if something's wonky.

Using a fine saw-blade and all the skills at your disposal, remove a U-shaped bit from between your guidelines. These cuts should be started parallel to your upper guidelines and, working your way around to ensure even progress, gradually angled down so that the cuts don't extend too low on the opposite side. This doesn't make much sense in print, but the first time you try to cut the "U"s in pairs, straight across, you'll find out that it doesn't work. You will end up with impossible-to-remove grooves in the inner areas of your claws and it will serve you right. In an ideal world, it should be possible to cut these across so that they are the correct shape right off, but I don't live in such a world and neither do you.

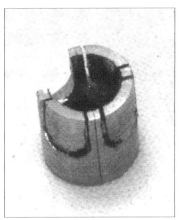

Wrongolini

As far as the final shaping and finishing of the claws, it's primarily a matter of staying flexible. The exact shape of the claws will be determined by their number and angle. Just remember to finish them up so that the sides of each individual claw are parallel, yielding a square or rectangular cross-section, not a totally useless triangle as shown here.

You'll notice, however, that this particular setting has five claws, which is kind of cool. You can use any number you like, within reason, to achieve the desired effect. Granted, an odd number of claws will tend to complicate the parallel finishing thing, but that's part of the fun.

Now, it's just a matter of cleaning up between the spaces so that they achieve that lovely parabolic shape of which I am so fond. This is done with files and sandpaper at first as these are easiest to control, but slow. Later, various burs may be used with discretion to speed things up a bit, but for now, we'll keep it simple. Take the time to make sure that these gaps, and the claws that they form, are symmetrical seven ways from Sunday and are delicate enough at the top without being spindly. What you have here is sort of a heavy, hand-made version of a commercial low-base or belly head, but now it's time to turn it into a work of art.

Take one final look at the upper zone of the head to be absolutely certain that it's straight and that your guidelines are still in place, 'cause we're not going to touch them anymore 'til we polish. Since this is a four-claw head, it is convenient to use a pin-vise to hold it while doing the next few steps. If it has a different number of claws, a small shellac stick is the way to go.

Using a square file, attack the base of the setting at the guidelines, gradually deepening the cuts and angling them out until they almost meet. Keep them even, and you will see where we're going. By feathering the cuts down and out along the guidelines, we are creating the illusion of four perfect, parabolic "U"s joined at the top.

Keep removing material in an organized manner until you have the nice, delicate effect you desire. You can tidy the cuts up with a square or triangular graver, but be careful not to extend the cuts too far up the claws, lest you give the impression that the claws are separated at the top. In some cases, this can be a desirable look, but for now, we'll keep it clean.

Incidentally, this is a neat way to fancy up a commercial low-base or belly head. They're so boring, otherwise.

By playing around with the proportion and depth of cut, and by using different numbers of claws we can create many different effects using this method.

Should you want more of a tulip or tiffany shaped head with a sharper taper, for example, it's necessary to start off with a fairly tight collet, separate the claws, and then stretch it out to the appropriate angle. Attempting to form a thick collet at such an angle will cause you no end of grief, so don't try. It

is vitally important, however, to ensure that the rough claws, and the openings between them, be absolutely the same thickness and length in order that they open up accurately. Any tiny inconsistencies will be exacerbated by the process, so it's best to make absolutely certain early on. Remember, it's easier to keep than it is to get back. God, I'm starting to irritate myself.

Once it's opened up and checked scrupulously for symmetry, the finishing process can begin. Since we so carefully marked the centerline of each claw on the outside of the collet, it will be a simple matter to take each down to the appropriate thickness, all the while maintaining perfect balance.

Truth be told, the shaping methods vary as widely as the style of the setting. One of your various needle files will have the correct curve and certainly the barrette file will help the process of getting the upper sections nice and parallel. Various burs and abrasives, used in moderation, make finishing the bases of the curves sweet and consistent. Be careful with burs, though: trying to get the sides of the claws flat with a small round thing is virtually impossible. You will end up with irritating waviness that will not go away.

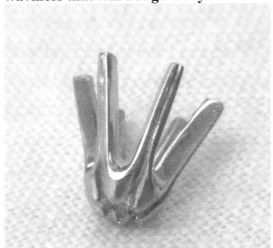

As with the standard antique head, make sure that the tops of the claws are perfectly finished before doing the scallopy bits at the base. Keeping things crisp at each step of the operation is most crucial; if it starts to look sloppy early on, it'll never look right.

Oddly Shaped Collets

I know, I know, the title is cumbersome as hell, but it's a working title, okay?

With the increased popularity of fancy-cut stones comes a quandary; how do we create bezels and collets for the goofier shaped stones that we have access to?

Having delved into the subject of round collets, the next logical step, in terms of popularity, would be ovals. I have not had a lot of luck using commercial bezel mandrels for constructing oval collets, primarily because they tend to be too big for most of the stones I regularly deal with. The other problem is that, when precious gems are cut, the primary concern for the cutter is often conservation of weight, not formation of a perfectly calibrated oval. This means that the standard oval mandrel seldom, if ever conforms to the exact shape of a given stone.

With all this in mind, what I generally end up doing is making a rough collet by bending the material to conform as closely as possible to the shape of the stone, soldering it, then rounding it up on a tapered *round* mandrel. Once it is nicely round, it is a simple matter, after annealing, to squeeze it back into a uniform oval using pliers, adjusting the shape to suit. This seems to be a profound waste of time at first glance, but it actually results in a much more uniform curve. In addition, the collet (or bezel) is already tapered and ready for bearing cutting.

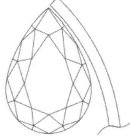

The next most common fancy is the pearshape. The important point to remember when we make a collet for one of these is to start the curving process with ample excess material to provide leverage, and then cut it to length. Remember that it's always easiest to achieve an accurate curve when there is a bit of extra material to provide leverage. There are two schools of thought on the actual shaping process.

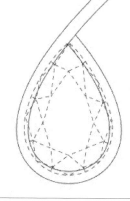

Giving the entire bar a slight curve before starting the actual bend will make the rest of the operation a bit easier.

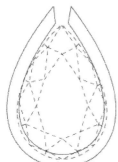

Starting at the point of the stone and bending the bar around until it reaches its own end seems to be the simplest, but the position of the solder joint is, to me, problematic. Add to this the built-in asymmetry, and I don't like it. That being said, it is simpler, and therefore quicker, so it's good to have as an option. My preference, which is, of course, the fussier of the two, results in a symmetrical bend and a concealed joint.

Having established the initial curve, the whole piece is bent in the middle around some round-nose pliers, and the two ends trimmed and filed to fit, closing it up as you go. A substantial amount of cutting and fitting is necessary, but that is the case no matter what, so it's best to plan ahead.

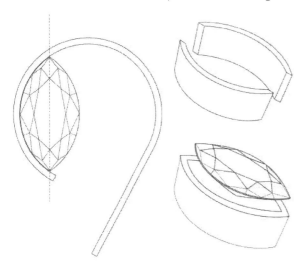

The construction of marquise collets is quite simple compared to the pearshape, in that it's made up of two identical sides, so that symmetry is assured as long as everything proceeds according to plan.

Start by bending the bar to the same radius as the stone, leaving ample material for both halves and a little excess for leverage. Finish the two sides so that the stone just about drops in and the sides match up perfectly and you have a collet.

Triangular or trillion stones are getting quite a bit of attention recently, so they bear mentioning. Notice how logically I'm approaching this subject? No pointy bits, one point, two points, now three points. Cool, huh? I just do this self-referential stuff to drive my editor crazy.

These stones, ideally, are cut so that the arc of each side is centered on the opposite corner. Check it out; it makes for a very pleasing shape. If they make a mandrel for trillions, this is the pattern upon which it will be based. That being said, there are a million variations on the shape which render the mandrel useless, so we may as

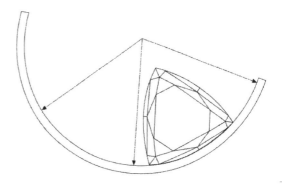

well start from scratch and save the twenty bucks on the mandrel.

Once again, start off with enough material to ensure an accurate curve, a curve which matches more or less exactly the arc of the sides of the trillion. Near one end, cut a notch with a square file or graver about two-thirds of the way through the metal. This will allow you to bend the metal to match the angle of one corner of the stone. Solder this point once it's perfectly fitted and step back and think about what comes next.

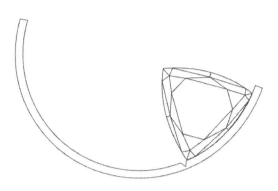

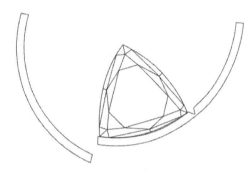

If you made the notch too close to the end, tough darts, start over. If it's okay, you can cut the long end to the same length and end up with an equilateral triangle. Basic geometry. It's probably not the right size right now because we didn't measure anything, but there's ample extra to play with. Using the stone as a reference cut the sides to equal lengths appropriate to allow the stone to drop in. This is easy to check because the two parts can be held together during the process.

If you're feeling real confident, you can save a step by notching the bar in two spots and bending it around. The fitting's a bit fussier, but one external solder line can be eliminated in this way.

Cushion- or antique-shape stones are fitted using a variation of this idea, but making the bezel double height, then sawing it in half, can save time. This ensures that the two halves of the bezel are exactly the same, just remember to flip one or you'll end up with some sort of weird rhomboid thing.

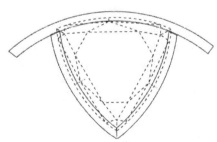

Mostly what I'm advocating here is an imaginative approach to building these things. The simple concept of bending a ribbon of material around the stone and soldering it doesn't hold up once you've left the basement and decided to do this for a living.

For example, the intellectual exercise of computing the exact length and angles necessary to create a bezel for an emerald-cut stone is best left to the hobbyist or prison inmate. Even with perfect technique, enough inconsistencies creep in to render the finished product a pale imitation of the shining concept. I've been known to use a heavy sheet of metal, pierce out the hole for the stone and, using a graver, fit the stone perfectly. Then, once it's sitting pretty, I cut out the bezel and finish it up to the appropriate thickness. Granted, this only works for fairly small stones, but it has the advantage of yielding a one-piece setting. It won't work with emerald-cut emeralds, but nothing works with emeralds. I know I shouldn't.

This is an example of a little one-piece string of box settings for some very scary princess cut emeralds. One's first idea would be to build five perfect platinum boxes, figure out some way to hold them together for soldering, and solder them together at the perfect angles. I could probably do it that way, but I have better things to do with my time. Limiting the number of components in a given piece is a topic that I keep returning to because not doing so has given me some of the biggest headaches of my life.

Once again, what I'm advocating is an imaginative approach to the construction of various heads and settings. Using some extra material to ensure accurate bending and forming is always important. Putting components together with the hardest solder

practicable to avoid future problems is also advisable. There's nothing worse than solder lines reappearing at inopportune moments.

What I find a lot in this business is a tendency to cut things just a bit too fine. Now I understand that it's a fussy old business that is primarily concerned with precious metals, but my problem is time. In a great many cases, a ton of time can be saved by simply using a little more gold. This stuff is eminently recyclable, after all, so if you make up an extra bit of wire or bar, for example, it can be reused later, either as it is, or melted down into some other form. Unlike gold, wasted time cannot be melted down and reused.

Marquise Head

Once we've figured out how to build a marquise collet, we're halfway to making the more complex style of head, based on the split box setting. (There's always a ton of crossover in techniques, which I'm hoping excuses the scatter-gun approach that I tend to take to the various processes.)

As usual, we're going to start off with a strip of material wide enough for the projected depth of our underbezel. This will be a little thicker than that used in the collet we made before, and will be bent so that the outer radius of the curve matches that of the stone. Make enough for both sides, of course.

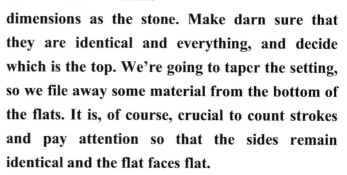

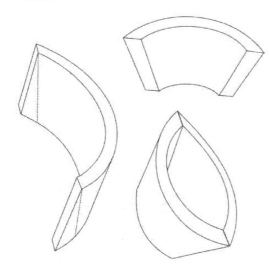

File the ends flat so that they fit together perfectly and are the same dimensions as the stone. Make darn sure that they are identical and everything, and decide which is the top. We're going to taper the setting, so we file away some material from the bottom of the flats. It is, of course, crucial to count strokes and pay attention so that the sides remain identical and the flat faces flat.

Clean up both sides and remove any burrs left from filing, and solder them together. Hard solder, of course. Then file the top of the assembly flat, to eliminate the peak formed by the angle we've filed into the two sides. This also reduces the size of what is now a lovely underbezel for our marquise. The little dotted lines show the placement of our V-claws. "What the hell are V-claws?" you may well ask. They'll come into use in pretty much any pointy-stone setting, so let's go.

Start off with a bar about .5mm x 3.0mm, straight, flat, and perfectly parallel, and long enough for the projected height of the setting. Make enough for the job at hand, and then some, because we need a little bit of extra length during the process.

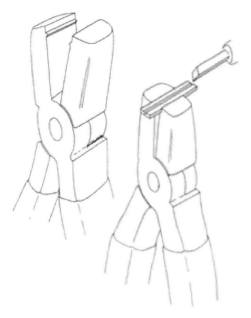

Holding this sort of long, parallel piece is always a puzzle, so I've modified a pair of cheap pliers to provide a notched platform which works quite well. It also comes in handy for holding onto those slippery little marquise sides while filing.

What you want is to cut a groove down the middle of the strip so that it will bend easily and accurately to form a right angle. The groove should be about 2/3 of the way through the bar, and at least 90°. In the course of making a lot of these things, you will discover that a 90° angle in the strip does not necessarily translate into a 90° angle in the bar. This is because the slot does not close perfectly, no matter how carefully

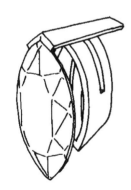

you've cut it. Just the way it is, sorry.

This is okay, though, for our purposes here. The angle on the end of a marquise is not quite 90°, so we're laughin'. When working on princess cut stones, we'll need right angles, but that's for another day.

We could simply solder this onto the end of the tapered underbezel, but that tends to yield a very heavy looking head. No style points for that. So what we do instead is to saw a groove through the underbezel halfway between the top and bottom, or wherever it looks right, then solder on one of the claws, of course taking all the necessary precautions to avoid fireskin and checking for fit. Remember, we're using hard solder here, so the joint is, in effect, permanent.

Clean up, open the slot in the underbezel the rest of the way, and affix the second end, and you're done. Don't use too much solder, so it'll be a snap to clean up. Don't try too hard to convince the solder to flow (there's always time to reflow).

This particular style of head is a little frustrating, at first, because of the angles. It takes a bit of practice and skull-work to make the underbezel the correct size to place the stone at the correct height. Just take your time with the fitting and visualize as you go. It's a major part of our business, this visualization thing.

Looks a little rugged, don't it? That's because some bozo didn't borax it up well enough. Probably in some sort of hurry.

This ring is an example of the use of the split-box marquise head, adapted to pearshape stones. The only difference being that the underbezel is, naturally enough, pear-shaped. The side stone end pieces are integral with the underbezel. That is, in order to minimize the number of components, I made more of a collet for each stone, then cut off the excess and added a "V" tip. I suppose that I could have eliminated the V-tip as well, but then the underbezel would have been visible from the top. I don't know, I just make this stuff up as I go.

Bezels

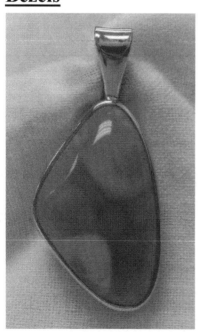

A bezel is like a collet, only different.

Whereas collets are primarily used to set round, faceted stones, and not very large ones at that, bezels come in handy when we bang up against the weird-shaped or huge ones. Cabochon stones, for example, are usually really tough to set into a collet with any success so, unless it's fairly tiny, it's best to go with the bezel.

To build a bezel, we start off with a strip of material as wide as the projected height of the bezel, if that's not too obvious. Bezels needn't be as thick as collets as they won't be supporting the stone but simply holding it in place. Many goldsmiths err in that they figure that a thin bezel will be easier to fold over the stone. This would be true if we were, in fact, folding the metal, and if the gold would just stay folded.

What happens to gold when you attempt to fold it inwards over a stone is that it compresses. This stands to reason if you think about it: the top of the bezel is being forced to assume a smaller circumference, so it must, perforce, become either thicker or taller. Meanwhile, it's also getting harder and stiffer due to the same compression. What happens then is that the material gets springier and springier the more we try to smash it down against the stone until the stone breaks and it just doesn't matter anymore.

Better we should use the characteristics of the metal to our advantage. This starts with avoiding false economies. Make the bezel thick enough to begin with and it will all go much easier. This is because we can taper the overly-thick metal towards the top of the bezel, so that the setting pressure will be applied more to the metal than the much more fragile stone.

How thick that is, of course, depends on a great many factors. If the top of the stone is a fairly tight curve, then you can get away with a thinner bezel as it only needs to be compressed a little to meet the surface of the stone accurately. If, however, it's a high-crowned cabochon, the metal needs to be compressed a fair bit to get it to the point where it contacts the surface. For this type of stone, it's also important to keep the height to a minimum so as to lessen the effect of that compression. If the bezel is properly fitted, not a lot of metal needs to be moved over the stone. Most of this will be covered in the setting section if I ever get around to it. Read the chapter on collet-setting in the meantime. It relates.

Making a bezel is somewhat more complicated task than making a collet, in that it requires more fitting and soldering. However, most of the complexity stems from the fact that you're usually not dealing with a small, round stone as you often are with collets.

In any case, the steps, broken down into logical bits are a lot easier to manage. This is why the bezel is the first choice for cheap, basement jewellery; it just seems so simple.

Me, myself, I like to complicate things early on so as to make it simpler down the road.

Since bezels really come into their own when it comes time to set a funny-shaped stone, why don't we start with a free-form opal? This particular stone is treacherous in so many ways that it's not even funny. The shape  is unusual but nothing special; the girdle is where the real fun begins. At the tip it is so thin as to be non-existent, whereas the rest meanders up and down, thick and thin all the way around. This situation requires special attention, but first we'll make the bezel.

Bending the bar should begin somewhere logical, in this case at the bottom or at the top. Once again it's important to start intelligently and not screw up the first step. Start bending the bar close to the end, matching the radius of the stone, and then cut it off. This means that you are using leverage to achieve the proper radius at the end, but immediately eliminating the area that is marred by being squeezed in the round-nose pliers. At the end of this process you'll be matching that radius, but for now, work your way around, fitting the curves as you go. That way if, all of a sudden things don't fit, it's something that happened in the last couple of millimeters and you needn't go back to the beginning.

Carry on this way all the way around and voila, the stone, she fits. That last little curve is crucial, so get it right before cutting it off. Oh, I grant you that there will be some tweaking later, but for now it's important to make certain that the outline is right before soldering.

Sooner or later you have to commit to it, so solder it with the hardest solder you dare. Make sure that the whole piece is annealed completely to remove all stresses because they'll be back to haunt you soon enough.

If the bezel is flat enough, file a nice flat on top to make it easier to visualize the next steps. If not, carefully whack it flat on a steel block, and then anneal it again. Then file it flat. This makes it much easier to visualize the crucial final tweaking.

You will notice that I tend to go on and on about the annealing thing. This is because it's important. The stresses build up in the metal with all the bending and whacking and we want to keep the process as predictable as possible to avoid things getting out of hand; changing one area of a closed curve such as we have here will affect other areas.

Using bending pliers and half-round pliers, tweak the bezel this way and that until it's the exact shape of the stone. In the case of this tapered bezel, we want the stone to just start dropping in, whereas with a standard, non-tapering one it will be desirable to have the stone drop right in with almost no space left over. Looking through the bezel at a light source will allow you to easily determine where, exactly, the stone is hung up. Do some filing as the last step, but only as the very last step, because if you start filing away at it, it won't be a consistent thickness throughout and will cause no end of difficulties.

Once the stone is perfectly fitted, it's time to make a bearing. In the normal course of events, we would bend a piece of wire to the exact shape of the inside of the bezel. It is important that it fit well because we're going to solder it in and spaces are bad. Irregularly shaped stones need to have a bearing that follows the curvature of the girdle of the stone. (I spent a goodly proportion of my early career making perfectly fitted bearings for perfectly awful shell cameos and the like, but it was good practice.

Of course, every opal is an exception, and in some cases an otherwise poor quality opal can be vastly improved by using a closed back and covering the inside with black or dark blue enamel. The opal shown here was a fairly transparent, unremarkable jelly opal with a little bit of colour play. Having been properly foiled (for indeed, that is what the process is called) it became a beautiful stone. The back also presented a nice plain surface upon which to engrave some classy initials.

I know I told you to file the top of the bezel flat, but that was before. This is now. Now we need to match the height of the bezel with the topography of the stone. Life's like that.

What we're looking for here is a bezel that's about a half to three-quarters of a millimeter above the edge of the stone. If it ain't a flat stone, it ain't gonna be a flat bezel. Should we attempt to fold a great deal of material over the stone, it will inevitably build up or fold and cause wrinkles and ripples that will be impossible to remove in the finishing process. Or they'll cause so much pressure that they crack the stone. In which case, it doesn't matter.

One way to avoid this problem is by relieving the top of the bezel. This is simply filing a bevel on the top of the bezel. Bevelbezelbevelbezel. Stick with me, here. The angle of the bevel depends upon the material used, the thickness of the material in relation to the stone, whether it's a sharp curve or long straight section. All kinds of complications.

Setting is not a process conducive to print instruction, since every stone and every setting is different, but if you refer to the opening section of the setting section, some of the basic principles will be laid out there. The main point to remember is that the metal responds better to compression than to bending in cases like this. Gold is very malleable but when it's worked it does get quite springy and intractable, so the minimum amount of material should be dealt with at any given time. Rather than starting at one point on the stone and working your way around, compressing as you go, it is best to start out at two opposite points, locking the stone in place, then halving that distance at opposite points, then quartering and like that. This way, the metal won't build up in a breaking wave all around the stone and cause one big monster of a gap when you get back to the start. There's also the chance that the stone will be forced off level, but the quartering idea sort of alleviates this difficulty.

One technique that I picked up from the raising process in silversmithing is to move the metal over the stone in progressive divisions; quartering, eightthing, sixteenthing, and like that. At some point in this process, you will end up pushing down on the top of a wrinkle a little wider than your pusher. This is good. Straightening out a curve in this way compresses the metal in a controlled manner, moving it outward along the radius of the stone rather than forcing it in over the crown. This is very hard to visualize, so I'll try a series of pictures when I get around to it.

Often it will be necessary to file away a bit of metal to alleviate the inevitable buildup that occurs. Make sure that the bezel remains a consistent thickness all around before doing any filing or you will cause yourself no end of grief. Most of the problems that arise during bezel-setting are the result of the bezel being inconsistent in thickness or height.

The final round of compression takes place almost parallel to the crown of the stone, in effect pushing the material down and outwards. This serves to force the last little bit of material tight to the stone. If you were to attempt to push the gold directly down towards the crown of the stone, you would come to a sorry end because, in order to make the gold come to rest in a given position, it is necessary to force it beyond that position so that it will spring back to the desired position. This would mean forcing it past the surface of the stone, which is not going to yield. It will break. Better we should use the compressive

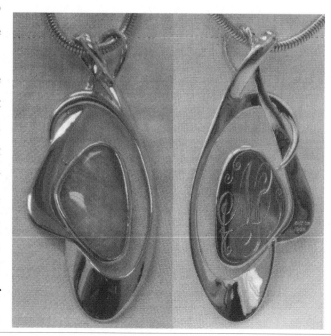

tendencies of the material to cause it to thicken downwards onto the crown. Like I said, hard to visualize.

Finishing is fussy work and is made more difficult by far if the process is not carried out consistently throughout as those nasty wrinkles and ripples only get worse. It's best if you can use the pusher to shape the material as much as possible before starting to remove material. Take your time and gradually eliminate the bumps and ridges until the whole thing is perfectly lovely. Good luck. I still kind of suck at this part because I am so reluctant to remove too much material. Use all the tricks at hand, gravers, rubber abrasive wheels, and tiny shreds of sandpaper, whatever it takes. Just remember that the chances are that this stone is far softer than the grit in sandpaper. Hell, it's probably softer than a good graver, so be careful.

At some point it will be necessary to commit to polishing the thing. Try not to over-polish to remove inconsistencies, as this just makes it worse. Most of the important finishing should be done at the bench. Once again, good luck. As mentioned earlier, I kind of suck at these things. So why, you may ask, am I writing this? Good question.

Wing Ring

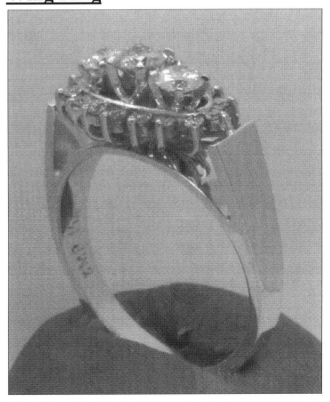

Never mind why we call it a wing ring. We just do.

The first time neophyte goldsmiths see a wing ring, they figure that the shoulders are added to a band. They just can't for the life of them... Okay, it was me. I couldn't figure it out. How do you balance the shoulder plates on the outside of the band while you solder? Never mind the fitting. Filing a perfect arc on the inside of the flat plate is impossible. I did try filing a notch in the band so that the plate would sit in place long enough to solder, but there was always that irritating solder line on the outside of the shank.

A commercial mount gave me enough information to go on, and the rest is history. It's a very adaptable concept and innumerable variations are possible, but we'll keep it simple for now; a flat untapered mount for a quarter carat diamond. I've made a hundred of them....no two identical (unless they were supposed to be), but all based on the same techniques.

Start off with a bar of gold just over four millimeters wide and about a millimeter and a quarter thick. Don't be stingy. Check it for straight and unflawed and anneal it. Don't worry about fireskin right now; it will actually help in the layout process.

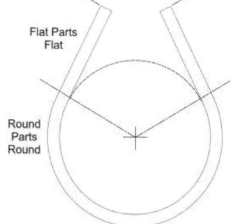

Flat Parts
Flat

Round
Parts
Round

Start bending the bar about 10mm from the end and keep bending 'til the end almost touches the bar. Cut it off there and reserve the rest of the bar. It should be at least close to a size six, so's to avoid dicking around later.

We weren't too concerned with the ends before, but we will attend to them now.

By adjusting the bend, determine an appropriate height for the shoulders. All this should be clear in your head based on the style of the setting and basic design needs.

Now, cut the ends off accurately and check everything again. Make certain that the blank lays flat on your steel block and that the sides are at perfect right angles to it. Check to ensure that the ends are absolutely parallel to one another and perpendicular to the block. I use the end of my steel ruler as a square for checking this sort of thing. Seven ways from Sunday is the byword. Remember that mistakes never get smaller, only bigger. So if you make it perfect now, it won't be a problem later.

The distance between the shoulders should be about four millimeters, that being the approximate diameter of a quarter carat.

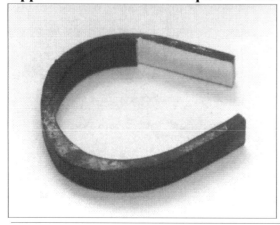

We have to extend the flat, inner surface of the shoulder to create a nice consistent surface for fitting. If the shoulder is as flat as it is supposed to be, then we can simply extend the line inwards until we create a notch about a third of the way into the shank. The length of each shoulder is identical, so the notches will extend equal amounts into the ring. Best we should check, though. While you're at it, mark this distance on the outside of the shank to ease the process of measuring the underbezel. The notches should be perfectly flat and square, of course. And equal, don't forget equal.

Slide the outer unit onto a mandrel and give it one last check. Slide the extra bit down the mandrel next to it and line up one end next to the mark on the shoulder. Mark the other point and cut it off there.

Now you can see more or less what we're shooting for.

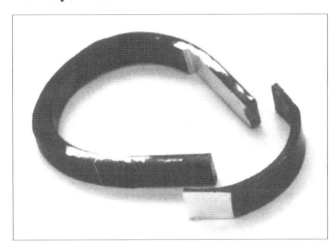

So now you take the bit of gold left over from the shank, and bend it to a size six arc and tidy up the end. Which end, I don't know. Just wing it, stud. This thing will be the underbezel, or at least that's what I call it. It will fit inside the shoulders as a support for whatever setting we decide to use for our stone.

Cut off the underbezel to the required length and clean up the ends to perfect right angles. What you need to do now is simply file flats where necessary to allow the underbezel to snap into place. Now remember, the outer piece is perfect, so we aren't messing with it at all. If the underbezel manages to get buggered up, we can easily make a new one and not be out too much time.

By alternately filing and fitting, the piece will soon be nestled into place and ready for soldering. If there is a bit of overhang, as shown above, it'll be removed afterwards. Right now, though, the fit's the thing. There should be virtually no space between the flats, so solder will be able to flow evenly by capillary action. Give everything one final check and clean it to remove any traces of grease, dust, or filings that would inhibit solder flow.

The best way I've found to solder these things is to do one side at a time. No matter how little you've stressed the gold in the process of fitting, there will be a bit of residual tension in it. What happens then is that the two units give a little and your carefully fitted joint no longer fits. Being as how hard solder is being used, this can be catastrophic as the pieces become as one, aligned or not. Scary!

So, to avoid such pitfalls, we clamp the joint in place as shown.

Usually, I let the thing cool down once the first side is locked in place, just to make sure that nothing has shifted. Call me paranoid.

Don't try to be a hero and flow the solder perfectly if it doesn't appear so inclined, as this is the ideal time to set it aside in preparation for a reflow. Put it in the pickle overnight, and do something else. Maybe make a nice wire setting for your quarter-carat.

Next day, take the ring from the pickle and give it a good cleaning in the ultrasonic and

steam it well. Dip the ring in boric and set it afire. Heat the boric up until it foams up and then settles down a bit. It's best not to heat it right up to the point where it fuses, just yet, as this may cause oxidation where the boric has not yet reached. Let it cool, then apply another layer. If your boric is too thick, you will barely be able to see the ring at this point, so add some more alcohol to the mix to bring it to the consistency of milk, not cream, milk, maybe skim milk.

When it's cool again, apply a third coat and heat it up to the melting point of the solder. You will be amazed to see the solder flow perfectly into the joint with no ugly gaps. At least you will if the goldsmith gods are smiling. They do not reward inattention to detail.

One of the more confusing aspects of this little game is the difference between borax and boric acid. Borax is a flux, meaning that it promotes the flow of solder by inhibiting the formation of oxides in and around the joint. Boric acid, dissolved in alcohol, is applied to the surface of a piece, once again to inhibit oxidation, but it actually also inhibits the flow of solder. However, boric acid is used to its best advantage in the reflow. It protects the finished surfaces and allows the solder to flow freely within the joint by capillary action. It seems to be a bit counterintuitive that a solder stopper should act thus, but it does. Go figure.

The remainder of this project is just finishing, so we'll leave it here and, hey, maybe make a wire head to go into the ring. Chronological ordering of things is not my strong suit, since I generally have several things going on at once.

Wire Head

At its simplest, the wire head is an underbezel with a bunch of claws attached to it. At its most complex, it becomes a cluster setting, and a marvelous thing to behold.

For now, though, we'll begin at the beginning.

First, make a ring of wire just a hair smaller than the diameter of the stone. This can be of round or square wire, though I prefer square. I've seen a lot of this type of head made by mutts, and they are almost invariably of round wire, so I tend to be biased. Besides, square wire makes for a much cleaner look, and you can do tricks to make it even more impressive. More on that, later.

Now lay out four equidistant points on its diameter. You can do this in any number of ways using dividers or rulers, but the best way I've found is to place one tip of the dividers on the solder line and lightly scribe a couple of lines approximately 90° around the ring. Get it as close as possible. Now place the tip of the divider in the center of each of the marks thus made and scribe a mark another 90° around. If you were real accurate, then the two marks cross one another and you've found the exact opposite of the ring and, by doing so, you can mark the ring at perfect 90° increments. Even if you missed by a hair, you can fudge it a bit and get your marks absolutely even. Like everything else, it takes practice. Make sure that the final marks are indeed absolutely accurate or you will be mightily sorry later.

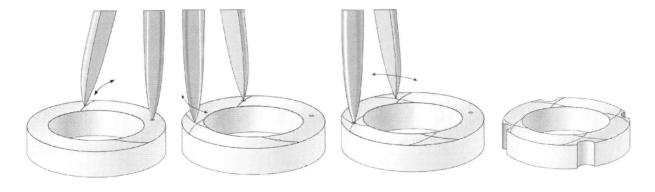

You will notch the ring at those four points. How you notch them will depend, of course, on whether you used round or square wire. If round, a small needle-file will do the trick. I like to use a diamond dental bur of the same diameter as the wire, but that's because I have one. It tends to wander a bit if you're not careful, so be careful. I have shown the grooves cut pretty much parallel with the side of the underbezel, but they should actually be cut at a slight angle inwards at the bottom. This is so that the groove will accurately line up with the wires we're about to make.

We'll be using round wire for the claws, so we may as well do that before we go any further. Cut two pieces of nice, straight wire a bit more than twice the length that you envision being necessary. It's always nice to have a little too much, rather than the alternative. You can always cut it shorter. Give each piece a sharp bend in the exact

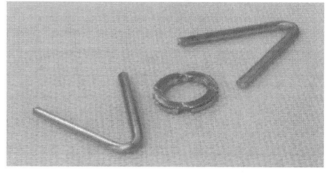

middle, forming a "V". The top of the "V" should be a little larger than the diameter of the stone.

For now, though, we're going to keep it simple. The fit isn't as important because the claws are made in pairs. Thus we balance the underbezel in the angle of the "V" that we made and solder it in. Of course it's in perfectly straight, right? I thought so. It may be necessary to adjust the angles of the grooves in the underbezel so that the surfaces line up for soldering.

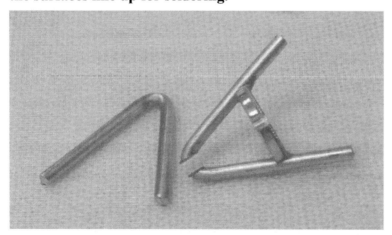

So now we just have to fit the other pair. This can be very simple if we don't care too much about the exact angle, but we do care, so we cut the base of the first pair so that the new "V" fits in. It's easy, trust me. I usually use a cut-off disc, as it's simpler to make the slot fit the second wire. First of all, make certain that the cut is perfectly centered, and then fit the new "V" in gradually. Use hard solder as there is precious little risk of melting it down there. Besides, we have to solder a post in if we want to do a good and proper job. Check the alignment of the claws and go ahead and solder the claws at the top.

Oh yeah, just a point about soldering these things. You don't want to be bothered with trying to boric up these little bastards, then scraping them where the solder goes. What we do instead is heat the individual units up a little and dunk them in borax. Repeat this as necessary 'til they're nicely coated. This will protect them from fireskin without stopping the solder from flowing. It's quick and effective. Just remember that I said borax, not boric, as boric (dissolved in alcohol) bursts into flames when you dip hot stuff into it. Embarrassing and dangerous.

Now that you've got the claws and underbezel put together as a unit, you can go ahead and add a post to the bottom. The post is necessary, in my opinion, because we want to avoid, at all costs, the dreaded "balancing act" when soldering it onto the ring. Just trust me on this. This is also an opportune moment to modify the height of the setting to suit.

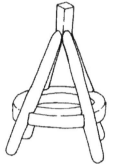

First, make sure that everything is lined up all hunky-dorily and symmetrical and then determine where the center of the setting is. This may seem simple, but if any step leading up to this has been fudged even a little, then the whole shootin' match is going to end up crooked. So check it carefully.

You can either drill the junction at the base to accept a post, or cut the junction out and snap in a square post. This latter is an option if the claws don't line up exactly, on account of you can cut and fudge a bit.

A square post is kind of nice because it allows the solder to flow freely if you're going to be applying solder from the inside of the ring and hoping that it will flow up to the base of the head. A round post is preferable if soldering the head isn't the very last step in your little construction job, as it is very unlikely to move in subsequent soldering operations.

Of course, this basic concept can be extended to oval settings or what have you, any number of claws (within reason), and any size stone. Simply make the underbezel the shape of the stone, only smaller. Claw positioning is fussier, but you'll figure it out. Just remember that if you can solder them on in pairs, it makes life a lot easier.

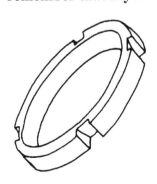

If you're making a head for a larger stone, it may be inconvenient, or just downright ugly to have the claws meet in the middle with a somewhat useless post dangling down. Therefore, we can use a double underbezel.

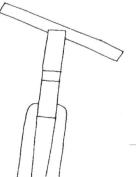

Now, the way I usually do this is to perform a balancing act wherein I cut the grooves in the underbezel and fit square claws individually. Then I make a smaller underbezel and solder it a suitable distance from the upper one. This distance will usually be about equal to the depth of the stone but will vary according to the desired appearance. I'm keeping this deliberately vague because the exact appearance will vary so much according to the shape, size, and proportions of the particular stone.

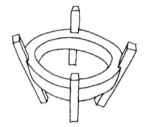

This method is easy if you're fastidious about fitting the claw to the slot so that you don't have to rely on a balancing act to get the claws in the correct position. Most of the time though, you'll end up poking the claws into position at huge risk to your mental health. Just be certain that they are lined up perfectly before you go to solder the underbezel on. This last should be done with the hardest solder you dare to use, as the setting will be put through the fire several times before you're done and you don't want to worry about the bastard falling apart.

The last thing to do, one which makes the setting process easier, is to bend the ends of the claws closer to parallel, or vertical, so that the claws aren't all splayed out where the stone will sit. The arrangement of the claws is covered in the claw-setting section, if you want to look it up

The trick is to avoid making the angle of the claws too steep as this makes for a weak setting. If the claws have to reach way out, almost parallel to the pavilion of the stone then there is no practical way to lay proper tips down. Never mind the fact that the claws tend to trap a lot of gunk against the pavilion, thereby affecting the beauty of the stone. And we are here to show off stones, after all. Some stones will fight you all the way, though. The transparent ones will be rendered ugly because the underbezel is visible, the badly cut ones will look crooked no matter how carefully you lay everything out, the emeralds will break… The emeralds always break.

There are myriad variations on this idea, so you get to be flexible. Just stick to some nice simple guidelines and the job will go easier, trust me.

Three Stone Head

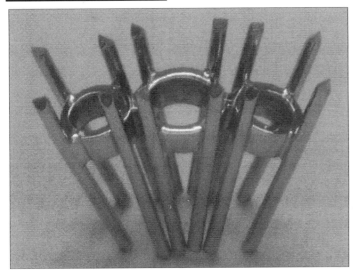

One of the main problems that we run into in the construction of wire heads and the like is that of the dreaded balancing act. How does one control the position of a multitude of claws in order to solder them? If there is ample space between pairs of claws, then each one may be positioned individually, most especially if the underbezel has been notched to accept said claws. It's not a perfect solution, but it is the one that seems to be the most intuitive, the first one to occur to most people. The concept of soldering the claws on in pairs is just a little twist on the balancing act, a little stability and symmetry built into the system.

Situations arise all the time where one-at-a-time soldering or even soldering in pairs is simply impossible. This is where investment soldering comes into its own.

Investment is a type of plaster of paris which has been formulated to withstand high temperatures. By using this stuff in crafty ways, miracles may be performed. I was introduced to the concept by Joe Parnoutsoukian (not Crazy Joe, the other one) back at Dunn's, and have since added some twists of my own.

Pay attention, now, 'cause it's weird at times, and always fussy as hell.

For this demonstration, we will construct a three-stone head for an anniversary ring. These are quite common and commercially available in many different sizes, but that doesn't concern us because we are manufacturing goldsmiths. Besides, the commercial heads are generally kind of crude, having been put together in a factory or, worse yet, cast. The cast ones are nice in that they are one-piece units and thus will not fall apart when soldered. Problem is; they are invariably so rough that finishing them takes an inordinate amount of time, or they have been polished by mass-tumbling, thereby rendering them shiny and all but useless. You will never have the correct size on hand, either, or the supplier will send you the wrong one the first couple tries, better you should learn the process. You can give a man a fish...

Starting with a piece of white gold plate about a millimeter and a half thick, lay out your stones so that they are touching and in a nice straight line. There is no need for an allowance between them, as we will be curving the plate later and this will provide ample clearance. Mark the center of each hole and drill out a hole about half the diameter of the stone. A small pilot hole may be used with a tapered bur to correct for any inconsistency in drilling, but whatever the method, ensure that the holes are exactly the same size and positioned accurately. This is the first step and the last place to be compromising.

Now cut out the area around the holes, leaving three little rings slightly smaller in diameter than the diamonds. Finish up the outside edges so that it looks like three perfect little rings welded together by God. Actually, three little rings could conceivably be constructed and soldered together to make an underbezel like this, but God himself couldn't make it look right. It's always best to limit the number of components when possible.

A narrow notch is cut into the underside of the junction between the rings so that it may be bent. The amount of bend that is introduced depends on the ring size, the stone size, the intended height of the head, and all kinds of things. It's important that you have an accurate picture in your head before starting a project like this, so just follow that. Usually, a curve that will be more or less concentric with the ring is good. Not too high, though, as the stones will actually sit a bit above the underbezel and we don't want it to look outlandish.

Make the notches deep enough so that the underbezel bends easily. We'll hard solder it after determining that it is bent perfectly, so strength needn't be an issue for now.

Clean up the gently angled underbezel and fine sandpaper it, but don't worry about polishing unless you're better at this that I am. Some fireskin is inevitable later in the process, but it's still important to have the piece as clean as possible to avoid problems later.

Make a bunch of wire about .75 mm. in diameter and, after the last annealing, pull it straight. This is done by clamping the end in the vise and giving the other end a tug. A little bit of a nudge is all it takes. Nudge is the only word I could come up with to describe the feeling of yanking wire straight. It's like a nudge, only inside out, or backwards. Try it; you'll know what I mean. If you give it more than a nudge, it'll break. That's how you know.

Fine sand the wire and cut it into equal pieces about nine m/m long. I'm kind of assuming quarter-carat stones here, because that seems to be the most common size that I run into. 8-10 mm. long will cover most situations.

Here I run into a bit of a quandary. I make most of these things in 14K white, and have gotten pretty good at it. Lately, however, I've been using platinum for the claws as it eliminates a number of the problems that plague an operation like this. It's also easier to set the stones in, and it wears like stink. What more can I say? The process is the same regardless.

The next technique involves the use of Rodico One-Touch®, a putty-like substance. Joe used plasticine, but it is oil-based, which caused some problems. So what I use is something called plasti-tac or Fun-tac or some variation thereon. Originally, I used Rodico One-Touch, which is used by watchmakers for cleaning up fingerprints and such from the innards of watches. It's blue and costs a mint and is identical to Plasti-tac in every way except that it is a watchmaker's tool and is priced appropriately. Well, maybe not appropriately. Just high.

What you do with this stuff is to flatten it out on one side by squashing it on your steel block or some such. This presents a smooth working surface upon which to build your cluster.

Place the underbezel on the plasti-tac and press it into place. There's no need to push it right into the stuff, just make sure it won't move. Of course, due to the curve that we've introduced into the underbezel, the putty has to be pre-shaped a bit, but this is a moment's work. There will be ample clean-up after the plaster sets, but a little care now will minimize it. I find a little pushed-in dimple in the middle works well.

Once the underbezel is in place, the claws are poked into place at the appropriate angle. Take your time on this step, as any extra time spent now on the preparatory work will be more than repaid later. The claws need to be in contact with the underbezel and perpendicular to it at the point of contact. Pictures help here. Some fudging is necessary on the inner claws, where the underbezel is bent, but it will make sense as you go. The example in the photos uses four claws for each stone, but a shared claw may also be used, if the size of the wire is increased appropriately. This actually works better if the center stone is larger than the side stones, more like an engagement ring, but this takes some different engineering. Later for that.

Just be sure that all the claws are in contact with the underbezel as solder becomes downright stubborn if you try to convince it to leap across gaps. It just won't, and that's that.

Let's see, now; perfect underbezel; claws perfectly aligned; good contact for soldering; yup, that's about it.

Here comes the part that makes me mental. The preparatory stuff becomes all the more important when all your work disappears into a dollop of cristobalite. That's investment, in case you were wondering.

I'm a stove-top kind of cook. I like to witness the process, keep an eye on things. This concept of putting something in the oven, setting the timer, and waiting just ain't in my world-view. I'm a peeker.

The claws have been positioned and checked and rechecked; now it's time to invest them. This is done by encasing the whole issue in plaster (investment). Because the investment is runny, however, we must confine it somehow.

My usual method is to take a piece of scotch tape about two inches long and turn it into a ring big enough to go around the claw/underbezel assembly with a bit of room to spare. Make certain that it is in contact with the plasti-tac all the way around so that your investment doesn't get all over the place.

Mix the investment up to about the consistency of cream, whipping or otherwise, and pour it into your little scotch tape tube. You don't need much, just enough to cover the sticky-up wires with about 5mm to spare. Notice how I switch effortlessly between metric and imperial. Irritating, huh?

Let the investment set for a half-hour or so and oh so carefully remove the plasti-tac. Don't pull it straight up and off as it may yank out your perfectly positioned wires. I generally kind of hold the plasti-tac at its outer edges and poke the setting out from below with my thumb. This bends the plasti-tac open from around the claws at the same time as it forces the assembly out. It works for me, what can I say?

Now you have a smooth layer of plaster with a bunch of little wires poking out. Only trouble is, the investment, being liquid, has insinuated itself into the gaps between the claws and the underbezel. This must be removed as it will impede the flow of solder.

The tip of an Exacto knife works slickly for this as it is very narrow and can remove the plaster without weakening the support that it offers. Be thorough, now, as we don't want this stuff coming back to haunt us. It's like flossing your teeth. No, more like having your teeth cleaned with one of those painful pointy things. And you're the dental hygenicist person. Except they're your teeth. Christ, I don't know. Just do a good job.

Cut away the excess investment from outside the working area, leaving enough for support and to protect the ends of the claws from the high temps that we're about to subject them to. Leave a nice smooth cookie of plaster that can be held, not too tightly, in a pair of good heat-proof tweezers. Cross-locking tweezers are quite necessary, as you don't want to have to concentrate on holding this thing while soldering. Some books I've read suggest wrapping the whole unit in iron binding wire to keep it from collapsing, but I haven't found this to be necessary. Try it, though, you may like it. Don't be afraid to experiment.

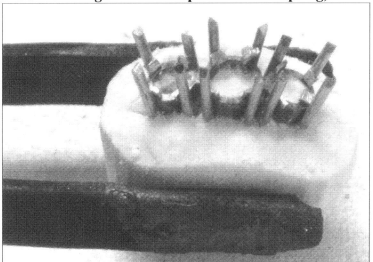

Once it's nice and clean, blow the crumbs and dust off and get ready to solder. Cut up a bunch of vanishingly small snippets of solder (white hard as we're going to be putting this puppy through the fire repeatedly) and mix up some borax. First of all, we must protect the surface of the gold to an extent, from fireskin. Heat up the little plaster cookie gradually with a soft flame and brush some borax onto the surface of the plaster and the exposed gold. Don't sweat it too much as some fireskin is inevitable and will be dealt with later. It's more of a superstitious thing with me. Just don't heat up the cookie too much first go, as your flux brush will stick and burn and we can't have that.

Apply the little bits of solder to the junctions between the claws and the underbezel. Make sure that there is ample borax in and around the joint, as the soldering process is very gradual, and we don't need any fireskin in there.

Holding this whole unit together during the soldering process is a bit of a challenge since the investment gets a bit fragile when put through the fire. I use a pair of old soldering tweezers that have been bent out to a nice curve that will hold the cookie without too much tension. The tweezers get pretty much buggered with the repeated heating required for investment soldering, so don't use your favorites.

Start heating the cookie gradually to allow the moisture to dissipate in a controlled manner, otherwise what you get is a little explosion and a lapful of hot plaster as the steam pressure blows the bottom off your cookie. This isn't always a disaster, but it is often enough to warrant some caution.

Heat the whole unit evenly from below 'til it's a cheery, scary red, and then move the flame around until everything is the same temp. If you rush the process and heat it too much from the bottom, what happens is that you actually melt the ends of your wires, even though they're encased in plaster. This is important, as the bases of your claws are in there. Once the whole issue is up to soldering temp, you should be pretty much beside yourself with anxiety. It is a tricky operation, so you should be. All at once though, the solder will flow exactly where it is supposed to and you can relax: Or not. Often the solder will crawl up the claw, if you haven't heated evenly enough, or the solder won't go anywhere at all because there wasn't enough borax, or you nuked the tops off all the claws. In the latter case, you're on your own, but a little solder can be convinced to go in the proper direction. Just remember that this puppy is HOT, so don't use your favorite solder brush to apply the extra solder as the pretty sable hairs will get all singed and curly looking.

Once the solder has flowed more or less as we wish, the cookie is allowed to cool and the plaster is quite easily chipped off. Pickle the whole issue overnight and take a look.

What you will probably notice is that it looks like shit. The high heat and insufficient borax has left the poor little thing all fireskin black and the solder hasn't flowed all the way through in some spots. This is just the way it goes with investment soldering; it's not pretty, but it's all we got.

The best bet for the latter problem is a reflow. Pickle it overnight, clean it up real well and steam it off. Boric it (notice I said Boric, not borax) and, once it's nicely glossed over, stick it into a charcoal block 'til the underbezel just clears the charcoal. Now that the claws are held steady you can carefully reheat the unit reflowing the solder just so. The excess solder will flow towards the heat and into the joints. We hope.

If the stars are in their proper alignment, it's done. After re-pickling, the trimming and finishing process is fairly straightforward, keeping in mind the delicacy of the structure. Once it's soldered onto a band or, better yet, a wing ring, of some sort, it will be safe as houses.

Cluster Head

The cluster head is simply a variation on the wire setting, in the same way a Porsche Carrera is a variation on a '56 Beetle. It's just a bit more complex and finicky. It epitomizes the difficulties which can and will arise with any inattention to details. The more perfect you try to be, the smaller any given error can be to completely screw things up. For this reason, I cannot over-emphasize the importance of making each step perfect before moving on. Mistakes never go away; they get bigger; always bigger.

The other rule we must remember is to limit the number of components necessary to do the job. This generally takes a great deal of skull-work to avoid having things go blooey. It's surprising, really, how easy it is to actually reduce the potential problems in a job by thinking ahead.

The major component, the building block of the cluster head, is the underbezel. The first time I really looked at one of these (a factory-made piece of crap), I assumed that the underbezel was a great multitude of tiny ring-shaped tubes, all cunningly welded together as a base for the stones.

While this may well have been the case in the beginning, we have since discovered the truth to be, well, otherwise. What you have to do is fool the eye into believing that the construction is more complex than it really is. You have to give the rubes some magic.

On an annealed white gold plate about 1.5mm thick, begin by laying out the stones in the appropriate pattern. If there is to be a major center stone surrounded by smalls, as it is in the majority of cases, arrange the stones so that the smalls, when viewed from directly above, contact (or even tuck under) the main stone. This gives a pleasingly tight arrangement, enhancing all the stones, and giving the impression of one big sparkle. If it's a remount job, where the custy has supplied you with a dog's-breakfast of mismatched stones, just do your best to make it look good.

Ideally, the outer stones should entirely fill the circumference, but this may take some adding and subtracting, and/or dicking with the sizes of the stones. In my experience, the fewer and smaller the spaces between the stones, the more impressive the overall effect.

Use the techniques outlined in the bead-setting section, and a bit of setter's friend to establish the positions of the smalls and mark the centers. Drill out each spot with a drill 1/3 to 1/2 the diameter of the stones. While you're at it, drill a hole somewhere in the middle area 'cause we'll be cutting that out as well.

What we're doing here is removing everything from around the holes so that your underbezel will, in effect, disappear when the stones are in position. Do your piercing carefully (of course) so that a consistent border is left around each. Kinda looks like a bunch of little tubes all cunningly welded together, don't it?

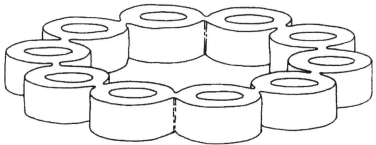

Now we need to think about claws. I hope you don't think we're going to try to attach individual claws at each appropriate spot. I didn't think so.

We're going to get back to the investment soldering technique as outlined in the previous section. This is simpler, in that the claws will be laid out parallel and are thus easier to check. Granted, there are a great multitude of them. You win some...

Place the underbezel on the plasti-tac and press it into place. There's no need to push it right into the stuff, just make sure it won't move.

Cut off a bunch of little pieces of wire, round or square, it doesn't matter much. I prefer square, but it's easier to draw round. The diameter should be about right for the job. Say .9mm for the inner claws, versus .6 for the outer claws, which will make up the "basket".

Another thing to consider is whether you want to use four of the inner claws as claws for the main stone. If so, use even heavier wire for these as some of the material is cut away to hold the smalls in place. This is advanced stuff but, as I said earlier, most of the skull-work should have been done already. Unlike the way I do things, apparently. For example, I have drawn this as a ten-stone cluster, which is just fine even though that's not what I had intended. Whatever works. This is why custom design is fun. If it needs to be an eleven stoner, make it so. This would make it difficult to use shared claws as a center stone setting, being as how we're dealing with a prime number, unless we use all the claws to set the center stone, in which case we needn't make them too heavy, there being so many of them. See what I mean?

Start placing the inner claws between the little rings, ensuring that they make contact with both rings, and are perpendicular to the setting. I forgot to mention length. Make them about twice as long as the desired finished length, plus the thickness of the underbezel. This extra length is necessary to hold the claws in place in the plasti-tac, and later, to hold the wires in place in the investment. The claws should be evenly spaced and parallel. This is fussy work, so take your time and don't be afraid to start over if it gets away from you. Any extra time spent getting it perfect now will be repaid in spades, later.

I was originally going to try to apply all the claws in one go, but I seldom do that in real life, so why would I do it here? It gets way too complicated and, besides, it's real hard to draw. One step at a time. If you have booked yourself to do a cluster head from scratch, then you should perforce have booked yourself enough time to do a proper job.

Make your little scotch-tape dam and pour the investment, as before. When it's set, clean away the excess investment and get it ready for soldering, placing the solder carefully in contact with each claw and the underbezel.

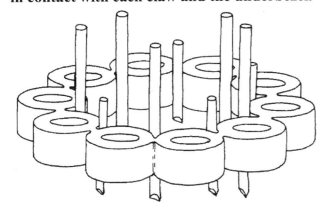

The trick when heating this thing up is to do so gradually. This is both because you don't want a lapful of hot plaster due to a steam explosion, and because the tops of the claws are inside the plaster where they can't be seen. If you overheat the plaster, you can actually melt the claws inside the plaster, and this is tough to fix without starting over. You'll be using hard solder, so things are going to get hot.

Once the solder has flowed more or less as we wish, the cookie is allowed to cool and the plaster is quite easily chipped off. Pickle the whole issue overnight and take a look.

Chances are it will need a little reflow to tidy things up, but let's say it's just right.

Clean up the fireskin and fine-sandpaper the whole issue. Nip away the excess metal that protrudes from the bottom of the underbezel and file it flat. Fine sandpaper that, too, and boric the whole shooting match up real well. When it's nice and glossy, scrape away the boric from the points of contact where the outer claws will be placed.

Stick the whole unit claws down into the flattened plasti-tac and do the whole routine again, this time with the claws on the outer edge of the underbezel. The wires protruding from the plasti-tac are way longer than before, because these will be the "basket". They will be soldered on with medium solder so we don't screw up the long, delicate wires or get everything all fireskinny again.

This stage of soldering is touchy because of the high heat necessary. It's hard to get the whole cookie up to soldering temp without overheating the bottom of it, thereby melting the wires which are imbedded in it. Truth be told, I'm a coward with too little time, so I cheat. I use platinum claws. This seems expensive at first look, but consider how much finishing time is saved if you don't have to worry at all about fireskin, or melting claws. Plus it's so easy to set stones with platinum claws…Crazy not to.

Then again, if you take too much time in the heating process, the borax is burned away and affects the solder flow. It's a major pain, but is basically the only way to achieve the results we are looking for. It's really tough the first ten or twelve times you do it. After that, it's just frustrating.

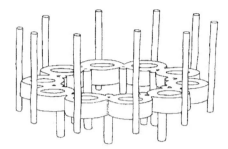

In any case, make certain that the solder has flowed enough to secure the claws, as there is the virtual certainty that a reflow will be necessary. Chip off the investment and clean the piece. Reflow as before, but remember that the inner claws are basically just hanging there on hard solder. The capillary action of the solder is usually enough to hold the inner claws in place, but why take chances?

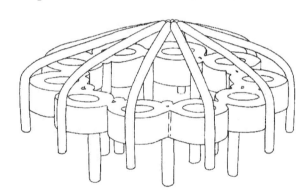

Once the solder has flowed sufficiently to permit some careful manipulation, the claws are nipped off to exactly the same length and bent inward, 'til they meet in the middle. I make this sound so simple, but it is one of those visualization things I go on about all the time. These claws, which will make up the baskety bit underneath, need to be long enough to meet in the middle without making the head too high. In some cases, the wires need to be bent in two stages so as to create a more rounded basket. Sometimes it will look best if they come in straight to the base. You decide.

The base is soldered with hard solder, or if you're real brave, you can fuse the ends together, but that's just showing off. Once the ends of the wires are nicely connected, a hole can be drilled and a post hard-soldered into place. Pretty cool, huh?

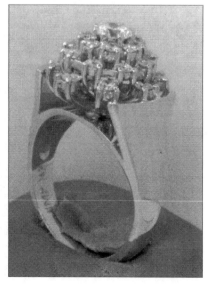

Now, I'm the first to admit that this is complex stuff, and it's frustrating as hell in the early days, but it's a very adaptable system that will be rewarding when it starts going your way. Multi-tiered clusters are possible and a real kick to put together, the only problems arising through flawed planning or sloppy layout work. Experience and experimentation, that's where the real creativity comes in, otherwise it's simply a technical puzzle.

Slap one of these on a modified wing ring and you have yourself an impressive piece of work. (In retrospect, it's ugly as a busted blister, but it was well done.)

Split Box Head

One of the most useful styles of setting for smaller emerald-cut stones is the split box. I just decided this moment that that is indeed the appropriate moniker for this puppy. So mote it be.

It is a good choice for such stones since they need a fairly solid underbezel to prevent them from twisting. Twisting is bad enough when you're considering a round stone, but if one of these twists by as little as ten degrees, it falls out. This is very bad. I tend to make my heads a little bit too heavy, but I'm working on this.

Deciding how high to make the box is always a mystery, as the proportions will vary according to whether the stone is to be set into a shoulder, or will be the main event. Let's say the stone is about four by six millimeters. Using a box four mm high seems about right, so let's start with a strip of material four mm wide, about one mm thick, and as long as you like. You'll want to make quite a bit so that you have a handle. Make the bar nice and straight and flat and square up both ends real well.

Now mark a line on the bar parallel to each end and equal to the width of the stone. Make a second line parallel to this about and about a mil further in. A picture, I think.

What you're going to do here is cut a groove with a graver or a square file between these two lines. Because you're working on the two ends at the same time, you can be fairly certain that they will be identical. Make sure, of course, that the grooves are straight. That is, that the sides are equal and at the same angle and like that.

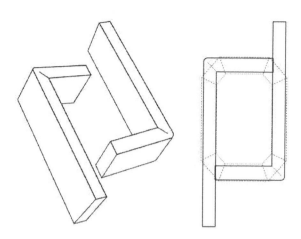

Now bend the ends up to a nice right angle. I mean a real nice right angle. Check the angle with a small machinist's square, if you have one, or do what I do and use a steel rule that has itself been ascertained to be a perfect right angle. Sometimes it makes sense to solder the ends so that you don't have to worry about screwing up these nice angles. I usually don't, because I'm a hotshot and think I'm above all that. I'm not.

At this juncture, it behooves us to cut the bar into two equal halves. Don't sweat the measurement too much, just somewhere in the middle is fine.

Now you see what you have. No? Well, you have an adjustable rectangular box approximately the width of your stone. Cool, huh?

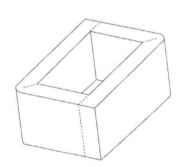

If it's too wide, then you can file equal amounts off the ends to bring it to perfection. Then slide the two halves against each other 'til the length is right and solder it, holding it in tweezers or laying it on a charcoal block. I'm not a big fan of the block method as I think it lacks control, but that's just me. However, make sure you don't use too much pressure in holding it; you're using hard solder, after all, and you don't want to collapse the whole issue.

Now you can cut off the handles and clean up the sides, top, and bottom. Don't worry about making the corners sharp 'cause we'll be taking those off, anyway.

Mark a line on each side a little way in from the ends. Use dividers to ensure that the lines are all equidistant from each end and side, as these will provide our guidelines to establish 45° angles at each corner.

After filing these corners nice and flat, check them against the actual stone to make sure that the claws will support the stone. Probably they won't, because I want to do this right, and I didn't tell you what I was up to. What we'll do is use a flat graver to cut a seat for each claw so that, when we solder, we won't have them sliding around and causing trouble.

The claws are simply lengths of square wire. (I used to notch the wire to sit on the corner of the box, but then I found that the claws were very weak where they met the box and had an alarming tendency to fold back and snap off at the most inconvenient moment.)

Before we solder on the claws, though, we come to the reason for the name. Split box, remember? Using the block and scriber, scratch a pair of lines a saw blade-width apart

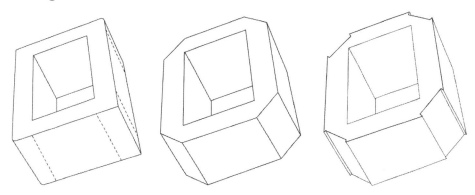

halfway up the box, and all around. This is just for style points, y'know.

Using a brand-new saw blade (trust me), tuned and ready, carefully cut halfway around the box, all the way through, and stop.

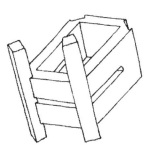

Boric up the box and solder two claws on where you've cut through. Steam it off, cut the rest of the way through the box, and repeat. Neat, huh? If you used nice hard solder, and not too much of it, you have precious little finishing work to do.

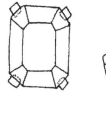 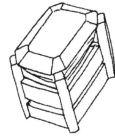

Often, though, the solder hasn't flowed perfectly. Chuck the whole assembly into the pickle and do something else, you're done for the day.

Next day, clean the setting real well and boric it up real well. Carefully reflow the solder at each claw. It's a beautiful thing. Well, it is unless you heat up the entire setting to soldering temp and collapse the whole issue. I did say carefully, did I not? Just remember to heat only half of the setting at a time, and you'll be fine.

As far as determining whether the size is correct, it should support the stone with a half to two-thirds of each claw showing so that the bearing for the stone will be neither too deep nor too shallow. In many cases, the underbezel will need to be cut away some to permit the pavilion of the stone to drop in without resting on the underbezel itself. I have seen many heads where the claws have no bearings supporting the stone, but are simply bent over to hold the stone snuggly into the underbezel. This may hold the stone in place, but it puts it at risk of chipping as the area under the claw is unsupported; should the claw get whacked, off comes the corner of the stone.

The other reason for keeping the underbezel away from the pavilion is that dirt and grease will collect in the narrow space and be difficult to remove. Emerald cuts are especially vulnerable to dirt buildup.

Variations on the basic design can include tapering the underbezel before attaching the claws, but this is hard to do and I don't want to talk about it.

Halo Settings

There is a peculiar style of setting popular right now that I have dubbed the Halo Setting. It's a goofy looking thing with a ring of material around the diamond and two round bars holding the diamond suspended over an otherwise plain band. It is quite effective if sufficient care is taken to ensure that the various components remain highly polished and unsullied during the whole process of construction. Problem is, the process itself is kind of counter-intuitive, in that it takes place in reverse. Disclaimer: I don't know how real people do this.

First, you set the stone. This is accomplished by, in effect, flush-setting the stone into a thick ring of metal. How this is done in the real world is beyond me, but here's how I do it. Take a look at the picture and see if this makes any sense.

First glance might suggest that you start with a ring of gold the correct thickness and moosh the diamond into place...Somehow.

How 'bout if we start with a huge collet, something about 1.5mm thick and high enough to clear the culet? Solder this to a convenient scrap ring and get it ready for setting. The bearing needn't be terribly substantial as the setting is virtually indestructible. Go ahead and set the stone as you would a flush-set or collet, mashing plenty of material over the girdle. Burnish it down nice and smooth, but don't trim it right now as we're going to put it through plenty of hell before we're done.

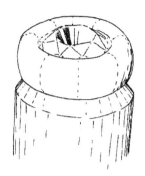

Now mark a line on the outside of the collet a distance equal to the thickness of the collet. If you can visualize what I'm shooting for here, you will see that this lumpy old collet is simply a ring of metal like in the finished halo head, but with way too much height. So cut it down, already.

Before you cut through, take the time to do some shaping of the ring as it will be tough to do this later. Make it as ring-shaped as you can, paying close attention to the transition between the top and the sides. Once you sever it from the base, you can fine-tune the shape, fine sandpaper it and such. See, it kinda looks like a ring wrapped around a stone. Keen, huh?

Something that you should do now is mark the solder line. Actually, you should have done it earlier, but I forgot to tell you. It should be visible inside the collet. Make a mark on the outside of the ring so you can find it easily.

Now to the support bars. First glance would suggest that these would be soldered into holes drilled into the band, then the halo head soldered in between. But this would be wrongolini; the problem being that it is unholy difficult to drill accurately into an oblique, curved surface such as the one we're presented with here. Better we should establish our parallels first, and then work our holes out gradually to fit. Well, I think so, and it is my book, after all.

So let's bend a nice, clean piece of wire into a big ol' "U", with plenty of extra to provide a handle. It's also easier to check to long lines for parallel than short lines… greater parallax or something. Remember, straight lines straight, curves curved. If the wire was evenly annealed, it should bend perfectly and remain straight where it's supposed to be straight. (Also, by holding the wire at the curve, you avoid marring the pristine cylinders that are effectively impossible to correct later.) Cut the U off nice and even, still leaving ample excess, but so that the U is perfectly perpendicular. Checky, checky, check. The distance between the bars should be such that the halo head will fit between with a bit of overlap. We'll be notching the outside of the ring so that it will be held securely by the bars.

May as well do that now. Use a round file close to the diameter of the bars and cut the notch about a third of the way through. Maybe less, maybe more, it's a vague quantity that varies with the size of the stone and such. Make sure that the notches are equal and perpendicular. Fit the ring between the bars and marvel at the glory of it all. Make sure that it sits in there securely and squarely and that the bars remain parallel. Checky, checky, check.

Now we can concern ourselves with those pesky holes in the band. This is where it can all go blooey if we're not careful. However, nothing that we do to the band will screw up the hard work that we've already put into the rest of the head. Pretty cagey, huh?

Mark the distance between the centers of the two bars with your dividers and transfer this to the band. If it's a seamless band, use the spot 90° around from the hallmark on the karat stamp side. (I usually size rings 90° around on the opposite side, that is, on the trademark side, but this makes no sense at all in print.) Otherwise, opposite the sizing line. What I'm trying to say is, "Decide where the top is and make it so."

Now, with a drill somewhat smaller than the bars, drill into the band at such an angle that the two holes are parallel and the correct distance apart, and at equal angles so that the bars will place the diamond straight and level. It's as tough as it seems. Miserable, in fact. You need to use all the tricks to open the holes so that the wires will fit in perfectly. I generally taper the very ends of the bars so that I can gradually work my way up to the correct size. This is no time to get aggressive. Once it slides into place nicely, it's time to start putting things together.

Usually, I solder the halo thingy in between the bars as it is easy to check it for straight and level. The tops of the bars can be pre-shaped; then the excess wire cut away.

Once this is assembled, it can be cleaned up and polished and made ready for soldering into the band. Saw off the rest of the U, as it has done its job; just be careful not to cut it off too short. Boric up the whole issue, scrape it where the solder is supposed to go, and fit it into the holes. Check it very carefully one more time as it would be a shame to screw it up now. The solder can be placed inside the ring where it will do no harm.

This construction method, while only suitable for diamonds, is quite effective when you have a very simple style that will allow even the tiniest imperfections to shine through and drive you crazy. Hopefully, it also removes some of the mystery from the process. Granted, this is still a fairly dopey style of mount, but it does serve to illustrate some cool stuff.

See, what we've learned here is that it makes a lot of sense to leave some excess material in place as a handle in the early stages. This comes into play in a big way when piercing, as well. I often find myself trying to make an accurate cut in a too-small sheet of gold, attempting to hold the little bugger down with a fingernail while the sawblade chatters away, and inevitably breaks.

Hinged Bangle

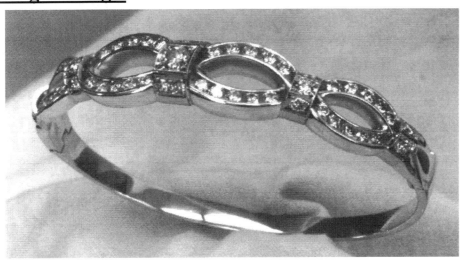

This section is not so much a treatise on hinge-making as it is a philosophical exercise which brings together all the skills and fussiness inherent in the bizz. However, in the process it will give you the lowdown on how to make a real cool hinge/clasp combination.

We start with a bracelet. Actually, we start with a bar. Actually, we start with... oh, you get the idea.

The bracelet, whether through strategic rolling of the bar stock, or forging after soldering, will have two slightly thicker areas at opposite sides at the positions of the clasp and hinge.

Having trued up the shape of the bracelet to the appropriate size, plus five millimeters or so to allow for the material removed during this process, we saw through the midpoints of the two lumps. It's best at this point to mark the ends of the two halves of the bracelet so as not to mix up the two hinge ends versus the two clasp ends. It could be important.

Life skill number one: Make one part perfect, and then make the other part fit.

Let's say, for the sake of argument, that there is a top to this bracelet. A flat surface for engraving. This will be the stable base upon which the hinge hinges. Theories differ on which part of a hinge should be the stable part and which should be the pivoting part, but for our purposes we will call the top of the bracelet the female part, for reasons that will become uncomfortable later.

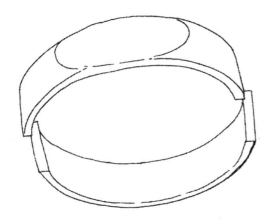

First of all, since nobody saws perfectly straight, we true up the ends of the pieces; perfectly perpendicular and flat like that. Put the two pieces together to confirm that the ends line up, are flat, and that they form a straight line. Stand them up on your ever-present steel block and ensure, one last time that they are, indeed, parallel, straight, and perpendicular. Just make them perfect, that's all.

Pick one side and mark it in some appropriate manner so that we don't get all mixed up later, and make ready to establish the hinge.

There are two ways to go from here. One is to drill a pivot hole now and establish the round end of the hinge to suit. If you do everything exactly right, it's a perfectly good method, but in my experience, it doesn't work as well, or as consistently, as the other way.

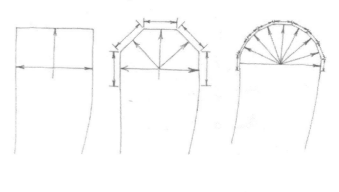

This is the other way.

For a starter, what we want to do is make the end round while removing a minimum of material, at the same time maintaining a perfectly perpendicular end as an axis for the hinge. Start by filing 45° facets on the end, removing the sharp corners and stopping when the facets are equal to

the bit remaining on the end. It's a bit zen, but it makes perfect sense and is the basis for most exercises in symmetrical filing, 'cause what you have now are three flat surfaces exactly equidistant from your axis. Think about it.

Now, simply remove the corners again, mindful to keep the facets equal widths and without removing your nice flat end: your reference.

Now, in theory, you just keep removing corners evenly until you have a smooth curve. This will take, in theory, forever, Zeno, so what you have to do is file the curve. Make sure that the surface of the curve is even and concentric with the axis. Check your end markings often. Finish it off with your finest flat file, and there you go.

Okay. As I said before, this is the female part of the hinge, so we'll be removing the middle bit. In effect, we'll be taking almost half of the width out of the middle. Not quite half, but more than a third. Just enough, but not too much. You know the routine.

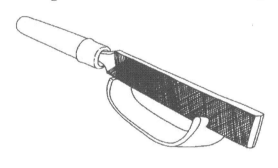

Mark lines to this effect and very carefully saw out the offending bit (*inside* the lines!). The amount of material you take out at this point sort of depends on how far you want the bracelet to open. If you saw only to the depth of the axis, you can make a perfectly fitted hinge that doesn't open at all, whereas if you cut it to the same depth as the thickness of the bracelet (or the diameter of the round end) you'll have a hinge that flops way, way open, but looks like shit when closed.

Fudge it. Somewhere in between is good, just as long as it's neat.

A great way to ensure that the inside edges are straight and parallel is to use your pillar file, the big hand file, not the needle file. By placing this brute in the slot (safe side down, of course) and lining it up on the opposite side of the bracelet, it is much easier to line up the file for straight cuts. Clean up the cut out to the lines with a fine, square file, always maintaining perfectly parallel sides, and a nice square shape to the opening. This is muy importante, 'cause once again, we're going to get Zen.

The base of your slot, at this point, is flat. This is not good as you require clearance for the male bit when it's fitted, so you're going to have to dig it out.

A flat graver works well for roughing out the groove, gradually shaping it into a concave depression. When you get to the edges of the slot, however, it's impossible to get a nice, crisp inner edge on the slot. You will find that the upper edge of the graver buggers up the pristine inner surfaces of the hinge.

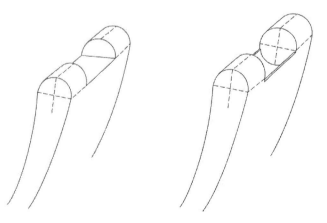

If you do a lot of hinges, you could theoretically modify a graver so's to have the leading edge wider than the following edge. This is technically okay, and I have one, but being as how you're also a setter, you will have at your disposal two small, offset gravers, one left-handed, one right-handed. These can be used to excellent advantage to clean out your inner edges.

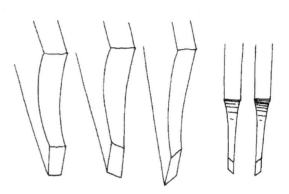

What you want to end up with is a perfectly cylindrical void in between the two sides of your hinge.

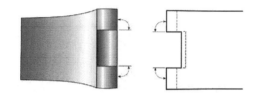

This is just about the hardest part of this whole ordeal, so take your time, do it perfectly, and looky, it's done and everything else will be so much easier.

Not easy, mind, but easier.

Okay, the female part is perfect. Eyeball it, measure it, do whatever you have to make you certain that it is so. Now don't fuck with it.

The male end is laid out in much the same way except that you'll be cutting away the outside two-thirds (or half, or what have you) so's to fit snugly (snuggly?) into the female bit.

Cutting the male end is a bit less esoteric than doing the female bit, as all the cutting is on the outside and is done to fit, not to some vague, idealistic plan laid out in little dotted lines inside a solid piece of metal. It does, however, illustrate two valuable life-skills: do the hardest part first (This is a corollary of the "Shit Sandwich" rule. See glossary.); and make one part perfect, then make the other part fit.

The layout of the male end is done in much the same way as the female. Just remember to cut on the outer sides of your layout lines. I usually start with just a slight taper on the little pluggy bit that constitutes the hinge.

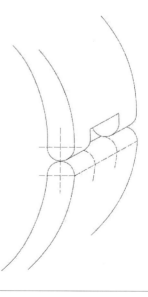

The male part, y'know, which sticks out (oh geez, now I'm blushing). It's just an analogy, relax. This way, you can sort of feel your way in. Is the piece centered properly? Is it perfectly square at the other end? This last can be determined by gently fitting the hinge together and checking to see that the opposite ends of the bracelet will come together accurately. Now is the time to find out as a tiny mistake at this end turns into a huge mistake at the other.

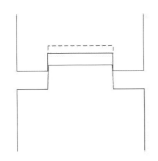

So now, without thinning the leading edge of the piece, reduce the taper 'til it chunks into place. As it does, you will round out the end so that it snuggles into the female end. The outer parts of the female end will butt up against the flats on either side of the male end. This is not a process that lends itself to verbal exposition.

By this point, it should be fairly obvious where the metal is to be removed. From. Which.

Just take your time and open out the curves where the female end will fit, keeping in mind the way the hinge will move, and soon it will start to look right.

What I usually do while fitting this part is to hold the female end in my left hand and sort of operate the hinge a few times under a bit of pressure. This causes the binding areas to burnish each other so you can see a little shiny streak where they touch. This you can remove without too much risk. Remember, we're only modifying the male end. The female end is already perfect, right? RIGHT?

The trick is to remove just enough material so that you're not making things worse every time you touch file to metal, or a graver, for that matter, as we are going to be using our offset gravers to cut out the roundy bits.

This job is time-consuming as hell the first thirty or forty times you do it but, as with most things, the more you do it the better it gets.

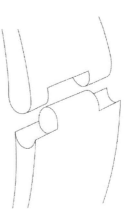

With repeated cutting and fitting, the hinge will eventually rotate properly about the axis that will eventually be the hinge pin.

This is easy if you do everything exactly right.

The appropriate size of drill is just a bit smaller than you would think, certainly less than half the diameter of the hinge itself. Best to start with something very small, as the first couple of tries at this are inevitably off a bit and we want to leave ample material for adjustment. Besides, if the hinge is fitted properly, the pin doesn't add much strength to the whole unit. It just provides a stable pivot and a bit of shear strength. As long as everything else is set up properly, there is very little stress on the pin.

First, sharpen your drill. It's important. You want to ensure that the bastard is going to go in absolutely straight. The bracelet I've drawn here is quite wide, for illustration's sake, and this would make it very difficult to drill accurately unless you're real good at it. Try drilling through a piece of scrap of the approximate dimensions of the end of your bracelet for practice, if you like. It will let you know whether your drill is tracking true. You have your centre lines laid out on the outside of the female end, so simply establish your centre divot with a round graver and drill the holes.

Start at the marks and drill towards the middle. This minimizes directional errors which are sure to develop. (We're only drilling the female end right now.) You will break your drill if you get too aggressive, so use plenty of oil, take your time and check your progress often. The drill end will come through nicely centered on the inner curve.

This also illustrates why we don't drill the hole first, then round up the end to suit. If you're good enough to drill accurately all the way through a wide piece of material, you probably don't need me.

If the holes are off at all, you can use a slightly larger drill to correct it. Just open the hole enough to be sure it's straight. Clean up any burrs on the inside of the female end and insert your male part (Yikes). At this point you can use a very slim pointy thing to mark the locations of the holes on the male end. This is a perfect opportunity to check whether the male end goes in far enough and the holes are centered. If they need adjusting, it's best done before drilling. Look through the drill hole as you rotate the hinge to see whether the mark stays in the center of the hole. If it doesn't, it means that the hinge isn't fitted quite as perfectly as you thought and adjustments will have to be made. If we don't do it now, the hinge will put stress on the pin every time it operates and cause a lot of premature wear. Trust me, this is the time to do it.

Once it's all ready, drill in from the two marks towards the middle. The moment when the two drill holes meet in the middle is the precise moment that the drill will break, so take it easy and go slowly. But not too slowly, as the drill is more likely to grab and break. Nervous yet?

Should the worst happen and the drill does break off in the hole, all is not lost. If you can't find some way to punch it out without damaging the end of the hinge, put it in a sealed plastic baggie or a 35mm film container, if such things still exist, with a strong solution of pickle and suspend it in the ultrasonic. Make sure that the acid doesn't leak out into the tank as it will cause nothing but trouble. As with reflowing solder, it's best to find something else to do and leave it overnight, as it takes a while. It takes even longer if you don't use the ultrasonic, so don't complain.

Now, I didn't mention this earlier, but to avoid confusion I generally hold the top unit in my left hand and run the broach in from the right, looking at the outside of the hinge, as in the picture. This allows you to use a bit of pressure on the whole thing as you open out the tapered hole. The other advantage of always reaming it from the same side is that, a few years down the road, when you have to replace the hinge pin, you will know which way to punch it out. No guessing.

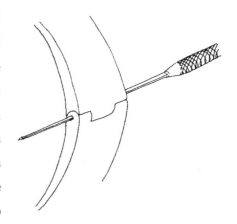

Keep reaming it until the broach is cutting all along the length of the hole. This provides a nice, long bearing surface for the pin.

Once it's cut all the way smooth, pull the hinge apart and just take another turn or two through the male end so that it won't fit quite as tightly on the pin.

Basically, once the pin is fitted, it will be solid with the female part, while the male part pivots. This makes sense for reasons of wear and posterity. Once again, down the road a piece, you'll have to repair this puppy, and it makes a lot more sense to replace the simplest bits (male end and pin) rather than the whole issue. If more manufacturing goldsmiths felt this way, life would be far simpler for more repair goldsmiths.

You'll be using a piece of hardened white gold wire as a final rivet, but for now, just taper any old piece of wire of the correct diameter and force it into the hole.

By this point, you should have the hinge operating quite smoothly and, as you operate it, the pivot wire (pivot rivet?) should remain motionless. If the wire rotates in the holes in the female end, you're going to have to open up the hole in the male end a bit more.

There. The hinge is more or less done. It's time to build a clasp.

I've been using this clasp for a lot of years, now, and it seems to work quite well. At first, it takes an ungodly long time to construct, but that's understandable on account of the fact that it's gotta be perfect.

Before we get into the construction of the clasp, we'll go into some of the philosophy behind the hinge/clasp combination and why I see it as a successful system.

As you've seen, the hinge is constructed so that there is virtually no flex in any direction other than that intended. Once closed, the clasp is also completely inflexible. This means that, as worn, the bracelet will not be subject to any internal wear at all.

You can be confident, therefore, that anything that causes the system to fail is not your fault. Maintenance is important, of course, and has been rendered quite simple to carry out, thanks to the simplicity of the system. If the hinge starts to get sloppy, for example, it will put a strain on the clasp and vice-versa, so everyone has to work together to make this piece last a lifetime or two.

Naturally, most custies are boobs, and you will not get to see the piece again until they've thoroughly fucked it up. That's life.

So, anyway, here's how to build a Kenny Paulson clasp.

Some of the work can be done while the hinge is dismantled which is why we just fitted a piece of tapered whatever into it.

The first step, after ensuring that the two ends line up straight and flat, is to make the receiving side of the clasp. We may as well call it the female end, for consistency's sake, even though there's not nearly as much of this "insert male part" stuff that got us so sweaty before.

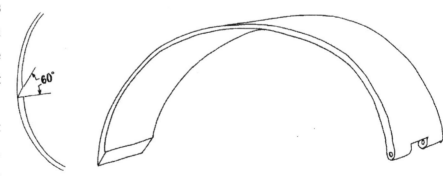

The end is cut off to a 60° angle. The reason for the 60° thing will become apparent, later. Make the cut straight and flat, and clean it up nicely.

As you can see in the picture, we have to create a notch of some sort. What I want is for the notch to be based on 60° angles so that I can use a triangular file for finishing it up.

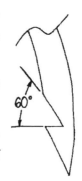

Did I mention that all this cutting is done on the inside of the bracelet? Well, it is. That's why we illustrate with pictures.

Now we do the same thing on the outside of the male or bottom side. The fitting is fussy, but you want to make it perfect, so take your time. If you keep all surfaces flat, parallel, and sharp, the job will be easier.

What you're shooting for is a perfect fit with no light showing through at all.

Good luck.

Now you'll see how happily it snaps into place. When closed, it should be under no tension and perfectly lined up before the next step.

The clasp is nice, now, but it slides back and forth a bit. We can't have that. Wear, you know. So we must stabilize it.

To accomplish this, we're going to insert a pin into the top part. A pin that runs parallel to the bracelet and, since it is in the undercut section, is concealed so it won't look ugly.

The other reason for putting the pin in this section is that it will be soldered, and therefore the whole section will be annealed. The bottom section, which will not be heated, will retain its woing and provide a little snap when the clasp is closed.

I suppose we could have drilled a hole in the top before notching it, but that creates a whole different set of problems.

This, however, is a process for which I have developed no efficient method. Next time, I'm going to drill the hole first. I'll get back to you and let you know how it went.

Once again, a sharp drill is crucial. I know I keep going on about the whole sharp thing but, Christ, it's important. I've ignored a dull drill and paid the price often enough to know.

So, refer to the pictures for this. You start your hole in the female, top, undercut, whatever side of the clasp and, after it's cutting in, but before it gets in too deep (say, a millimeter), gradually lower the drill so you're drilling parallel to the bracelet. Needless to say, you will have centered this hole in the bar.

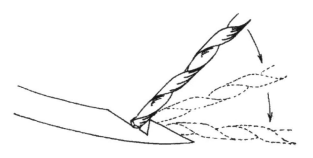

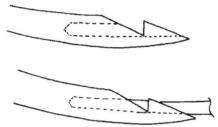

As you lower the drill, it will cut into the notched bit. This is good. This is where the pin, which goes into the hole, will be soldered. If the drill doesn't want to cut away enough of a notch, you will have to use a round graver to remove a bit of material so the pin will settle nicely into place.

Once the position is established, you'll want to drill in about five millimeters or so. The pin will not be soldered all the way into the hole, but it will be secure, so it doesn't have to go in a great distance.

Okay, now switch to a drill one size larger and recut the hole so it's nice and clean. Clean up the surrounding area with a triangular file or graver.

Grab a piece of wire just a hair larger than your drill and file a very slight taper on the end of it, testing it in the hole 'til it's snug and goes in almost to the end of the hole.

Now, clean the whole top section to remove any residual oil and boric it up well. Clean the drill and use it to clean the boric out of the hole. Jam your tapered wire into the hole, cut it off flush, and solder it at the end. Use the minimum amount of solder practical as you don't want any creeping into the sharp angles and screwing up the fit. Clean it up, file the end flush, and you're done.

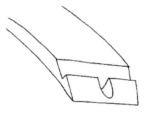

Next, you'll have to notch the inner portion to fit your stabilizer pin doodle. This is a straight-forward cut-and-fit kind of thing, done with the hinge reassembled. Since it fit perfectly before the pin was installed, it'll drop into place once you've cut it properly. It's a thing of beauty.

Now, we need a way to keep it closed. Usually, what I do at this point is to file a flat area on the top part of the bracelet so as to form a stable pivot area for our clasp. Take a look at the picture of the finished piece, and you'll get an idea of the fitting and geometry that's involved. I'll try to hit the high points here, but, rest assured, there's a lot of picky work to be done.

The trick is, as I've said before, make each stage perfect before moving on. Your clasp already snaps shut beautifully, and nothing you now should change that. If you bugger up the first attempt on this swively bit, start anew. Don't do anything at all to the bracelet itself. Get it?

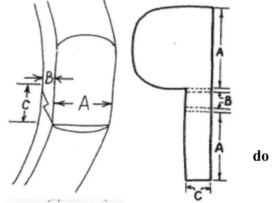

do

So, you need to start off with an "L"-shaped piece about .75 m/m thick.

I generally make the short bit the width of the brac and the long bit the width of the fitted area. This provides plenty of strength and also covers the cracks where the ends come together. Pretty and functional, who could ask for more?

How long to make these ends is another question entirely, and this is where the geometry comes in.

The long bit is going to be bent around so as to hold the clasp together, so we may as well fit this. First, we notch the underside of the piece so it will bend at a clean right angle. Then, we make a second notch that is the thickness of the bracelet distance from the first notch. Check the picture. We want to make a "U"-shaped clamp that will hold the clasp shut.

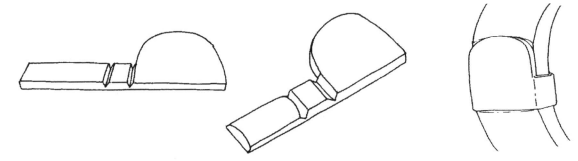

Usually, I file the end of the piece to a slight arc before bending, as this is the bit that goes inside the bracelet. It's real hard to file this arc once the piece is bent. Trust me, this I know.

Bend the piece at the notches and check that it will clamp the bracelet the way it should because it will be easier to adjust it for fit before soldering. Make sure that the top and bottom are parallel and at right angles to the side piece. Solder the joints and clean the inside up nice. Don't sweat the outside right now as we will be messing with it quite a bit and there's no need to worry about cosmetics at this point.

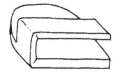

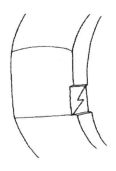

This piece can be left to clamp the clasp as is or we can notch the bracelet slightly to make for a neater job. Might's well do it right.

Now that it clamps nicely, we have to create a pivot point so that this thing will open and close properly. I find that it's best to centre the pivot on the bracelet, but it still has to be positioned so that the clasp will open as shown. You will generally only run into trouble if the bracelet is really wide.

Simply hold the clampy bit in the closed position and mark the center line, then swivel it out to its most open position and, once again, mark the center line. This should give you an accurate point at which to establish a pivot.

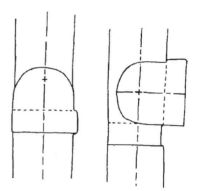

Y'see, you want to have a clasp that opens and closes in the most efficient manner possible. Too much movement either way just creates headaches with catching and bending. (Actually, truth be told, I just came up with this little formula. I've been by-guess-and-by-goshing it for way too long, but this seems to make sense.)

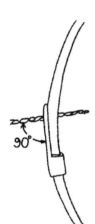

The hole for the pivot rivet has to be drilled perpendicular to the flat surface we filed on the outside of the bracelet. First, drill the swivelly clampy bit, then, with great care, the clamp is placed in closed position and the hole drilled through.

This hole is cleaned up with a tapered broach, at the same time testing the accuracy of its range of motion.

A tapered wire is inserted in the hole in the clamp and soldered there once it's fitted and cleaned up.

At this point, it's best to do any final fitting and adjusting. Then the piece is

rounded off so it's not so ugly and so it won't catch on stuff. Clean up the end that's inside the bracelet so it's comfy. Don't take too much material off the base of the "U" (outside of the clamp), as this is the area that takes the strain and provides strength.

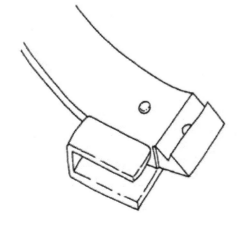

Before proceeding with the riveting of the pivot, pull the hinge pivot rivet out so that you have easier access to the inside of the clasp.

Counter-sink the hole inside the bracelet just a bit with a ball bur and fit the pivot wire. Cut the wire off with 1/3 of its length exposed and carefully tap it with a ball-peen hammer. Be cautious, take your time, and there's a chance that you won't leave ugly peen-marks on the inner surface of the bracelet. Don't over-peen the end as you will freeze the pivot, thereby rendering the clasp useless. This would be a bad thing. Clean it up with a large beader from your setting tools. You can use the handle and rotate the beader to shape the rivet, or if you feel like taking a chance, you could hammer it to shape. This is quite risky and not recommended. At least not by this cowboy. The chance of freezing the whole unit is just too great. Better a slightly rough-looking clasp that works perfectly than completely useless thing of beauty.

Now we're going to fit a permanent pivot wire in the hinge.

Take a piece of white gold wire which has been drawn down to just a hair larger than the big end of the tapered hole and, without annealing it, hammer it straight on a flat steel surface. By twirling the wire and tapping it gently with a polished (slightly convex) hammer, the wire will be straightened and further hardened.

File a slight taper on the pin (same taper as the broach, naturally) and reduce it 'til it goes in the hole. Test it to make sure the hole in the male end pivots on the pin.

Without changing the taper, fine sandpaper and burnish the pin so it will be smooth and friction-free. Burnishing the pin hardens the surface and polishes it so that friction is reduces.

Use a ball bur to create a slight counter-sink in each end of the tapered hole and insert the pin. Snug it up nicely by pulling it through from the small end.

Cut it off and clean it up so that each end protrudes a distance equal to 1/3 of its diameter. This leaves just enough material to form a good head for the rivet. Both ends, of course.

Using a ball peen or cross peen hammer, carefully tap the end of the pin while resting the other end on a steel surface. Take your time and work from both ends, flipping the bracelet often. You don't want to leave peen-marks on the polished sides of your bracelet.

Sometimes the rivet will be perfectly formed just by hammering, but a large beader from your setting equipment can be used to give a lovely round shape to the ends. There's no need to check the function of the hinge because it was perfect before. Right? Okay, another option is to counter-sink the hole just slightly and hammer the rivet flush. This makes it a lot easier to finish, but lacks that je ne sais quoi of the latagne little rivet-end.

There. You're done. Polish the whole issue and revel in the glory of it all.

Post Script: Doing all this in metal has many advantages, but is ungodly time-consuming. Making the whole thing up in wax is way quicker, but can go horribly wrong if all the rules aren't followed. And there are no rules.

Square Shank

Okay, now, I'm the first to admit that I know little about the repair business. Not my juju, y'know. However, my experience in manufacturing has forced me to develop some novel techniques, mostly based on the teachings of Bert Cruse.

For example, I seem to have created a market for square shanks. To the uninitiated, these little buggers seem to be a bit more trouble than they're worth, but my custies like them a lot. So I gotta do 'em.

Problem is, as with any other piece of jewellery, they eventually wear out. Truth be told, this hasn't become a problem, yet, being a relatively new development. What actually happens is that people like the feel of the square shanks and want their old rings retrofitted, and, by cracky, I'm just the bucko to do it.

The extra bit of weight also provides a bit of balance. For example, a diamond solitaire ring will remain more nearly upright with the addition of such a shank.

The other detail that I'll be touching on is Bert's method of installing shanks. Once again, a method that, at first glance, seems to be a profound waste of time, but on further consideration, makes infinite sense.

We'll assume here that we're not dealing with a ring that's too far gone. That is, the shank is worn, but there's still structural integrity in the head. We should all be so lucky.

The first step is to determine where, exactly the new shank will start. This is as much an art as anything else in this bizz as the new shank needs to blend smoothly into the old shoulders, while retaining the maximum amount of original material, and still allowing the shank to be of a sufficient weight to make the whole ordeal worthwhile. What I think I'm trying to say here is that it's gotta be right. I hate the repair business, too many compromises.

So, having made the decision as to where to lop off the old shank, we make a tapered bar whose ends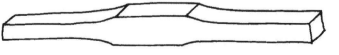

of are the same dimensions as that point. I suppose we could measure it, if we were so inclined, but that seem kind of useless, considering the fact that we have no clue as to how long to make the bar, nor how fat the fat bit should be, nor the length of the fat bit.

Well, one thing about the repair bizz is that it's always nice to have spare parts around, so if we blow this first effort, the result may be useful somewhere down the road.

That being said, the piece needs to be long enough to make a weird little tapered band about size two. Before bending it, though, we'll do some pre-shaping to make things a bit easier.

Using a cross-peen hammer, whack the middle of the fat bit thinner. At the same time, it will become wider, but we can deal with this later. Now bend the blank into a ring and pound it round. See how the two remaining fat bits form a couple of little bumps? These are the beginnings of your squared-off bumpy bits. This point can also be reached by simply forging the tapered bar, rather than pre-shaping, but this method has its advantages.

In any case, through various forging processes, we finally achieve the nice squared-off shape which we so desire. If your blank was too short to make the shank the correct size, it's quite acceptable to cut it and do the remaining shaping with it open. The whole top is scrap, anyway. It simply provides a handle for the shaping process and will be cut off.

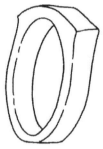

Now it's time to commit. Having boric-ed up the old ring well, cut off the shank at the predetermined point. Slide the new piece of shank down the mandrel to the appropriate size (you did remember to note the size, didn't you?), and place the now-truncated head and shoulder of the old ring next to it. Center it carefully and make marks a millimeter and a half or so past the ends of the old shoulders.

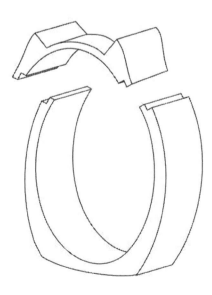

Perhaps a picture. Check that the angles of the cuts line up all straight-like and perpendicular so that things will line up properly when things get hairy, 'cause that's what is about to happen.

Carefully cut a notch on the inside edge of the old shoulders, a step, as it were, for indeed, this will be known henceforth as a stepped shank. Make the notches as clean as possible, right-angled and about halfway through the shoulders. Make one part perfect, then make the other part fit.

Now notch the new shank, on the outside, of course, to line up with the shoulder notches. This is fussy work, so it's probably best to be cagey and work the notch up to the right size, rather than hacking in there and cutting off too much. As you get better at this, most of the work can be done with the saw, just a little clean-up with a file or graver. This is how Bert did it and Bert, of course, is God.

So, if things are going your way, the two parts fit together so well that no tricks are necessary to hold them for soldering. If, however, you live in the real world, they need to be wired. Bert would make these cool wire harnesses that could be reused many times, but I never quite figured out the technique. I 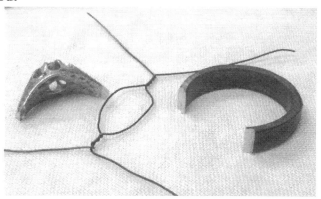 end up making a new one each time, each one just a little different from the last. Sort of re-inventing the wheel repeatedly. Highly inefficient.

From this point on it's fairly straightforward. Use the hardest solder you dare out of consideration for the next goldsmith who works on the ring 'cause, after all, it may be you.

The basic rules of repair apply; don't modify the original portions any more than necessary and do no harm. No, wait. That last bit is the Hippocratic Oath, or something. Never mind, you get the idea. Just do a good job.

The stepping technique can be applied to regular shanks, as well, and is a useful thing to know if you are having trouble visualizing a soldering job, particularly if you can't figure out how to hold pieces together for soldering. If they can be held together by tension or simply stay in place without any precarious balancing acts being necessary, then they will be better solder joints from the get-go.

This is the word according to Bert.

One quick note: The first time I did a stepped shank, I had already cut off the old shank, had already melted it down and recast it into a bar (we did that, then), when Bert leaned over and said, "What size was it?"

Of course, he knew, but a lesson learned in the face of terror is often a lesson well-learned. Bastard.

Hinged Shanks

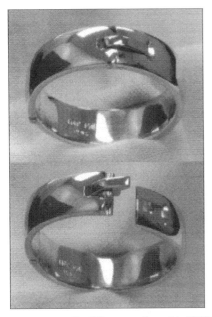

A little gizmo that I came up with a while back has become a boon to arthritis-sufferers everywhere. Well, everywhere within hailing distance of me.

It's not a new idea, just an improvement on a commercial product. It simply involves the installation of a hinge/clasp combination on a ring to allow it to fit on the finger without going over the knuckle. My record, thus far, is a size 4 1/2 finger with a size 11 1/2 knuckle. The usual tricks simply won't suffice in a case like this.

I've been asked why I don't patent them and the only real good reason I've come up with is that, realistically speaking, they're totally impractical. All the anal fitting and zen eyeballing makes it difficult for normal people to accomplish.

The snapping part of the system, which in a bracelet is angular and very solid, is rounded off with a less positive snap. The smaller diameter of the ring, and the mechanical advantage this affords, makes it impossible to get the ring on and off otherwise.

A workable yet durable clasp system is also important, of course. We have to remember that, for the first couple of weeks at least, the ring is going to be opened and shut several times a day until the novelty wears off.

A clasp which has delicate or protruding parts is out of the question, for obvious reasons. This is a ring, after all, and will be put through all sorts of delightful punishment. For this reason, it behooves us to strengthen the areas of wear as much as possible to avoid problems down the road. A clasp that swings out the way our prototypical bracelet clasp device does is to be avoided.

Therefore, we go to a more concealed, flush style of clasp. It works well on bracelets, as well, so keep it in mind for narrower or thicker half-round bracelets where swing-out clasps won't do.

Obtaining an accurate ring size in this sort of situation obviously calls for some special preparations. My original method for this was to lay in a supply of sheet brass cut into a variety of lengths and widths and bent into rings. Working with, or next door to, a machine engraver can prove a boon because such strips are scrap to them. So suck up to your local engraver. Exchange favors, whatever.

One of these strips, of the appropriate width, is fitted around the finger 'til it feels right and, by marking it, the correct size is provided. Cool, huh? (Recently, hinged ring sizers have become available that greatly simplify the process. So never mind.)

Naturally, being who we are, the shank is going to be square so we can always put the hinge in one of the bumps, and the clasp at the junction between the old ring shoulder and the new shank, using the shoulder as an integral part of the clasp.

Generally, I join the square shank to the old shoulder with a nice, strong step joint on one side, and a butt joint on the other, since we're going to be cutting this joint out later to make the clasp.

While pre-shaping the square shank, be sure to leave an extra bit of thickness on one side to allow for the cutting of the hinge. Now it can be hammered up to the correct size, thereby rounding it up nicely and at the same time hardening it.

Of course, making it round now means that it won't be perfectly rounded after we've cut out the hinge and clasp. This isn't a big deal in most cases as we'll be doing a fair amount of dicking around during the fitting process and can tweak it all into shape at that point. All we're doing now is strengthening the shank through hammering, paying special attention to the hinge area as this is where the strength is needed most.

Cutting the hinge is carried out in much the same manner as laid out in the hinged bangle section. The confined spaces just mean a little more care and attention are necessary to ensure an accurate fit and smooth operation.

The amount of travel necessary in the hinge depends, to an extent, on the severity of the problem. That is, the difference between the size of the finger and the size of the knuckle. Some need only open a bit to provide some relief over the knuckle, whereas others, like the case mentioned earlier, have to avoid the whole knuckle entirely. The basic idea is to limit the travel of the hinge as much as possible. More extreme swings mean greater wear and a greater chance of catastrophic damage due to catching and such.

This provides another reason for placing the clasp and hinge as far away from each other as possible. If they are on opposite sides of the ring, in order to open far enough to completely clear the finger, the hinge needs only to swing through sixty degrees. Whereas, were you to put the clasp at the other bump in the shank, it would have to swing through a full ninety degrees.

Once the hinge is done, and a temporary pin fitted, we can take a look at the clasp.

As mentioned earlier, the action of the clasp needs to be a little less positive than that used on a big, floppy bracelet. This means that we can use round gravers and files for the fitting, more of a jigsaw kind of look than the on-and-lock of the bracelet. I've put together shanks that snapped together rather loudly and wouldn't come off without the judicious use of pliers. This is bad. The system is dependent on a sort of belt-and-suspenders cooperation between the clasp and the little lock we're going to make next. So I guess this is a hinge/clasp/lock system. Whatever.

The trick to building one of these little gizmos lies in the fact that the strength of the system relies on the combined strength of the components. If the hinge flexes, the clasp won't click into place accurately enough to allow the catch to catch. Therefore, the likelihood that someone will try to force it becomes a virtual certainty. Besides, the system is supposed to be a solid unit when closed; otherwise wear becomes a major issue. How soon do you want to see this pig again?

That being said, how do we make this as solid as possible? Well, considering that it already snaps together quite nicely, anything that's done from this point on should avoid screwing up what's gone before.

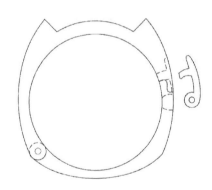

A catch, in this case, is meant to immobilize the joint, and it is important that this is kept in mind while finishing this little project.

The catch itself will be made from a work-hardened chunk of white gold. The reason for the white gold is strength, of course. Roll a white gold plate down to about 1.2-1.5 mm and you're ready to start. This is muy hard to describe, but we have pictures, so look closely and dig your heels in. It's going to be a bumpy ride.

This next bit gets a little scary because you're going to drill a hole in the ring, first on the male side, to provide a slot for the pivot of the catch.

Check out the final shape of the catch. It will fit into the slots we're about to cut, holding the clasp shut, providing some lateral stability, and staying out of the way when it's closed. If it's fitted properly there is little stress on the pivot pin because the catch itself is holding everything

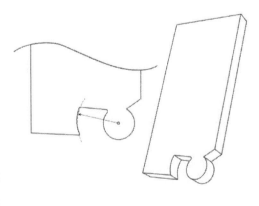

together. The tiny bit of overlap at the end of the hooky-bit provides a little click, a positive closure.

Creating this miracle usually starts with a rectangular hole just long enough for the pivot end of the catch. How long is that? Well, I generally start out with a tapered hole and widen it out until the corner of the bar just starts to fit in. Then I rough out the basic shape of the catch.

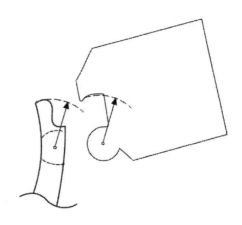

This starts out as simply a wedge-shaped piece that fits snugly in the hole, keeping in mind the fact that it'll be filed into a nice, round pivotty kind of thing. I suppose a bit of preshaping can be carried out at this point. Try it, you may like it. In any case, leave yourself an allowance as insurance and as a handle.

It's best to keep this hole fairly tight to the clasp because the longer the catch, the more likely it is to get bent or broken in use. Leverage, don't you know.

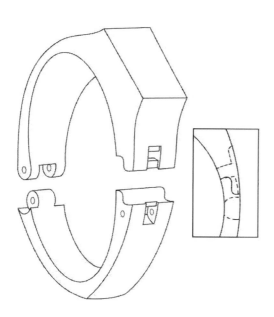

Having determined the proper distance and angle for the catch, the hole can be drilled in the ring. Carefully. Great care must be taken to get this hole perfectly straight, otherwise the whole exercise has been for naught. No pressure. Just make sure the drill is absolutely perfect and take your time. The hole needn't be very big. Hell, it *can't* be very big considering the thickness of the ring, but it must be well positioned. The hole should extend straight through the center of the pivot hole, of course, and be broached out before drilling the pivot.

Once the ring is drilled, the pivot can be marked and drilled. Don't drill it until you're certain that it's centered perfectly. There has to be ample material around the hole for strength and function. Check that the hook end will snap nicely over the end of the male end. Cut away the excess material to form the hook and the little lever that makes it work.

Now you can drill and cut the corresponding rectangular slot in the female end. The hole should allow the hook to enter easily and be relieved so that the catch holds the female end firmly. This part of the trip is the fussiest and can take the best part of an afternoon, but it needs to be done right.

Only after it functions properly do we even consider cutting the catch away from the handle. This little pig is tough enough to work on with a handle, never mind trying to grip such a dinky little curl of metal in pliers.

By this point, the rest of the fitting process should be fairly obvious. Just make sure that the catch is slightly recessed so that it can be strong but unobtrusive. The very last step is usually left until just before the final polishing. This would be using a scrupulously sharp flat graver to cut a little fingernail relief. It seems a shame to work so hard on getting everything flush, only to create a groove defeating the process, but the clasp needs to be functional, and this little notch needn't be all that deep to work. It's a hell of a project, a day or two to complete at first, but a satisfying one nonetheless. Just remember to charge a lot and you'll be okay.

As an afterthought, sort of a mental exercise, I discussed with myself the possibility of reversing the clasp. I know, I know, I went on at great length about what I thought the correct method was, but one of the most valuable skills you can develop is that of a flexible imagination. I think I'll try it the other way next time, 'cause it's a crazy idea, and it just might work.

Speaking of crazy ideas, here's a design that incorporates a hidden hinged shank. It is actually way easier to create perfectly functional hinged shanks when you're putting the whole ring together from scratch, because you aren't limited in the location or the method of operation.

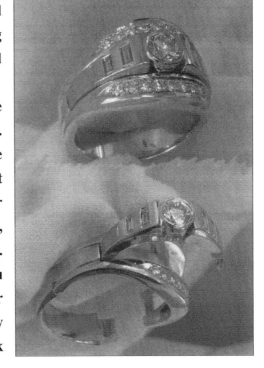

This one works by grasping the entire white gold section, which acts as the catch, and pulling. Then the shank is tugged to open the whole issue up. It's incredibly strong, as it is an integral part of the ring, yet easily operated. Y'gotta remember that the customer probably has arthritis, otherwise they wouldn't need a hinged shank. Starting from scratch on a job like this frees you from the constraints imposed by a repair job. For example, making a wax hinged shank is way quicker than all this piddling about in gold. Check it out in the wax-carving section.

Pendant Loop

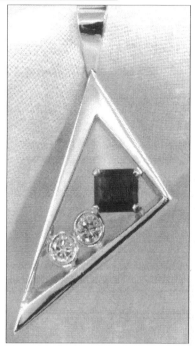

This is just a little project that demonstrates how much easier it is to let the properties of the metal work for you, rather than against you.

First of all, I'll touch on the philosophy behind this sort of loop versus more boneheaded versions. Or are my biases showing?

The simplest form of pendant loop is a jump ring stuck through a hole drilled in the pendant. The problem here is that, not only does the chain wear on the ring, but the ring wears on the pendant, which wears on the ring, so it's a dead heat as to which part gives out first. In addition, the ring quickly establishes a favorite point of wear, or rather two, top and bottom, so that the process accelerates.

In my world, it is a given that things are going to wear, and we're going to have to fix them, so let's make the process as painless as possible. Therefore, the perfect loop should be an integral part of the piece, large enough to move freely on the chain, and heaviest where the greatest amount of wear will be concentrated. Oh, and attractive, I forgot attractive.

And here's how to make one.

Start with a bar, oh, let's say three millimeters square. Roll it down flat to about 1.25 mm thick, and anneal it. Cut off about 12 mm and roll it,

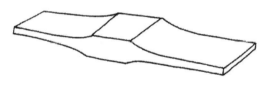

inward from either end, down to .75, leaving a bit about 4mm long in the middle unrolled. Now, what you have is a flat bar almost 3.5 mm wide (due to spreading while rolling) with a thick, annealed bit in the middle.

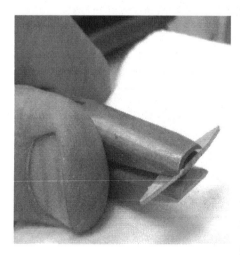

Now, when you go to bend this bar, it will bend at the annealed point, the ends having been hardened by rolling. Had we done it another way, the fat bit in the middle would have remained stubbornly flat. You can't blame it, though, that's just the way metal is.

Cut off one end of the bar about 8mm from the bend. This will be the height of your loop. File the end of this section to an angle so that the gap will close up accurately, and clean away any fireskin in the vicinity.

Close up the loop and solder it with the hardest solder you dare.

Once it's pickled, the handle, as it were, may be bent, and a center-line established. At this point, the loop can be filed to a nice taper, straight-sided or curved, split, engraved, whatever.

What you have is a loop of more-or-less the right shape, and looky, it comes with its

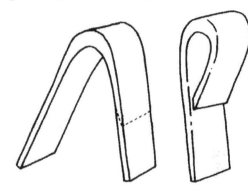

own handle. The handle can be used to make a peg for attachment. If it's filed to a peg, it can easily be inserted into a conveniently placed hole, thereby avoiding the dread balancing act. If it is left as a flap, it can be soldered to the back of a flat pendant, without too much difficulty. Quite adaptable, really, and quick, too. After the first thirty, forty tries.

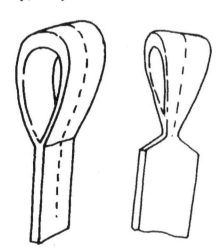

That all having been said, here's an alternative method that works well if you're piercing out a little pendant or two and only need a delicate little loop. It's largely predicated on the fact that I have a new digital camera and can use it to document some of my projects. Whatever works.

In this case, I pierced out a couple of little engraved pendants from a sheet of one millimeter metal and have enough

left over that I can also cut out the pendant loops. The sheet itself is all annealed so that once we've cut out the appropriate shape, it's an easy matter to roll the ends thinner and thus harder.

The initial bend in the bar is accomplished with these cunning bending pliers. Once the bend is established, some round-nose pliers are used in conjunction with a pair of heavy chain-nose pliers to close up the loop the rest of the way.

At this point, we can decide whether the loop will be best attached directly to the top of the pendant or fastened to the back. I say fastened partly because, way back in the darkest past, before I learned to solder, I used to make up loops this way and rivet them to pierced pendants. Hey, it was the best I could do at the time. As far as I know, some of those pendants are still around.

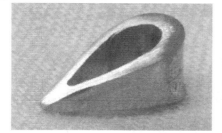

It's simply a matter of deciding whether one or both of the legs of the loop are bent. Legs? You know. The top one will be soldered to the back of the heavier pendant, leaning somewhat forward, while the bottom one will be soldered to the top of a delicate script "J".

Solder the loops closed using the hardest solder you dare and pickle them off. The bottom one, of course, will need to be clamped shut while soldering. Clean each up to a pleasant shape and fine-sandpaper finish. Sometimes I polish them up prior to soldering, but today I'll just solder them on as is. The pendants themselves are pretty much polished, so it will be easy enough to clean up the solder fillet and the pendant loop itself at the same time.

Here are the pendants and loops all boricked up and ugly with the areas to be soldered scraped clean of boric acid. The pierced J has a small divot drilled into the top to provide some stability while soldering and strength once it's finished. You may already be aware that I am not a big fan of butt-soldering anything, most especially when it's something that is

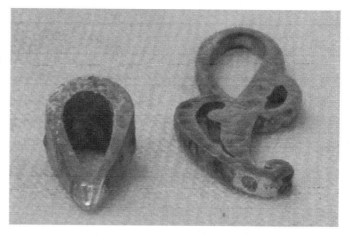

structurally integral to the piece, so we will try to avoid the appearance of that. The other loop is just about ready to fit onto the back of the other pendant.

The tab at the back allows you to hold it in place while soldering, thereby avoiding the balancing act often necessary in such cases. The J pendant, I'm sorry to say, does rely greatly upon your skill at two-handed soldering. I didn't take a picture of that because that would make it a four-handed soldering job. Balancing is made easier, however, by the little hole at the top of the pendant. If you take your time and control the heat cleanup is a breeze. Do not, I repeat, do not try to rush the process or you will surely end up melting something. (The solder didn't flow perfectly first try on the larger pendant, so I left it in the pickle and will reflow it on Monday.)

The reflow, as I may have mentioned before, is the magical process of correcting nasty solder flow. If the solder stops flowing along a joint it is sometimes possible to "convince" it to flow, but this is often a risky proposition. Instead, I like to drop the piece into the pickle overnight and do something else.

In the morning the piece can be thoroughly cleaned and then covered in at least three layers of boric acid, each fused on and cooled. On the last coat the piece can be brought up to soldering temperature and, if there was enough solder to begin with, it will flow neatly along the joint. If it still just sits there, you may not have used enough solder and, after scraping a spot on the joint, add a little more and some borax. Don't rely on heat to force the solder to flow and you won't have any unpleasantness. And we don't want any unpleasantness, now, do we? I will keep reminding you of the reflow thing because, well, I like it and it works.

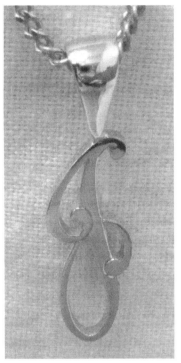

Butt-Soldered Chain

One fussy little problem I run into from time to time is that of performing a neat solder job on a rope or wheat-style chain.

With a curb-link chain, it is usually a simple matter to solder a single link as there is ample space to confine the heat to the joint without glomping up the whole vicinity. The fancier chains, including the rolled ones like the serpentine or herringbone, present some difficulty in that the links are in virtual contact to begin with. This means that capillary action tends to carry the solder along the chain no matter how carefully the heat is controlled.

One way to avoid such a problem is to melt the end of the chain first, thereby limiting the extent to which the solder can flow up it. Simply nip the end of the melted area off flat and there is a lovely surface which provides a nice strong junction point to which the jump ring or whatever may be soldered. Of course, it's still important to confine the heat to the specific area to avoid flooding the solder, but this method at least decreases the tendency.

Truth be told, I suck at chain-soldering, so I shouldn't be giving advice.

Alloys

An alloy, by simple definition, is a mixture of two or more metals. They are mixed for the express purpose of improving on the properties of one or the other, usually ending up with something better than either.

Gold, being very soft, needs to be mixed with other metals to make it less so. Silver and copper do the trick quite well, thank you, but sometimes we want more. By varying the proportions of the silver and copper in the mix, we can control, to an extent, the colour and the hardness of the resulting alloy.

In general, the higher the proportion of alloy in the mix, (the karat), the harder the alloy. So 10K is harder, in general, than 14K, which is harder again than 18K. This is not to say that 10K actually wears better than 18K, but that's a story for another day.

Once we've established the karat, the proportion of silver versus copper in the mix will also affect the properties. In general, a higher proportion of copper will yield a pinker or redder alloy which is also harder. Increasing the silver gives a softer alloy which tends towards a greenish tinge. In between are myriad shades of yellow gold of varying hardnesses.

The addition of nickel to the mix is where it starts to get weird. The addition of just a small percentage of nickel to the alloy makes white gold.

Originally, white gold was developed as a substitute for the other white precious metals; silver and platinum. Silver is very white but doesn't stay that way for very long. Left to itself, it tarnishes. It is very workable, although it is quite soft.

Platinum is miserable stuff to work with in a lot of ways, but is beautifully white and will remain so under all normal conditions, a truly noble metal. The fact that it costs a ton causes some problem, however.

Nickel white gold, our standard alloy, is hard and bright. Oddly enough, the eighteen karat white gold is much harder and whiter than fourteen karat. This goes against the logic that higher karat gold is softer, but this is jewellery, so logic doesn't apply.

The problem with eighteen karat nickel white gold is that it is so hard as to be almost useless for some purposes so the metallurgists came up with palladium white gold. This stuff isn't as hard and shiny as nickel white, but it does have a few characteristics that recommend it.

The colour of palladium white is closer to that of platinum, specifically iridium platinum. It's kind of grey, which is nice sometimes, especially if someone likes the colour of titanium.

This is a major subject of irritation for me; what is the goddam deal with titanium? It's grey and feels flimsy as hell in spite of being so hard as to be completely unworkable by regular folks. The same problem arises as with cheesy white gold, which is maintenance.

Let's say your ring gets scruffy looking, or you've suffered a cheesecake injury (major food-related weight gain) and it doesn't fit anymore. You want to drop in on your local goldsmith, and for a couple of bucks, and after a few minutes or days, it's more or less pretty again. You don't want to be told that your pride and joy, being titanium, needs to be subjected to some major industrial process or, worse yet, replaced.

Yes, replaced.

This is indeed the case with titanium rings. It's cheaper, in most cases, to simply replace the ring, titanium being so bloody cheap. Now, granted, titanium is expensive when compared to other industrial metals, but it's still sold by the *pound* for crissake. It's not a precious metal by a long shot.

Palladium white also addresses the flimsiness question. It is my feeling that heft equals quality. Perhaps it's just me, but heavy things are better than light things. Rolls-Royces weigh in at a couple of tons and that is good. Granted, Ferraris don't weigh hardly anything, but they're not actually meant for everyday wear. You could take the Bentley out on a Friday afternoon in Saskatoon, when the moron quotient is way high, and pound your way through several cheaper vehicles without slowing down. Perhaps a borrowed Bentley.

I'm rambling now.

So, if you have a custy who may be interested in a titanium wedding band, keep the palladium white gold idea in mind. Just be aware that 14K palladium white runs at about the same density and price as 18K. Did I mention that it's also expensive? Well, it is. Boohoo. All the more reason to sell it up.

The problem with the popularity of white gold right now is that, since the factories like to deal with huge quantities of any particular material, (economies of scale, don't you know,) they need a white gold that will respond well to the industrial processes to which it will be subjected. Palladium white gold ain't it. Nor, for that matter is the high-nickel white gold preferred by most folks. Both alloys have exceedingly high melting points and only a small window of opportunity within which they remain liquid once melted. This makes it difficult to cast large quantities of metal.

What does work for factories is an alloy which stays molten for the extended period of time necessary to fill the large capacity molds used. This is an alloy with an additional proportion of zinc to lower the melting point. The problem is this alloy isn't particularly white, more like beige. So what do the manufacturers, in their wisdom do with the crappy coloured beige gold? They plate it with lovely white rhodium, is what. This yields an exceedingly hard white chrome-like finish that ensures that the ring is going to get out the door of the store, that being the primary concern. What happens to it after that is most definitely not on the mind of the manufacturer.

What does happen is that the plating, being only microns thin, wears off. Then the beige gold shows through and, thanks to the intense contrast between the two metals, it appears that the ring is turning yellow. This leads to a maintenance problem.

Now, granted, if the first prerogative is to get customers through the front door, happy or not, then this replating necessity is a fine thing. If, however, it is satisfied customers you want, then telling them that they have to come in every six months or so and have their ring sent out to be plated, at about forty bucks a pop, is not the way to go. Jewellery is supposed to be worn and have an air of permanence about it. A lasting quality, not a temporary gloss.

Small casting lots and higher prices are the necessary sacrifices to be made if satisfactory white gold jewellery is ever to be acceptable to the discerning customer. And discerning customers are the best kind if they are treated with the respect they deserve.

Platinum

Okay, I have to admit that virtually all of my techniques are perfectly suited to platinum work. All the anal fitting, the pre-shaping and preparations before polishing?

These are all platinum things. However, I couldn't very well call this little tome "So You Want To Be A Platinumsmith" now, could I?

It's true, though. Platinum is muy demanding in all these ways and more. It's also exceedingly rewarding to those of us who find it necessary to make everything perfect.

I lie. The shit drives me crazy. Just when you think it's perfect, one tiny flaw shows up. One little scratch, a sandpaper mark, a solder line (and platinum solder always shows). Yes, some tiny, virtually imperceptible defect and, because everything else is so close to perfect, it sticks out like a pig in a punchbowl.

Okay, before I get myself all aufgeregt, perhaps I should begin at the beginning. Some sort of structure might be nice, for a change. You know me, organized as anything.

Platinum is a wonderful material with a great many interesting properties, not the least of which is its stubborn refusal to oxidize. This means that, try as you might, you will be unable to ruin the finish short of melting it. And that's tough to do on account of the fact that it won't melt until 1768.4°C. That's over thirty-two hundred degrees to the metrically retarded. Hot.

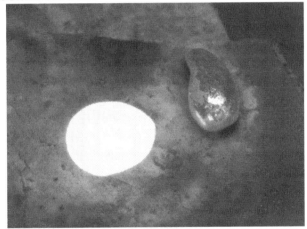

Granted, having to don welder's goggles just to melt some material can be a pain, but the hassle (and risks) are, in my opinion, far outweighed by the pleasure of seeing that bright, shiny smartie sitting there, all but permanently welded to the back of a crucible. You definitely need some tungsten alloy instruments to manipulate this stuff. Tungsten doesn't melt 'til 3422°C which, in Fahrenheit, is really hot.

If you decide to scrimp and just use steel, you will inevitably end up with an ugly coating of it contaminating your platinum. If the contamination gets melted into the body of the platinum, you are most definitely fucked. Or at least your platinum is. Oh, sure, you still may be able to turn it into something but, after all the initial labor is into it, it will be impossible to polish as the iron contamination will show up continually as an ugly discoloration on the surface, and it will *not* come out.

For this reason, it is important to keep all foreign matter out of the melt. Always clean up the surrounding area, both to avoid said contamination, and to avoid setting fire to everything in the vicinity. I repeat, this stuff is *hot*. The white thing in the picture is a glowing smartie.

Working with platinum is just like working with gold except that it's impossible to cast into a bar, so you have to use some tricks to render a smartie down to a usable chunk, be it bar or plate On the upside is the fact that you needn't concern yourself with fireskin during each step of the operation. Add to this the fact that, owing to its low heat-conductivity, platinum can be welded into itself at any stage of the proceedings, and you can start to have some fun. Okay, perhaps your idea of fun doesn't quite jibe with mine. No surprise there.

Y'see, the fact that this material is ninety to ninety-five percent pure gives it very nice working properties. Malleable and ductile in the extreme, it can be taken to great lengths without worrying about stress cracks and such nastiness.

Granted, the stresses will build up and cause problems if not attended to, twists and the like. Annealing is, naturally enough, done at a substantially higher temperature than would be considered prudent for gold, and for a more protracted period, as well. However, if you can look at it without goggles, there's precious little risk of melting through overheating, so fire away.

The real problem with platinum, the thing that makes us all nuts, is finishing the stuff. This is where it can all go wrong for you. Discipline is the word, here. If you try to rush through any particular stage, it will show up in a later stage, trust me. This is not the place for a "good enough" attitude.

Whereas gold is more or less ready to polish after being sanded; with platinum, you've only just begun. One trick is to perform each finishing operation at right angles to the previous one. This cuts back on nasty surprises. Nothing worse than finding the scratches you missed two stages late. Keep in mind how the next step is going to proceed, and it will go better for you. Besides, it is my opinion that scratches should never be removed by polishing, even in gold. They should be sanded out or, if they're more like gouges, filed, then sanded.

Once again, I must admit to being a bit of a fraud. I really have no clue how this is done in the real world, I simply make it up as best I can. Perhaps there are other methods more efficient than mine, but mine are all we have at this juncture. So be it.

One other indispensable in the finishing of platinum is a good burnisher, or a few good burnishers, depending on circumstances. These little beauties can occasionally eliminate the need for polishing altogether. When finishing castings in platinum, it is virtually always necessary to burnish the hell out of the surface so's to close up the tiny (and sometimes not so tiny) pits formed in the casting process.

Platinum is hard on burnishers because it's so tough, so the burnisher needs to be refinished often. A little oil or setter's friend will protect both the burnisher and the surface of the metal from the little bits of grit that can occasionally make life hell. Also, the oil will keep the surface of the platinum from contamination by the steel in the burnisher, although this isn't as much of a problem if the burnisher is sufficiently hard. Check out the section on burnishers in Tool Time.

Once you've entered the polishing room with the piece, the fun has just begun. It's important, as with gold, to avoid polishing in one direction as this will cause streaky little lines to form. These lines just get worse and worse if you attempt to polish them out, so don't try. At first, polishing platinum entails a lot of backing-and-forthing as you realize that you did, indeed, miss a spot. And get used to burning your fingers. If you ain't burning your fingers, you ain't polishing platinum.

I didn't want to get into the whole platinum thing in a big way except for a couple of tips. Platinum Guild International has a bunch of excellent publications that cover the subject in intense detail. They do tend to favour the mass-production end of things a bit, deep-pocket industrial techniques foreign to the low-rent systems I espouse.

One handy little nugget that I will leave you with is that your worn out files come in very handy when working with this stuff. You've probably noticed its draggy tendencies if you've had any contact with it at all. A new file jams up solid in no time at all on platinum; little pins of material clogging the teeth and scratching the surface of the piece. Irritating as hell. For some reason, though, an old file doesn't have this problem to the same extent.

Way back in watch repair school, the machine-shop instructor gave us some advice in a similar vein. Use your new files on softer metals 'til they're worn a bit before using them on steel. In that case it was more a matter of letting the teeth round off a little so that they're not as brittle. Same concept, only different.

Oh, you still have to clear the file often, old or new, it's just the way platinum is. A tenacious metal, it jams in the teeth with alarming frequency. I use a thin sheet of 14k tri-colour gold for no other reason than that it's more or less useless for anything else. Just drag it along the teeth until they're clear of the little nuggets that are causing the problems. Yeah, right, it's just that simple. Sure. Patience pays off, as one little pin of platinum clogging the file can undo hours of finishing work.

Textured Finishes

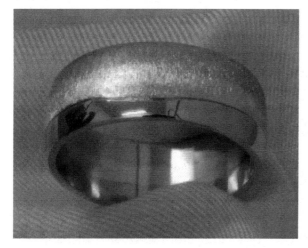

Just a few words about the many textures that are available to relieve the ennui induced by plain, old, boring, perfect polished surfaces.

First of all, textures are *not* meant to hide faulty surface finishing. They should be part of the design, not some desperate afterthought.

With this in mind, it's crucial to finish as you would for a highly polished surface. If the surface isn't perfect to begin with, fix it. Any decent texture won't hide much, anyway, so you had best pay attention to the details now, or they will most certainly make themselves known, later.

Oh, granted, if the surface is afflicted with the fine, frosty porosity that can affect 18k white gold, for example, a nice texture will render it less noticeable, but what if the custy decides, "Hey, maybe a polished surface *would* be nice after all?" They do this, you know.

Polish first, then texture 'til the shiny bits are all gone. This way, you're certain that the surface is perfect before applying the finish. Plus, you know when the finish is yet unfinished, as the shiny bits stand out quite distinctly from the textured.

Being human, of course, we all try to fudge this last bit, but in the long run, it always pays to do it right the first time. The plan, in most cases, is to create a uniform finish which leaves no clue as to how it was created. A little mystery, here, please. Actually, with a little extra care, it's an easy matter to dazzle the folks who already *know* how the finish is done, but have never taken the time to do it properly.

Don't be afraid to experiment. Ball-burs, bearing-cutters (hart-burs), cut-off discs, they all make cool finishes, but if you use them in a creative ways, remarkable results can be achieved. A hart bur can be used to make a real cool mac-tac kind of woodgrain effect, if you do it right. And a tiny ball-bur can create a sort of sandblast finish which I consider to be better than a real sandblast in that you don't need a sandblaster. I hate gizmos.

Future considerations are also taken into account, in that these finishes are easily renewed over the years. The concept of a factory-applied finish that cannot possibly be duplicated in a shop setting completely escapes me. This is my basic problem with the whole concept of rhodium-plating white gold, but that's a story for another day.

Finishing the finish is also important. If you just let the finish fade off into the polished area, it will look kind of lackadaisical. Sloppy, y'know. My favorite method is to make a razor-thin cut with a triangular graver to separate the two. If the two are on different planes, around the corner from each other, this won't be necessary, but I like to see a distinct transition in any case. Planning is important.

A properly executed texture is a lovely touch, providing another method of creating depth and movement in a fairly limited medium.

Burnishing

A textured finish, properly done, is a lovely addition to a piece of jewellery, but occasionally a texture shows up which wasn't planned. This would be the scourge of porosity.

Whether from a bad casting or a bad soldering job, sometimes the metal has been overheated to the point that bubbles form in the melted metal and remain there when it freezes. Starting over is not always an option, but there are ways to alleviate the problem without going all nuts.

Burnishing is the use of a highly polished metal tool to compress the metal in the porous area so that the holes, while not going away entirely, can be made to disappear or at least be less noticeable. You will find the method to make yourself a fine burnisher back in the tool section. The burnisher is applied to the surface of the metal with all the strength that your puny arms can muster,

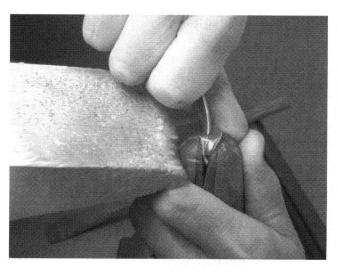

compressing the surface and, hopefully, closing up the major holes.

This leaves the surface more or less flat, but small-scale bumpy because of the variance in the density of the metal. Previous to this it was, in effect, foamy. There are other methods of burnishing using power tools, but I find that they make the surface so much worse than the porosity itself, that the cure is worse than the disease. That being said, try several methods to determine the one that suits you best.

File the ring flat to remove most of the irregularities, keeping to surface as flat as possible. After filing, go over the surface with

the burnisher again, but this time using somewhat less force. It will take several repetitions to achieve a smooth surface, but persevere and it will all work out.

The metal, now being nice and flat, is actually a bit of a skin, with the cavities still lurking just below the surface. The trick now is to avoid removing material in such a way that the variable hardness of the surface doesn't cause it to become bumpy again.

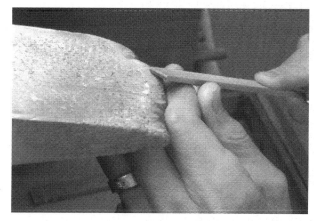

Using a soft medium such as Tripoli at this point would simply cause the cavities to reappear. Therefore, stick with fine sandpaper and, in order to keep it as flat as possible, sand the top of the ring by using a square of sandpaper and your bench block, or some other extremely flat, hard surface. Place the sandpaper on the surface, holding it steady, and sand the metal flat, being careful all the while to avoid rounding off the edges of the

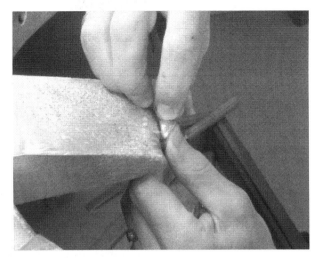

top. In this case, a small piece of extremely fine sandpaper (1200 grit) is rubbed in a random way in the middle of the surface. This further ensures that the edges remain sharp.

If you have access to a wonderful product called MicroMesh, the surface can be finished to such a degree that resorting to the polishing machine becomes almost unnecessary. Any excess polishing will cause the porosity to reappear.

This is not an ideal way to do things, but starting over on any job that isn't absolutely perfect is not the best way to run one's life. Expedience is sometimes necessary.

In the case of a poor solder joint, it is often quickest to cut out the offending, overheated solder and redo it, but if there are time constraints, the burnishing method will allow the ring to be finished quickly. Just remember that the final polishing should always be done across the solder joint to avoid any unpleasantness.

Burnishing castings as a matter of course is actually a good habit to get into, since the density of most castings is quite low, making the surface soft. The ring will take a much better polish and be less likely to scratch after the process. This is especially true of platinum.

So…

If you've been paying attention, then you will realize that what I've tried to give you here is an old-fashioned Chinese menu for putting together some pretty cool rings. One from column A. One from column B...

I admit that the rings made by these methods seem to lack any real sense of style, being very basic in design. Dull, really. All I know is that I've sold a ton of extremely fine engagement and wedding sets based on exactly these concepts. A little tweak here, a bit of a curve there, and by cracky, it does have style, after all. My stuff has been belittled by the more artistic of our brethren as "conservative" or "commercial", and I suppose it is. I don't know where you live, but around here getting married is still a very conservative affair, and making a living is a fine way to continue in your goldsmithing career. You work it out.

My experience has been that the best stuff is done when you've designed just a little beyond your capabilities. It makes you extend yourself in a controlled manner, with only a bit of the risk associated with the unknown.

As for commercial, if you don't think it's commercial, take a look around. Weddings account for a huge percentage of yearly retail sales anywhere in the world, and you ignore that fact at your peril. If you are not interested in making a living at this game, I wish you would go now, because this show will bring you down so much...

In the process, I hope I've instilled in you some of the joy of creation and a bit of the importance of detail that makes this job fun.

Setting Overview

The basic concept of stone-setting is, of course, to hold a stone in place while showing it off to best advantage and, if possible, providing it with a modicum of protection.

It is important to have several different methods at our disposal to achieve the best combination of strength, safety, and appearance. For example, small stones are not shown off to great advantage in four-claw heads because the claws, being relatively huge compared to the stone, cover up an awful lot of the crown and lessen the brilliance. At the other end of the scale, bead-setting larger stones is inefficient due to the amount of material that needs to be removed in relation to the size of the stone. Channel-setting is a very limited method and not one of my favorites. Invisible setting isn't worth mentioning. If you can't say something nice...

The engineering behind a proper setting job is, or should be, not immediately obvious. We're trying to provide a little bit of magic, here. Most importantly, the bearing's the thing. Almost all the setting problems one encounters can be traced back to the early stages of preparing the setting; mostly the bearing. If it's not right, nothing else will be. One of the best ways to make the process of stone setting more efficient is to limit the amount of cutting necessary to create a bearing.

The bearing of a particular setting is simply the support beneath the stone's girdle. In many inferior settings the stone is in contact with the bearing a goodly way down the pavilion. This has several disadvantages.

Perhaps the most important is that it is simply inefficient. Cutting away that much material takes a lot of time and is likely to result in a lot of burned out burs. Too many of my brethren find it easy to just power a bur into the setting, unheeding of the screaming of the overworked bur and the smoke as it loses its temper. This method has many disadvantages beyond the obvious. The chance that the stone is supported somewhere other than at the girdle increases the possibility of damaging it. Gemstones, as a rule, are possessed of great compressive strength, but relatively little shear strength. Diamonds are cleaved by taking advantage of weakness along the so-called cleavage plane, and if we're not careful, the same plane can take us straight to hell.

The other reason for avoiding deep bearings is one that will show up later in the life of the setting. As the ring, or whatever, is worn, skin oils and dirt of various sorts build up on the underside of the stone. This filth is easily removed by standard cleaning methods as long as there is ample room for it to be flushed out. Due to capillary action, however, it is common for junk to get into the narrow interstices of the setting and not want to come out.

The longer the bearing, the greater the capillary force in play, so you have this great whack of goop stuck to the pavilion of the stone where it rests on the claw. If it's a diamond and it's perfectly cut then this doesn't matter so much, but in a less than perfect world, it's our job to enhance the appearance of the stone as much as possible. Better we should limit the amount of contact between the claw and the stone as much as we can.

Next is the metal over the stone. This is the tip, the collet lip, the top of a V-tip, or the bead in a bead setting. The common tendency is to assume that the larger the tip, the better it will wear, so by cracky let's make it big.

Now, granted that we want to see some metal over the stone, but let's not get carried away. The problem with large tips is that, beyond a certain point, the dead weight of all that excess material is ugly. The most important area of a claw or collet is that just outside and above the girdle of the stone. If there is plenty of weight here, and the stone is properly fitted, nothing is going to get that stone out of there. Many commercial settings scrimp on this most important area and emphasize the metal on top of the crown of the stone. What you get then is a claw that is large enough to catch on stuff easily, and without the strength to counteract the leverage, resulting in the tip folding back at the most inopportune moment. I go into this at great length in the section on claw-setting.

So, to reiterate, the material on top of the stone is ideally not what is holding the stone; it's the metal compressed against the girdle, in most cases, that is the major factor in ensuring that the stone remains set no matter how long it's worn. Many are the times we would get a worn-out diamond ring back at Dunn's, the tips worn entirely away from the crown of the stone, but the stone still securely wedged into the setting. These would be stones set by Jack's grandfather, William Edmund Dunn, from whom I learned, indirectly, the whole setting gig.

Sharpening Tweezers

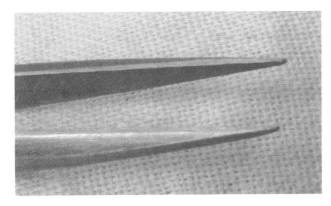

I suppose this belongs in the tool section, but you will have forgotten it by now, and it is important to the process.

Through use, the inner surfaces of your tweezers get worn smooth and rounded off. The tendency is to try to use more pressure, which just means that when the stones pop out, they will do so at a correspondingly higher velocity; expanding the search area in the process. Picking up a multitude of small stones is fussy work and it will be made even more so if you can't keep a grip on them.

For the sharpening process, we use a fairly coarse, small sharpening stone; sometimes called a penknife stone. Or penknife piece, fairly archaic concept nonetheless.

The trick when using this is to hold the inner plane of the blade of

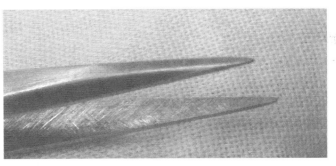

the tweezer flat against the stone while you slide it back and forth. Do this by pressing it down on the broad area up the blade a bit. It's a tricky little move to describe in print, but the broad area ensures that the skinny bit at the tip doesn't rock and simply make matters worse. Don't try to do both jaws of the tweezer at once, it won't work. When once you have achieved a nice clean surface on both inner faces, it is a simple matter to clean up the sides and the tip to present a sharp angle. I like to have a sort of chisel shape to the tip. Not razor sharp, but that sort of shape. The absolute flatness of the inner tips means that stones will be held securely without much pressure.

Another option is to use fine sandpaper, or, more specifically, 600 grit wet/dry silicon carbide paper. Hold the sandpaper in the tweezers' jaws, under a bit of pressure, and drag the paper through. It's best not to drag the paper all the way out under pressure, as the last little bit rounds off the very ends of the tweezers.

Bead Setting

Based on the primitive techniques I espouse throughout this little endeavor, bed-setting would be a good place to start the subject of setting. It's where I started, after all.

Okay, dead simple. We're going to set a stone into a square. Just a little stone, don't worry. Big stones are different. Way different. We're assuming that the square is atop a ring or otherwise secured, as it's tremendously frustrating trying to set a stone into a free-floating square of white gold like the one illustrated.

These are some of my oldest drawings for this book, so bear with me until I come up with alternatives.

First of all, is it a square? If it's supposed to be a square, make sure. Measure it seven ways from Sunday. Check angles. Measure sides. Whatever it takes, make sure because you'll hate yourself if it ain't so.

Now, lay out a couple of lines from corner to corner.

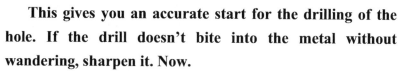

They cross in the centre unless you didn't use opposite corners. Do so. Mark this centre by digging out a small divot with a round graver.

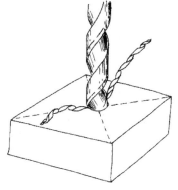

This gives you an accurate start for the drilling of the hole. If the drill doesn't bite into the metal without wandering, sharpen it. Now.

Switch to a tapered bur and ream the hole out to the diameter of the stone, checking often. If your hole wasn't positioned perfectly, you can move it around a bit with the bur, but you shouldn't have to. You risk making the hole oval, so be careful.

Now, before we go any further, I should mention that I do all this stuff under magnification. This is because I'm a genetic mutant who is left-eye dominant. This is covered in the intro, so go back and read it. We'll wait here...

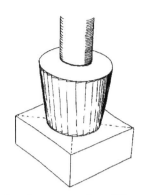

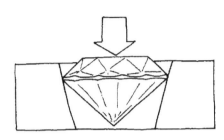

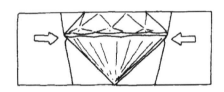

The stone should drop into the hole 'til it's almost level with the surface of the metal. It should actually be just a hair above, and, with a bit of pressure, it should bite into the sides of the hole and be left perfectly flush. Check the surface from every which way to make absolutely certain that this is so. Remove the raised burr from the edge of the hole so your view is clear.

Okay now. Things are going to get a bit Zen from here on.

You have to imagine a 45 degree angle from the girdle of the stone to a point on the metal. This will be a distance from the edge of the hole equal to the depth of the stone. Zen. Right is right.

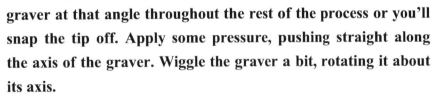

Place the tip of the small round graver on one of the diagonal lines, aiming towards the stone, of course. If the tip doesn't bite in right away, it's dull, sharpen it. Now.

Hold the graver at about a 45 degree angle, sort of aiming at the girdle. Scary. Keep the graver at that angle throughout the rest of the process or you'll snap the tip off. Apply some pressure, pushing straight along the axis of the graver. Wiggle the graver a bit, rotating it about its axis.

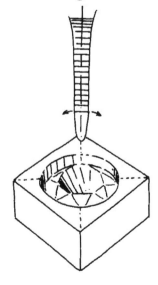

This isn't a twisting motion, but more of a vibration. What you're doing is using the outer edges of the graver to apply some additional leverage to the metal. It also seems to cause more of a slicing action, which results in tidier beads. Experience will help you figure it out.

The main reason for this apparently risky process (the aiming at the girdle thing) is that if you overshoot, you will knock off the bead above the stone, perhaps crushing the stone in the process. Contrariwise, if you aim under, the stone will be pushed up and out of position. Or, more likely, you'll simply snap off the end of your graver on accounta there's just too much metal to move. Just aim at the girdle and you'll be fine.

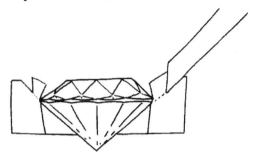

You will notice the edge of the hole being distorted in front of the tip, and at the same time you will feel an increase in resistance as you push the graver towards the girdle. At some time or another, you're going to have to stop pushing. Don't force it, but if you are indeed aiming at the girdle, it will be virtually impossible to go too far. The force of the graver has pushed the edge of the hole over the stone. This is your rough bead. (You will notice in the picture that the rough bead is not mashed down over the crown of the stone with the graver. Actually, it isn't even forced completely down until the very final step, after cutting up. This preserves the maximum amount of material so that the finished bead will be as attractive as possible.)

At the same time, the stone will be forced against the opposite wall of the hole. Hopefully, it remains level. If you've done everything correctly, it will. Trust me.

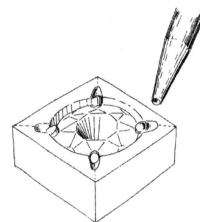

Do the same thing on the opposite side, then, check to make sure that everything's proceeding hunky-dorily, because this is probably your last chance to fix up any problems. Then, because we've done everything right, the remaining beads can be "raised". The stone is officially locked in.

Use a beader to give a bit of shape to the rough bead. There's no need to smash it down, just rock it around a bit. We'll come back to it later.

Trimming the setting starts behind the bead and tends to be a bit tedious, but you've got to pay attention. This is where the real graver-pusher can show off. Start with one corner of your flat graver on your diagonal layout line behind the bead, almost to the corner of your square. Now slice forward to your bead. You shouldn't have to use too much pressure because your graver is sharp, right? When you reach the bead, you can pop the curl off, but not the bead. You don't want to try to remove too much material at once, or you will most certainly fuck something up.

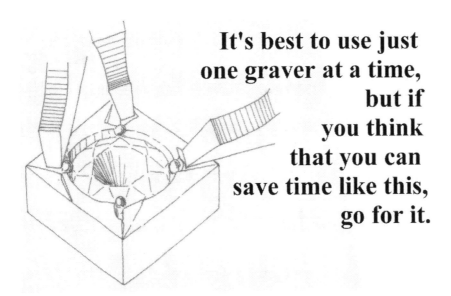

It's best to use just one graver at a time, but if you think that you can save time like this, go for it.

Cut away material behind each bead, gradually flattening the cuts 'til the back of each cut is parallel to the sides of the square.

Start cutting away the sides of the hole between the beads. First, cut towards one bead, then, work your way around the stone one bead at a time. You'll realize that you are sliding your graver along the girdle of a diamond, and the graver is losing. This is true, but it is only one corner. The other one is just fine.

Flip the graver over and trim to the other side of each bead. Once again, you gradually flatten the cut until it's parallel to the sides of the square. Sharpen your graver often. It's a pain in the ass, but it's a lot less risky than some other methods.

You should be noticing that the square is forming up nicely. The remaining work should be done with an extremely sharp, bright-cut graver.

The technique used in cutting starts out rather crudely, the graver being pushed straight forward as with a chisel. As you get into the finishing cuts, more of a slicing motion should be employed. Finishing is virtually always a gradual removal of the evidence of previous work, and this is no exception. As you slice one way, lines are formed by choppy cutting. By sharpening up and cutting in the opposite

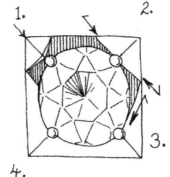

direction, those lines will be removed, or at least diminished. This process can go on forever, so at some point you have to admit that it's the best you can do. Never good enough, but the best you can do at that moment.

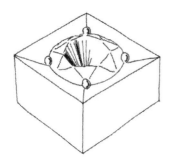

Once the square is smooth and bright, use the beader to finish up each bead perfectly. The word to describe a perfect bead is "latagne". I think it's French.

Something worth considering at this point is millegrain; another French word, I guess. It translates to 'thousand granules' or something.

In any case, it gives a very tidy, finished look to a bead setting, so I use it a lot. As usual, though, I have my own anal twist on the correct procedure. That sounds painful.

If you are possessed of immensely powerful hands, and superb control, then milgrain (an alternative spelling, probably American) will be no problem for you, Jack. However, it is generally best to prepare the area and leave less of the process to chance.

This usually consists of simply ensuring that the edge to be treated is sharp, consistent, and, if possible, at an acute angle. This makes it easier to keep the millegrain tool, which is just a little wheel with a bunch of little round divots in it, on the right track. It also makes the myriad little beads stand out a little more latagne, style points, y'know.

As you gain experience in the technique, you will find that setting the stone deeper will make cutting it up a lot easier. For the same reason, it is best to keep the square as small as possible in proportion to the stone. It is brutally difficult to cut a broad surface perfectly flat and smooth, but it is good practice. So I guess I should move this paragraph closer to the beginning of the section. I'm such a prick. If you are presented with a situation where there is too much space for the stone, read on.

Selby Setting

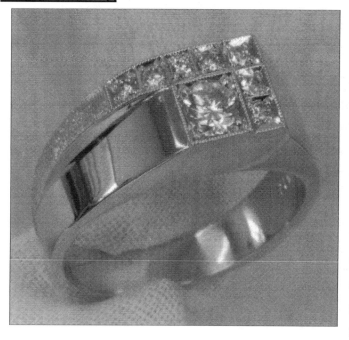

Another bead-setting method, the one mentioned as being more difficult, if not more risky, is one that comes in handy for bead setting larger stones, as well as more fragile stones. It also works real well when you're left with too much room and not enough stones. My buddy Selby sends me setting work where there's way too much room for the number of stones, so I need to use this method a lot. Therefore, we will refer to this style of setting as Selby setting. So mote it be. It's a somewhat more advanced method and yields very nice results when successful. When unsuccessful, it can result in a huge amount of extra work and interruptions in sleep patterns.

Basically, you're going to do virtually all the cutting-up before setting the stone. This means that you're not constantly grinding off the corner of your graver against the girdle of the diamond. At the same time, you aren't going to grind off the sides of softer semi-precious stones with the corner of your graver.

Drilling the hole and fitting the stone is done the same way as previously, although you can generally go a bit deeper, because you're moving a lot less metal and the bead should be a bit more prominent in this style of setting.

Now you lay out your corner-to-corner lines as before (having removed the stone from the hole) and determine where your bead should start from.

You do this by laying out small triangles, or 'A's on each centre line. These will be left standing after cutting away your square so think about them carefully.

The width of the 'A' will be determined by the size of the stone and the size of the graver that will be used in setting the stone. And how confident you feel that day. And the phase of the moon. You know, right is right.

Generally, the width of the 'A' will be about the same width as the end of the graver - a graver somewhat larger than what that used in regular bead-setting. The height of the 'A' is a bit harder to determine, but if you imagine that the bead will be started about half-way along it, you should be okay.

Now, with a nice sharp triangular graver, you start your cut at the top of the 'A' and just make a nice, light cut into the hole. Keep the cut to the outside of your layout line so's to preserve the entire width of your 'A'. Be careful that you don't try to go too deep all at once, as you'll just snap off the tip of the graver in the metal, or it'll snap when you come to the edge of the hole and plunge into the other side.

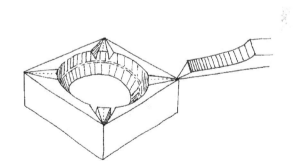

(The reason that I call it an 'A' is that, upon occasion, you will be starting the cut at the cross-bar of the imaginary 'A'. This is primarily with larger stones, so just keep it in mind and you won't be ending up with outlandishly huge beads when you don't need them.)

These cuts should be just deep enough to come to the girdle of the stone. This is easy to determine if you're setting a larger stone and have used a bearing cutter, but mostly you'll just have to feel it. With experience comes confidence. Pretty profound, huh?

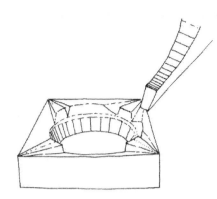

Now comes the risky bit. Well, the first risky bit, actually. You're going to bright-cut your square, leaving the beads (your little 'A's) untouched. Take your time and you won't cut off one of the beads and have to start all over again. There are tricks, but it's best to assume that, if you knock off a bead, the whole job's fucked and you have to start over. Terror keeps you focused.

Speaking of focus; on reflection, these illustrations bear absolutely no resemblance to reality. The scale is way off. For example, if this were a #10 graver (my favorite), then the stone would be about 12mm in diameter. This is way too big to bead set. Never mind.

Once the square's nice and clean, use the reamer to clean the hole up. Gently now, you don't want to enlarge it, simply clean up the burrs left by cutting the beads. Then poke the stone in and level it.

Raising the beads should begin just a little farther back than usual, with the cut just a bit shallower. You are still aiming at the girdle, but it will take a lot less pressure to move the requisite amount of material. Carefully observe the tip of the 'A' as it curls up and over the girdle of the stone. When the base of the 'A'

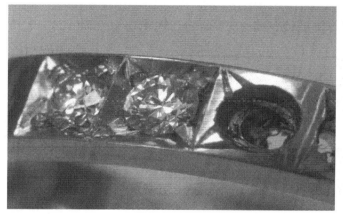

begins to move out over the girdle, stop. This is the scariest part of the whole trip. If you knock off a tip now, there's no metal left from which to start a panic bead. Oh yes, there's also the risk of smashing the stone.

Good fun.

Repeat this process on the other beads.

On smaller stones, the whole 'A' is used, which leaves this tiny skewed pyramid hovering over the girdle. On larger stones, when you start halfway down the 'A', the rough bead is closer to a cube.

Using the appropriate beader, shape the beads over the stone. You'll see that quite a substantial bead has been formed. That's the beauty of this method. Now simply clean up the area behind each bead, and you're done.

Using this method, most of the work is done early on, so it seems like a real timesaver, and other times it seems like a major pain in the ass. And sometimes no other method will do.

Star Setting

In this world of ours, there are a few tasks that are so simple as to be impossible to get right. This comes up in the wax-carving section in the construction of signet rings. In that case, it is the compound curves that cause the grief, here it is the crisp precision that makes the slightest flaw stand out. Making a perfect signet ring and star-setting a diamond in the centre is not for the weak of spirit.

Of course, the trick is experience. No, I don't make anything easy. Through repeated trials, the task becomes easier because the tiny errors are recognized before they get too huge.

The operation starts pretty much the way any bead-setting does; stone level with the surface and just slightly lower.

With the stone out, we use a desperately sharp triangular graver to cut into the hole. I don't mention layout at this point because, quite frankly, it won't help. The assumption here is that we're setting this stone into a pristine, highly polished surface, so any layout lines will be cut away in the process. You can easily scritch in some teensy guidelines at ninety degree increments around the hole using all the tricks at your command, and at least that'll get you started on the right track.

In any case, it's best to kind of nibble away at it so that any discrepancies will show up early enough to be corrected. If it seems that I'm going on about this, it's because it's important.

Another reason to take it slow is that, if you try to cut away too much metal at once, the following edge of the graver forces up an unsightly ridge behind the cut. Add to this the fact that you will surely snap a half-mil off the tip of your graver and it all adds up to a double plus bad idea. So don't do it.

Take your time and don't get carried away. The best looking stars, in my opinion, are nice and tight. Never longer than the diameter of the stone, certainly, and the larger the stone, the shorter the star in proportion. I find that, as in other styles of bead-setting, the result is generally more pleasing if the cutting is kept to a minimum. It's quicker, too. Also less chance of Hitlering it.

While working around the setting, I like to do something that seems kind of counter-intuitive. Rather than trying to bring all the points of the star to perfect symmetry by enlarging the small ones, I go to the biggest one and make it as perfect as I can. Only then do I try to bring the others to the same size and shape. This is assuming that they are all positioned more or less correctly. It's a maddening process, but if you keep your eyes open and don't rush it, you'll be okay.

The cuts should extend to below the girdle to allow light to bounce around in a pleasing manner and make cleaning easy.

Push the stone into place and make certain that this is so. Note how the stone seems to be suspended in the setting, this is good.

Using a round graver, aim at the girdle of the stone and carefully push a little bead of metal over the stone. It needn't go very far over the crown, so don't get carried away. If you try to move too much material at once you will end up knocking the stone off level. Or out, god forbid.

Besides, it doesn't take a lot of metal to hold a stone in such a tightly fitting hole, and we're looking to keep things very clean here. Too big a bead just tends to look sloppy.

To this end, it behooves us to make the beads as small as practical, all things considered. I just wanted to say behooves. I apologize for my appalling behooviour.

Once the stone is locked in, round up the bead a little with the appropriate beader. There's no need to form a perfect bead right now, we're just trying to define things so we know where to cut. Use a nice, crisp, polished beader, though, as polishing this style of setting should be almost unnecessary.

With your square graver, cut in behind the beads, once again taking small bites to ensure symmetry. Also, if you rush this, you will most definitely snap the tip off your graver. The cuts needn't be long, just perfect.

Now use your flat graver to widen these cuts 'til they're just about touching the previous star cuts. Style points are gained by having the inner points of the star meet so that they appear to touch the stone when viewed from above.

Thanks to all the prep-work, there's nothing left to do but tidy up the beads to a pleasant state of latagne and give it a cursory rouging with a short-bristle brush. Anything more and you risk losing the crisp definition for which we are justifiably famous.

It's a classic style of setting for some very good reasons. It's attractive, simple, and it wears like stink. I've worked on many a ring made at the turn of the century (the last one) where the stone is still intact although the rest of the piece is toast. In effect, the entire top of the ring has to be worn away before the stone is in jeopardy. Only problem back then, though, was that they tended to make the jewellery so ungodly thin. False economies, don't you know.

Preparation however, is the key to a proper job. The gravers need to be scrupulously sharp and the beaders tidy; otherwise, the results are destined to be no better than expected.

Shared-Bead Setting

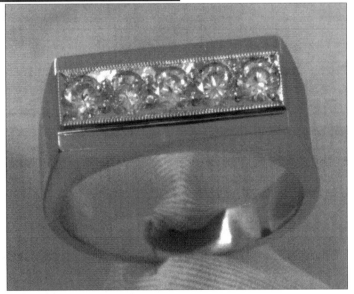

The next step on the road to setting fame (pavé) is to set some stones, generally small ones, in a straight line, with shared beads. Hence the name.

We're assuming that everything's already laid out so that a series of stones, let's say seven, will fill the space and end up just about touching.

First, make certain that this is true. This is where we are introduced to setter's friend. Setter's friend is a water-based protein solution with which we will temporarily fix the stones, face-down, to the surface into which they will be set.

Pick up the first stone in your tweezers and gently touch it to your tongue and place it in position. Repeat, and place the second stone right next to the first with just a shade of space between them.

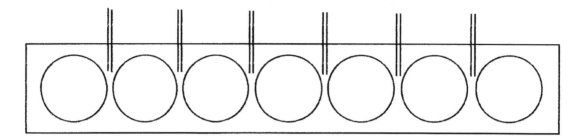

Experience will determine the correct spacing as the stones need to be far enough apart so as not to touch (they break, you know) but not so far that a single bead will fail to hold them both. Actually, each stone is held by four beads which it shares with its adjacent buddies. I suppose that I could call this covalent setting. Maybe I just will.

Move the stones around while the setter's friend is still wet and get the spacing perfect. I always rush this step and hate myself later.

Did I mention that setter's friend is spit? Well, it is. Quite disgusting, really, but it's always right there when you need it. Just remember to use it sparingly, as it defeats the whole purpose if the stuff spreads around and glumps up whole clusters of stones. Plus spinbarkite may develop and drag stones out of position. Avoid milk.

So you've got these diamonds stuck belly up in puddles of gob. Now what do you do?

First, pick up the second stone. Not the one on the end, the second one. Look, there's a little circle (an octagon, actually) left by the table of the stone. It may be barely visible, but it's there. So with your sharp, pointy scriber you make a little circle in the centre of your little invisible mark. Make sure that your scribed mark is directly and exactly midway between the two adjacent stones. If it is so, stick the stone back in position. Don't try to save time by trying to mark all the positions in one go. It will go badly for you, trust me.

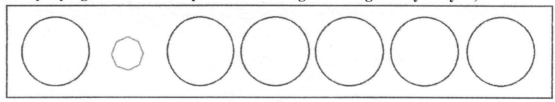

Now, grab the next stone (again, not the end one, which will be done last) and mark its centre just as carefully. Repeat. Do the end stones last. Now, place the stones in order on your little pan, remembering or marking which end is which. This is important because no matter how identical the stones may appear, there are tiny differences which will return to haunt you.

With a small round graver, mark the centre point of each stone's position with a little divot to start your drill in. A sharp drill, need I add?

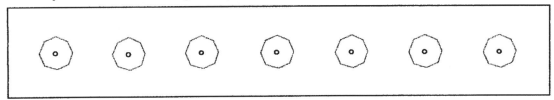

Pay attention, now.

Start drilling the second hole. When the drill starts to bite, stop and check to see that it's drilling exactly midway between the two adjacent divots. If it is, go a bit deeper until the hole is committed. Use a bit of oil to assist the cutting, but not too much, because you need to see what's happening.

Skip a divot and drill the next hole in the same way. Do the same thing in the next alternate space so that what you've got is divot, hole, divot, and like that, all perfectly spaced. Right? If not, now is the time to deal with it.

Now drill the other spots, the divots, again checking spacing. Then go ahead and finish drilling the holes through, using plenty of oil so's to avoid overheating the drill. Lovely little curls of metal all over the place. It's a beautiful thing.

Switch over to your tapered bur and open the holes, paying attention all the while to the spacing. If all goes well, the holes will all expand evenly until they're virtually touching, with just a thin web of material between each. Chances are, though, that you'll have to move the holes this way and that, just don't get carried away. Many times I've moved the holes so that the spacing was perfect, only to find that I'd made them all too large. Bummer.

Using a small, round graver, cut away the thin area where the holes touch. Cut down to a depth about twice the distance from the girdle of the stones to the table. Christ, I don't know, just make the notches deep enough. You want them deep enough so that there's clearance below the girdles. It'll become obvious as we go.

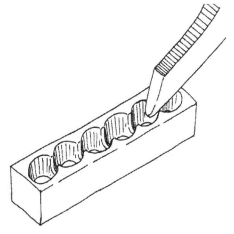

Clean away all the burrs from around the tops of the holes and clean up all the oil and crap so the area's nice and tidy.

While you're at it, clean up the pan of your bench a bit, put away surplus tools, and sweep up filings and cookie crumbs. You're going to be dropping tiny diamonds, trust me, and you want to have a clear field in which to find them

In most cases, the tapered bur is the only one necessary for this style of setting, but there are times when other burs may be brought into play. Flame burs, hart burs, even ball burs will sometimes come in handy, particularly when for some reason the hole does not go all the way through the metal or there is some obstruction behind the hole.

Grab your first stone and plunk it into the first hole. If it drops right in, congratulations, you're a genius. On this planet however, we have to expand the hole a bit. This calls for a great deal of patience; alternately burring and fitting until the stone drops to just below the surface of the metal. How much depends on the size of the stone and the crown angle, as well as many other variables, but for now just make sure that the actual table is slightly below the metal surface. Probably seventy-five percent of the problems that arise during bead-setting are caused by seating the stones too shallow. Granted, the other twenty-five percent are caused by setting the stones too deep, but there you go.

Once it looks right, put the stone back on your little pan thingy. Okay, that's it. I've simply got to name the sonofabitch and have done with it. A digression.

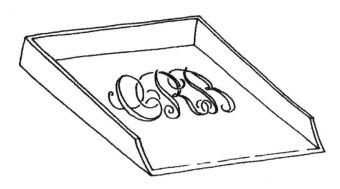

When I was back at Dunn's, I was doing a monster pavé setting job and had at my disposal every stone in the shop under about six points. In order to keep them organized, I also had every diamond shovel in the place. A diamond shovel, as you may gather, is a scoop-like device for carting around large numbers of stones. I ended up making one for myself because the commercial ones had high sides that made it hard to pick up stones. Tweezers bumped them you know. Anyway, mine is brass and has CRB engraved on it very nicely for reasons that we needn't go into here.

Take the second stone and fit it the same way, but before putting it back on the pan, take the first stone and put it back into the first hole. Make sure that they both sit at the correct level, I.E. a little below the surface. Remove the second stone.

Now, with your large round graver, which is used almost exclusively for this purpose, push the first stone firmly into its seat, ensuring that it stays level. Mind that you're not trying to sink the stone any deeper, that's for the bur to do. (How deep, exactly, that is is always the question. Eighty percent of the problems that develop in bead-setting are caused by not setting the stones deep enough. Granted, the other twenty percent are caused by setting the stones too deep, but there you go.) You're just squeezing a little groove the metal as a bearing for the stone. It shouldn't move now so grab the third stone and fit it.

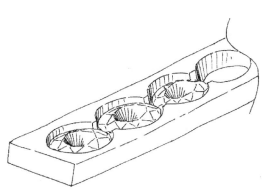

What you're doing now is sort of working in pairs. One stone that's already fitted and one that's in the process. This way you aren't trying to run a bur right next to a diamond (always fatal for the bur, and often for the stone). Also, you're not trying to fit all seven stones at once. This is cumbersome as hell and if you happen to bump the pan and mix up the stones you'll waste a lot of time and hate yourself.

So just do it my way and don't argue. It's my book.

The other advantage to doing it this way is that you've always got a reference point for stone depth just two holes back. Brilliant, huh?

When the third stone is fitted, put it back on the pan in its appointed spot and lock in the second. Carry on to the end until they are all firmly in place.

One little tip at this juncture. As you go along, burring away and locking stones into place, you'll discover a build-up of gold particles from the burring process. This crap gets in the way and affects the way the stones fit, so it behooves us to remove it. This is where Rodico One-Touch, or its cheaper alternative, comes into play. From time to time during the process, jam a wad of this stuff into the setting-in-progress. It lifts away the crap and, not incidentally, checks to see if the stones are indeed locked in. It's best to find out now.

I admit that all this toing-and-froing seems anal as hell just to set seven more or less identical stones but the point is that you seldom have such a straightforward time of it. Mostly what I run into in the bizz is remount work. This is when you're presented with a dog's breakfast of small single-cuts from a variety of rings and are expected to combine them into some sort of cohesive design. Then you end up with twenty different sized stones and a curved, tapered plate to set them into. Keeping track of the individual stones then becomes the most important thing in your little world, trust me. If you learn to do it the hard way, the simple jobs are a pleasure.

Lovely. It's time to start setting the stones in earnest.

In order to ensure that the stones remain level, we'll lay the beads down alternately across the row. Where to start the beads is, as usual, the big question.

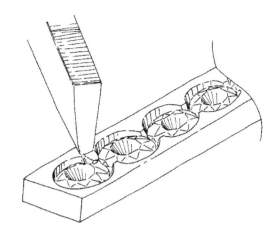

Using a medium size graver, place its tip just back of the point where two stones (first and second) meet. Visualize an equilateral triangle formed by the arcs of the two stones and your graver at the base. Zen again.

Since the stones are set more deeply than an individual stone, you'll be pushing your graver a bit more deeply as well. Slightly closer to perpendicular is what I'm trying to say. Aiming towards the girdles again, wiggle the graver in until the bead just starts to move in over the junction between the stones. It needn't move far, as beading it down will spread it out a bit.

Now go to the spot between the second and third stones on the opposite side of the row. This way, you'll lock in the second stone quite effectively while not taking too much of a chance with the stone ending up crooked.

Continue locking in the stones. Sometimes I'll move up the line until half the beads are done and switch to my small round graver to do the four end beads, then go back to the medium round and finish the shared beads.

Pick an appropriate beader, one that will effectively round up your rough beads, and do so. As with the single stone setting, don't mash them down, just take the corners off. Do the end ones with a smaller beader and get ready to cut up.

In picking the correct beader, it's handy to think of the cup as, in effect, gathering in the points of the little triangles, pulling them into a nice ball. If the edges of the cup mash down the triangle, the beader's too small. Contrariwise, if the cup engulfs the triangle and snaps the edge of the stone off, then you've got a real problem.

In the course of doing a lot of this stuff, you will fine-tune the sizes of your beaders to correspond to the size of gravers that you prefer. This is why I insist that it's best to know how to maintain your own tools. The other point is that, as mentioned above, you won't always have a bunch of identical stones and perfectly matching beads. A lot of setting jobs require that you use half-dozen different beaders as you go from larger stones to smaller.

Actually, cutting up this style of setting is dead easy compared to an individual setting as there are only four corners for seven stones. First cut away all the excess metal to leave a nice clean rectangle, once again making sure you don't knock off any beads. Bright cut, rebead and you're done.

158

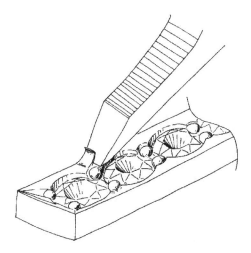

This is as good a time as any to mention finishing.

My basic rule is that if it's not already perfect and shiny, it's not time to polish it. Never try to remove scratches and file marks in the polishing room, you'll fuck it up. Your graver skills should be such that the bright-cut surfaces are smooth and flat. Your beader should be maintained so the little cup is round, sharp, and burnished so as to form an accurate shiny bead. Latagne, don't you know.

When you're done a job, the flat areas should be flat and the round ones round. Polishing tends to blur the differences. You end up with mushy, melted looking beads and wallowing, rippled looking flats that any mutt could achieve.

You're no mutt, you are a setter.

Get it?

Pavé Setting

Now we're getting into real old-guy territory. Using the skills learned in the previous sections, we are going to set a bunch of stones in a pattern with no detectable space between them, like paving stones. French paving stones.

Depending upon the space available and the configuration of the stones, we will have to choose whether to use a square or offset arrangement of stones. If we have a square design in which to set the stones, we will have them set in a rectangular matrix, whereas if they are, for example, set in a circular pattern, we will use the offset arrangement. In crystallography, these arrangements are called space-centered and face-centered, but that's not important here. The techniques are similar to shared-bead setting up until we start pushing metal around, so I'll decide later whether to use a separate section for each.

For now, though, we'll just roll along with a bunch of stones set into a slightly domed oval, because that's what I have pictures of.

The stones will be laid out in our pan and pushed about until they are in the most pleasing pattern for the given job. Then, using our old pal setter's friend, we arrange the

stones on the metal moving them this way and that until the spacing is perfect. Mark all the positions of all the stones, one at a time, replacing each one in its own little spit puddle. Once again, don't try to cheat and mark all the holes at a go using the little spitmarks or you will come to grief. Trust me on this. Divot and drill all the holes accordingly.

One more thing to keep in mind when pavé setting is that, as you will notice once you've drilled the holes, that there isn't much material between the stones. If you have done this in a plate that is otherwise unsupported, by the time you open up the holes to the appropriate size there will be nothing at all in the middle except for this foamy arrangement of holes. When you try to put any pressure on this during the setting process, the whole shooting match will begin to collapse in on itself and you are, as we are wont to say, fucked. Plan ahead by either using an extra-thick plate, or by designing some sort of substrate that will support the area during the process.

Back in the old days, when gold was apparently too precious to ever use enough of, setters would support a thin plate with shellac, do all the heavy work without worrying about anything collapsing, and then remove all the shellac. This would leave a very delicate structure that was lovely and magical to behold. I hate the bastards. Why I hate the bastards is that now, a hundred years later, I am occasionally asked to tighten stones in an antique ring with the stones set in just this way. This entails filling in the back of the setting with shellac and doing the job, then removing all the shellac. It's a pain in the ass, messy and time-consuming, and hardly ever works properly since the shellac flows into the setting and conceals the fact that the stones are loose, so you tighten them all, remove the shellac that was holding them and discover that they are still loose. I hate repairs.

Open up all the holes gradually on the assumption that all the previous stages were done accurately. When they all get very close together, the webby bits in between are opened up and the stones are fitted. This, of course sounds delightfully simple, but is generally anything but. The stones are fitted in gangs, rather than one at a time, so we must keep our wits about us. It is necessary to lock in the stones in an organized fashion so that we are not burring holes next to locked-in stones.

It is also undesirable to open up all the holes and hope that all the stones fit all at once. They won't.

In this case, I went so far as to start beading the middle stones before even locking in the outer ones. I was concerned because the combination of the proximity of the stones with the domed plate made for a scarily thin area underneath and I didn't want any trouble. Once the inner stones are set, they actually become an integral part of the unit and help, in their own right, to support the structure. Being a belt and suspenders kind of guy, though, I built a bit of an undercarriage to further buttress the whole unit once it was attached to the honkin' big ring of which it was part. The top unit was actually bezel-set once everything else was done. There was a ton of skull-work involved in this one, believe you me.

Anyway, back to the issue at hand. In this case, the beads are formed from the raised triangular section left uncut between stones. Rather than trying to simply bead over the little triangular towers, hoping that they will mushroom over enough to hold the stones, we must make the decision as to where the individual beads will come from, and where they will go. This is one of the major points in bead-setting.

In the case of the parallel rows of stones, you are left with a square area from which to raise your beads. Doing so with small stones is problematic in that the individual beads will be so small as to be almost useless, so it's best to choose a direction from which to draw the beads and work in pairs. In effect, you are choosing rows of stones to deal with, rather than a mass of stones. This makes no sense unless I add some photos or sketches.

With the offset style, you end up with strange little dog bone-shaped areas between the rows of stones. This works out well because we simply use half of it each area to create the bead for each row of stones. Simple? Yeah, right.

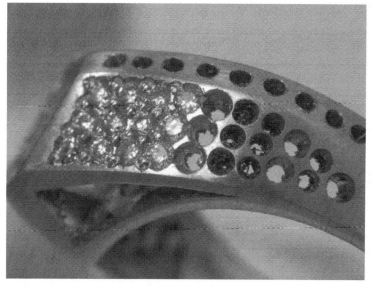

When you get into groupings of stones that fit into an irregular area, you have to pay attention not only to the layout of the stones, but to the areas between them, as this is where all the little beads come from.

Truth be told, pavé setting is probably a book all of its own, but I'm very busy right now.

V-Setting

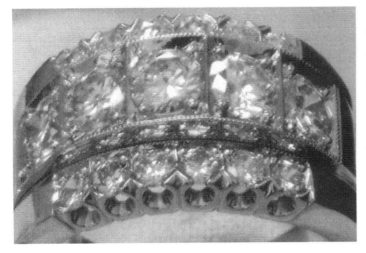

I don't know what else to call this style of setting, but it comes up often enough that, in order to talk about it, I am perforce compelled to name it. So mote it be.

First of all, let me admit that my favorite setting styles are, for lack of a better term, subtractive. That is, rather than building claws and bearings and soldering them on, I like to start with a smooth, flat piece of material and cut the setting out of it. Bead-setting, pavé, and flush-setting are like that. And so is V-setting.

This is an old technique that used to perplex me a great deal until I gave it some thought. It works well when you run out of width on a bead-setting job, by the way. Kind of an extended panic bead.

What you do is to lay out the selected stones along the outer edge of a prepared piece of material. The spacing depends upon whether you want the stones to have bead settings as an adjunct to the V-settings, and whether they are shared or individual beads. In the case of individual beads, there should still be relatively little space between stones or else the little "V"s, which are, in effect, split beads, will not spread out adequately to hold both stones. We'll go into this in greater specificity later.

Drilling and seating are carried out in much the same manner as with bead setting, the tables of the stones dropping to level with or just below the surface of the metal. If the beads are to be shared, then the area between the stones, the little webby bit, is cut away before finally seating the stones. At the same time the thin area at the edge of the metal is relieved to expose the girdle of the stone and remove the hair-thin bit of material there. Don't cut away too much as this is the raw material which will form the V.

Actually, I think I will break down the technique to the two different styles, shared versus individual beads, because it will get awful confusing otherwise. Hell, it's bad enough as it is.

So, we're going to use shared Vs in this example. It is set up in platinum and uses the entire width of the metal in the setting.

The stones are seated with a little material between them and the area cleaned up and readied for the process of locking them in. I use an old, exceedingly wide graver that I

inherited from Jack White a long time ago. I could never figure out what he wanted such a hefty graver for, and I'm still not entirely sure what he used it for. The belly of the graver, under the cutting face, is cut to such an extreme angle that it seems to be useless for any sort of regular engraving. It forms more of a wedge than a cutting edge, and it is in this capacity that we use it.

The edge of the wedge (it rhymes, you know) is placed at the exact middle point between the two stones and, by rocking it up and down just a bit, it splits the little triangle of metal and forces it over the adjacent stones. It takes a fair amount of force, so brace the ring well against your file peg. If the wedge isn't at the exact center, or the force is uneven, then the V will not be moved evenly over both stones, so now is the time to correct it. If it starts out crooked, it only gets worse and worse.

This is where the cunningly formed graver-type wedge is used to great advantage. Because it is not quite symmetrical, it can be turned upside-down and the force is applied in a subtly different direction. This is hard to explain verbally, or even textually, so I'll try pictures. Whatever you do, try to keep the force directed down the absolute middle of the metal. Use the cutting angle to change the distribution of material, rather than attempting to push metal towards one stone or the other. Upon occasion, it may be necessary to use a sharp triangular or knife graver to correct the position of the cut if it's gone badly awry. Care must be exercised in such a case as removing material now will come back to haunt you later.

It is best to proceed gradually, working your way along the line of stones, keeping each V identical to its neighbour. As in bead setting a row of stones, we'll proceed at alternate sides of the row, thereby keeping the stones level. The end stones, by the way, are usually done with a regular wide, flat graver. Because it cuts in a completely asymmetrical manner, it is perfect for finishing the ends. Sort of cutting half-Vs. Sort of. More on this later.

It is not necessary, at this point in the operation, to push material out over the stones. Like bead setting, the process of locking in the stone is only moving material. The shaping of the metal will come later.

If everything has gone smoothly thus far, it is now time to do some shaping to make everything pretty.

It will be seen that the Vs do not extend very far over the stones and the first step in finishing is to make them do so. So, with a small flat pusher, start forming the metal into wider Vs, while at the same time burnishing it down over the crowns of the stones. Once again, work alternately up and down the line to keep things even. It's a gradual process so take your time and you will see the shape of the final Vs developing. At this juncture it is time to decide whether the final Vs will be soft and rounded or quite angular. Sometimes the metal will decide for you, so go with it. Carry on smoothing things out, primarily by burnishing or planishing with the pusher because the last thing you want to do is remove a bunch of material and leave a stingy, wispy little V.

At some point, however, we will have to trim it to shape. May as get at it.

I usually give the final shape to the V-cuts by gently going over them with a fine (6-cut) square needle file, following up with the corner of the 600-grit sandpaper stick. This process will reinforce the need for real sharp corner on the sandpaper stick. A brutally sharp triangular graver leaves a very nice crisp line, although if the wedge-work has been done carefully this should not be necessary.

Finally, the bit of metal over the crown of the stone needs to be trimmed back to a pleasing shape. This is done with the trusty flat graver. Once again, the shape of the

finished product is a matter of taste. Sometimes I like to leave a straight edge, sometimes an arc concentric with the girdle of the stone.

As with bead-setting, this style of setting is very secure and wears like stink. The whole top of the ring has to wear away before the tips are at risk. Granted, the girdles of the stones are hanging out there a bit and can be chipped but, if we've done our jobs correctly, they won't be hanging out very far and will be somewhat protected by the projecting material in the Vs.

The second method, analogous to basic bead setting where the stones are left in little boxes, is going to be a bit fancier. This is the style that used to confuse me so. It looks like a bunch of little U-shaped settings all stuck together. Or something.

In this method, accurate drilling is essential, so sharpen up your drills and your layout skills. Since the stones are not going to be touching, there is a bit of leeway in the stone spacing, but you still don't want them terribly far apart. Start with a smaller drill than would normally be the case because it's going to get very weird from here on.

Once the holes are perfectly positioned, or even if they aren't, you can take your tapered bur and open up your settings, dropping the stones to about the same level as if they were to be pavé set. That is to say, the tables level with and just below the surface of the metal. Don't worry if the edge of the setting starts to bulge out and get thin, that's sort of the point.

Once the holes are pretty much the right size, keep track of the stones in their correct order, perhaps sticking them in some Rodico, marking it and the mount appropriately. Few things worse than fitting a bunch of stones, each into its very own individual bearing, only to inadvertently randomize them through inattention. Kind of like marking a favorite fishing spot on the bottom of the boat so that you can find it again next time.

Once the holes for the stones are perfect, we're going to drill corresponding holes in from the sides. It is common for the drill to grab and snap as it enters the existing hole, so be very careful. If the drill enters the existing hole straight, this is less likely, but that never happens, so

don't get too aggressive and you'll be okay. There is precious little room for error when doing this sort of thing, so take extra care.

At this point we need to remove any bits of material unnecessary to the finished setting. Don't remove the webby bits between the stones as these are necessary to the tidy appearance of the finished product. The outer edge of the setting, the one that has been rendered all wispy and useless as a result of expanding the holes to fit, needs to be dealt with at this point.

Open out this section so as to avoid the aforementioned wispiness, leaving a firm triangle of material with which to work.

The time has come to pretty up the sides of the setting a bit. Depending on the size of the stones, the height of the setting, and the distance between the stones, an appropriate bur should be chosen which will open up and shape the hole. What you're looking for is a bit of the old "hide the process". Properly done, this technique should leave the impression that the setting is made up of a bunch of little Cs all stuck together.

The main concern is to open up the holes to leave a clean, bright surface that will polish up easily and still be crisp-looking. Hart burs, flame burs, perhaps even a ball bur can be used, as long as they make a clean chatter-free cut.

Once again, we seat the stones and split the triangles into Vs, using all the skills at our command. The inner beads are, in this case, separated by the thin line of material that extends into the V. Use a small round graver to raise some nice crisp beads at the appropriate points. Use a beader to do the initial shaping and start doing some trimming. Most of the contours of this style of setting are suggested by the process itself. It only remains for us to tidy up the shapes thus formed.

The sides of the setting are trimmed up with a scrupulously sharp triangular graver, lightening up the appearance and giving that all-important fool-the-eye impression of a series of free-standing Cs. Vs on top, Cs on the side. It's a whole little spelling bee.

Claw Setting

I have major trepidations about getting into this because claw setting, while very simple as a concept, is one of the best ways to get one's self into deep, irreconcilable shit.

Cut the bearing, bend the tips over. Nothing to it, right? Well, if everything else is perfect, yeah, it's that easy, any mutt can do it; and does, with alarming regularity, and equally alarming results.

Doing it well and consistently is the point, though, and that's what we're after. I learned from the best and hope that I can pass on some of the wisdom so's to make the world a better place for us all.

This section (claw setting) comes after bead setting because some of the stuff you learned there comes into play in a big way.

We'll start off with a diamond in a four claw setting, which is the most straightforward. Y'see, as a rule, diamonds are cut consistently, have a distinct girdle, and are remarkably resilient. Also, this is the most common situation in which a setter finds him(her)self. (Most coloured stones being consistent in neither cut nor shape, they require major refinements of the standard setting procedure.)

If the claws are more or less vertical where the stone will sit, this is good. From an engineering standpoint, this gives the most stable platform on which to work. If the claws are splayed out a bunch, the tips have to be stretched way too much to give adequate support. We see this in solitaires where a four claw head is spudded onto a narrow band and the claws have to reach way, way out to grip the girdle of the stone. Bad idea.

Rather than drilling a hole and tapering it out to the size of the stone, we adjust the claws so that a minimal amount of material is removed in cutting the bearing. Some books recommend cutting away one-third if the claw leaving two-thirds to push over the stone (the tip). This is a nice rule if you always have a perfect setting. In the real world, we often have to make the setting perfect before moving on.

Ideally, the main strength of base with a smooth, tapering curve out under the pavilion and ending up almost vertical where the stone will be seated. Curves are strong, sharp angles are weak.

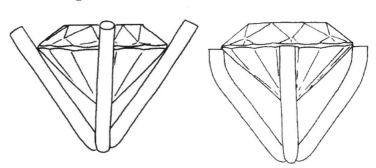

If you have to adjust the setting to make it so, make it so. If you've got the time, adjust the claws, then anneal the setting so as to remove any unnecessary stress points in the metal. For example, if you've had to bend the metal where your tips are, they aren't just going to bend over where you want them to. They'll fight you all the way. If you don't have the time, welcome the real world. Some settings fight you anyway.

So cut the bearing already.

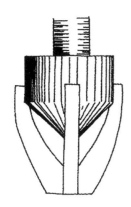

If you've adjusted the claws properly or, perish forbid, the setting was perfect to start with, the old one-third/two-third rule will apply. Simply choose a bearing cutter of the correct diameter and buzz it into the setting. If the claws are the least bit flimsy, the cutter will twist the setting into this cute little spiral and you are fucked.

It's best, usually, to work your way up to the correct sized bur. You won't twist the setting and, more importantly, you won't burn your burs by overheating.

Did I mention that you will never have the correct bur? You won't, but don't let it throw you. You are a setter. As a rule you have to tidy up the bearing anyway, it's just that with an undersized bur, you have to remove a bit more material. Sometimes you can use a slightly oversized bur and tweak the claws in a bit, but be aware that this is risky. Go undersized and use a graver.

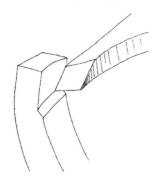

An offset bearing cutter graver is the weapon of choice to clean out the slightly rounded area where the girdle will be seated. You want a nice, sharp angle that will match the shape of the girdle perfectly. Fit the stone and make sure that it is level seven ways from Sunday, and doesn't rock. If it rocks even a little, not only will it most likely sit crooked, but when the tips are pushed into place, you will be attempting to bend the stone. Stones don't bend. Remember this and life will be good.

Now that the stone is properly seated, we come to the scary part. This is why we never let the customer watch. Ya, grab yer pliers. Big pliers. Big scary smooth-jawed crushing implements.

Don't worry, we're not folding the claws over with these bastards, we're just locking the stone in. Gently ease the tips in a bit, moving around the stone to ensure that it remains level. You should feel the pressure against the tip as it gives. If it doesn't give at all, don't squeeze, just adjust the angle so that you're pulling the tip gently over the stone.

Check that the stone is still level and that the tips are at the same angle over the stone. Grasp it with your tweezers and give it a gentle twist. If it moves, it's not really locked in, now is it? Make it so. Trust me. If you've done everything else right, you're at little risk of smashing the stone. If not, you're on your own.

Oh yeah, before we get into the Zen shit, I should mention squaring up the stone. This just means placing the stone so that the table is square with the setting. This starts out as a style thing, but actually has some important technical reasoning behind it as well. We'll deal with that later, but for now, just do it because it looks like you care. You do care, right?

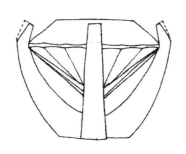

Now the usual routine at this point would be to use your prong pusher to bend the tips the rest of the way over the crown of the stone, mashing it down into firm contact with the stone with all the strength that your puny shoulders and back and arms can muster. Woof. (I do this from time to time just for fun with small stones, bending the tips down 'til they actually touch in the middle of the table. Looks funny as hell.)

No. What we do is to file away a good deal of the tip, shaping it so that the characteristics of the metal work for us, not against us.

Reduce the length of the tip to two to three times its thickness. File the tip to a taper, removing metal down to a point directly opposite the girdle. Check the picture, it will make more sense.

Here's where it gets weird.

One of my basic precepts is that it's better to compress metal than to stretch it. Granted, R. Buckminster Fuller contends that "tension and compression only coexist," but he's dead.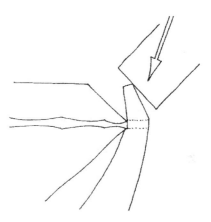

The fact is that bending the tip over the girdle creates tremendous stresses on the metal at the outside of the bend, in effect pulling the structure of the metal apart where you need the strength most. Never mind the amount of leverage that is being applied to the girdle of the stone.

This is a diamond, remember, tough and hard, but not invulnerable to mechanical stresses. And expensive, don't forget expensive.

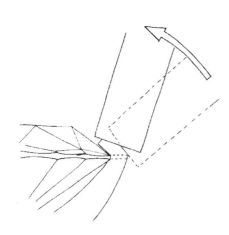

Better you should use the compressive tendencies of the metal to form a compact tip that is actually stronger than the original claw. Because of the shape of the tip that we've filed, a force directed down against the claw, not over the stone, will have the effect of compressing the metal over the girdle anyway. Check it out. It takes control and a well prepared pusher to achieve, but the result is actually more predictable and consistent than the old "cut the bearing and fold" method. Also, you're less likely to hear the pesky little click that says you've taken the side off a stone that you can't afford.

So you force the metal down in a kind of rocking motion that really needs to be felt but, hey, we'll try to describe it in words because this is a book. Sort of.

Place the pusher flat against the filed surface of the tip and, imagining the force to be directed down the claw, gradually raise the pusher, keeping the pressure on 'til the pusher is almost perpendicular to the table of the stone.

This, of course, takes some practice and chances are that the early efforts will result in tips that are a bit too thin. Stick with it, though, and increased control will allow you to move a surprising amount of metal over the stone. If you start off with earrings, say, which don't need very substantial tips, you can basically fuck it up and it won't much matter. It's expensive practice otherwise.

The ideal tip should be more or less flat on top. That is, parallel to the table with the bulk of its weight beyond the girdle of the stone. This is the area that holds the stone, and accepts the majority of wear. There's no need to have a huge glump of metal over the crown of the stone, particularly if the claw left at the girdle is too thin.

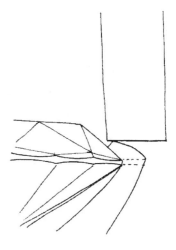

Also, because of the slight rocking motion as the tip is moved over the crown of the stone, the curved inner face of the tip (cut by the setting bur) nestles over the junction between the two girdle facets. Or it will if you've squared up the stone properly. Which you have, right? Well, it's too late now.

This further secures the stone from any twisting motion and strengthens the setting because it will take a huge blow to move that claw. A disastrous blow.

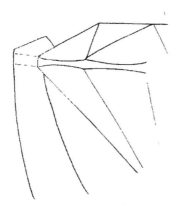

See, what you have now is a tip that is heaviest where it will do the most good, virtually flat with respect to the table, nicely tapered in cross-section, and compressed rather than stretched. This means that the crystal structure of the metal is tighter and stronger by far than would be the case had it been stretched to near-breaking. If you look at the outer surface of a folded tip under magnification, you can actually see the crystals pulling apart. It's scary.

Now we just have to trim the tip to its final perfect shape.

To trim, we're going to be using a 6-cut triangular needle-file and a small flat graver. (Some folks prepare their needle file by grinding the corners off, but I prefer to simply go ahead and use the file as is. The corners come off pretty quick in any case.)

What you want is, oh Christ, I thought that the shape that I was thinking of was a trapezoid, but a trapezoid has no parallel sides. Then I thought it was rhomboid, but a rhomboid is a parallelogram with no right angles. I will look it up and get back to you.

Shape the tip more or less like Saskatchewan.

Saskatchewanoid, we'll call it. You heard it here first.

Actually, the base of the tip, the American border, as it were, will end up somewhat rounded. Jesus, I need pictures. And an editor. A real understanding editor. (I looked it up, and it's an isosceles trapezoid: Ed.)

Anyway, brace the ring, which is firmly in its clamp, against the bench pin and hold the file so that your index finger is extended out along one face of the triangle. This allows you to hold the top of the file flat, thereby ensuring that the two other faces file both sides of the tip at a consistent angle with the crown of the stone.

First file the end of each tip to the appropriate length. This length varies a bit according to the style and construction of the mount and the crown angle of the stone, but if you take it down to the tip of the star facet, you won't go too far wrong.

Trim the end with a scrupulously sharp flat graver as the file always leaves a little feather where the tip is flat against the diamond. Check to make sure that the tips are all the same length.

Now we get into the goofy habit of counting strokes. The 6-cut file doesn't remove a great deal of material in one stroke, but we're not dealing here with a particularly massive structure.

What I generally do is file one side of each tip with, say, two strokes, turning the ring clamp so's to orient the tip to the file. Don't start trying to move the filing hand around too much; it should be machine-like in its precision.  Nice long straight strokes with a little tap of the file after each. It's a habit I picked up to clear filings off the file. If you leave them on, sometimes the file just rolls over them instead of cutting.

Now do the other side of each tip. Same number of strokes, same pressure, machine-like precision.

How they lookin'?

If they're consistent and exactly the correct proportions swell, you're done. Fat chance.

Clean up the angles, keeping all claws identical. Touch up any that are too big. Generally tidy them up. Don't get carried away and file them down to nubs or you'll have learn about retipping way too soon. This process of over-filing is referred to as "Hitlering", as this is how he ended up with that dopey mustache. A little off this side, oops, a little off that, oops, just a little more off this side... presto! A Hitler mustache.

Once they're nicey-nice, you can trim the feathers with your well-honed graver. You're sliding the corner against a diamond, bucko, it's going to get dull.

Clean up and round off the heel of the tips with some 600-grit sandpaper and use the same to clean the pusher marks off the top of each tip. Be careful not to round them off.

The best way I've found to polish tips is with a very short nylon brush on the polishing machine. Only rouge should be used, never tripoli.

Tips

Reluctant as I am to open the incredible can of worms that is the repair world, I should tell you about tips. Once again, this will be a bit of a pæan to Bert, but you'll just have to get used to that.

One of the worst tendencies in goldsmithing is forgetting about those poor schmoes who are to follow. All manner of atrocities have been passed on to the unwary in the name of expedience, and I think it serves them right when they get this crap back. I think we should be more like watchmakers, and sign our work in some unobtrusive spot in the piece, so that everyone else will know whom to hate.

Easy solder, for example, is a curse, sure to bite you on the ass the next time you have the misfortune to work on that particular piece. Badly fitted joints, in combination with the aforementioned easyflow, cause rings to explode into your lap in fiery chunks. And it serves you right.

One of the most poignant moments in goldsmithing has to be that moment when, while innocently soldering four tips on an old ring, all the other tips dissolve into shapeless lumps because they are composed entirely of easy white-gold solder.

Here in my world, we hate it when that happens, and try not to create situations where such a thing might occur. I sort of believe that what goes around comes around. Karma, y'know.

So, here's what you do. Try to make the new, replacement bits similar to, and at least as durable as the original. Sounds easy enough until you try it, but with some planning and forethought miracles can occur.

Planning, in this case, means determining exactly how far gone the original is. In some instances this is as easy as removing the old, worn tips in as organized a manner as possible and soldering some new tips on. In other cases, there's not enough metal left to solder anything to, and you have to do some backing and filling just to get started.

This is where I get into trouble and why I make such a crappy repair-guy. I always want it to be perfect, and in the repair industry, that's not always possible. Best you can do under the circumstances is more likely. Otherwise, you end up rebuilding stuff from scratch and losing a ton of money, and therefore wasting time. They're virtually equivalent, y'know.

We'll assume for the sake of this discussion that this ring isn't too badly worn and that there is still plenty of claw-area upon which to solder our new tips. Notice the distinction between claws and tips. They're different things, y'know, in spite of the fact that a lot of people use the terms interchangeably.

In any case, the thing to do is file the existing tips off 'til they're flush with the crown of the diamond, 'cause this *is* a diamond we're working on here. If it ain't, then what the hell are we trying to do tipping it in place? By the way, the ring should be scrupulously clean and properly boricked, as if you didn't know. Silly ol' me.

First of all, pretty much any stone is risky as hell to tip in place because of the high temperatures necessary, and even if it is a diamond, if it's dirty, the goop, usually grease-based, or at the very least, organic, is going to carbonize on heating and effectively bond with the surface of the stone which is, of course, carbon, never mind the smell and you will find yourself very deep in it. I forget what the second thing is.

So, the ring is all nice and clean and covered with several layers of boric acid, so now what do we do?

Well, as I said before we were so rudely interrupted, file the old tips off parallel with the crown of the stone. If it's not a straight extension of the crown, the new tip can't sit flat against the stone. And it should, so that the tip we're about to attach will lie flat on the crown. (Upon occasion, you will be presented with a claw that has so much material outside the girdle of the stone, an embarrassment of riches, that the seat for the tip may be notched. This makes it double-plus easy to fit, solder and finish. This hardly ever happens.)

Speaking of tips, here's how to make some.

This is one of those feats of sorcery that Bert pulled off from time to time, so counterintuitive in a way, but absolutely inevitable in retrospect. Genius is like that.

Start with a strip of flat wire, the width being equal to the length of your desired tip. I like to keep a number of strips handy, of varying widths and thicknesses to cut down on the dicking around when I'm forced to do tips.

Now, here's where it gets weird.

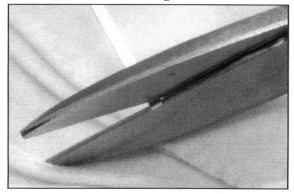

Using nice, sharp, shears nip a bit off the end of the bar at a slight angle. Now flip the bar over and make another cut, at the opposite angle keeping your finger over the little piece to keep it from flying away. The little piece, with any luck at all, will be shaped like a perfect little tip. Cool, huh? The natural angle of the cut made by the shears imparts a very pretty taper to the tip. You'll still have some finishing to do, don't worry, but the tidy shape of the rough tips makes it especially easy to line them up nicely. This goes to my basic premise of manufacturing that things work out best if every step is pretty and symmetrical. Kind of lets you

know that you're on the right track.

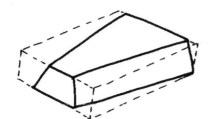

'Course, if it's not, the next one will be. I usually end up nipping off several extras so that I can pick out the best. The extras will come in handy someday, so keep them.

Now, it's just a matter of soldering the tips in place. Use easy solder and don't try to be a hero. The tips are put in place, a tiny piece of solder placed on the junction, and the ring heated until the solder flows. If the tip heats up first, the solder will flow up onto it and create an unsightly mess.

This method flies in the face of the common belief that the heat should be confined to the immediate area. People who use little tiny torches like to heat up only the claw in question and kind of poke the tip into place. I'm not saying this is wrong, it's just not the way I learned to do it. Oh, you'll end up doing a bit of poking to get recalcitrant tips to settle into place, but in my experience Bert's way saves time in the long run and does a better job. There's also less likelihood of overheating the solder.

Okay, it's a pain in the ass, I admit, but you have to admit that the elegance of the method is alluring. Besides, Bert would be working on four or five rings at once, seats cut on one, tips placed on the next, solder placed on another. It was astonishing, and not for just anyone to attempt.

The same basic process can be used for bead-set and pavé stones. There's nothing to it. Just use a small flat graver to cut a seat for each individual tip. Position the tip, which is

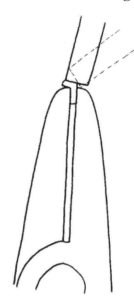

about the size of your smallest snippet of solder except pre-shaped, and apply a correspondingly minuscule particle of solder. Leave this to dry, because heating it up will surely knock the tips out of position, and then simply flow the solder.

I saw the old bugger doing up to sixty-four individually-seated tips on a single ring. This was not work for normal humans.

Upon occasion, it will be found that the claws are too far gone to simply solder tips on. In such a case, we must resort to fold-over tips.

Here, rather than sticking the tips on top, we do some judicious pre-shaping, and solder them so that they extend over and around the girdle of the stone.

Starting with some rather ridiculously long tips, we grip the narrow end, the tip of the tip, as it were, and, using a pusher, bend the tip over to the appropriate angle. This angle will vary with the condition of the claws, these having been prepared to accept the new claws.

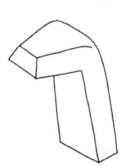

This preparation can take the form of simply filing a flat on the outside of whatever claw that happens to be intact on the old head. This is nice. Sometimes, though, it becomes necessary to do some fairly complicated notching and fitting to preserve as much of the shape as possible. In either case, it makes sense to do some shaping on the fat end of the tip. You know, while it's clamped in the pliers as it is. If it's a simple job as above, then file the end to a taper to reduce the amount of dicking around that we have to do after it's soldered. If it's the more complex case that I describe not quite so far above, you're on your own.

Using all the skills at your disposal, solder the tips in place and clean them up to remove any evidence of your sweat and patience. A perfect repair job is one where the problem is fixed, but the rest of the piece is unchanged. My problem is that I want to fix everything. This is why I'll never make any money on repairs.

Lately, I've been using platinum for tips. At first glance, it seems kind of wasteful, but consider the advantages; the stuff doesn't oxidize, so there are no concerns about fireskin buggering up the soldering process, and it burnishes down more smoothly, decreasing the risk factor, and it wears like stink, so the tips may well outlast the rest of the piece.

It all follows my basic philosophy that doing a proper job is easier than not, if you look at the big picture.

Pearshapes et al

These are your pointy stones; pearshape, marquise, trilliants, and princess cuts. As a group, they scare the hell out of setters because those points are fragile, but as with so many things, preparation is the key.

Since I'm not in the business of teaching anyone how to do commercial setting, I needn't bother describing the horrors that are visited upon the unwary setter in the name of commerce.

I will, however, help to set up a properly built head so that the stone will remain intact during the process, and secure for the foreseeable future.

First of all, it will be painfully obvious where the main concern lies in this style of setting. The damn points are where! We must protect these at all costs. In the construction section, I describe the preferred method of making the claws for these stones, and said claws are exactly what is needed, as far as I'm concerned.

I'll show a marquise on accounta that happens to be the one that I've drawn, mostly. First trick is to make absolutely sure that the setting is the correct one for the stone. It should sit in the claws level and, depending on the style, a proportion of the claw should be visible from above. Two-thirds or so higher, if the claws are fairly perpendicular. If the claws splay out a bit as in the settings we construct in the construction section, then it should basically drop in a little. Then the process of cutting the bearing will allow it to drop to the correct level.

In any case, I generally start by cutting down the angle with a triangular graver. This process will be repeated as we go and is important in protecting the tip of the stone. We want it supported near, but definitely not at, the tip. Some setters use a small ball-bur to open out the angle so that there is no contact between the tip of the stone and the claw. These people are mutts. Usually when I see this style of setting, it is because the stone has fallen out of the setting, the claw being so weak that the slightest mishap shears off the whole top.

Once you've got it so that the stone drops in nicely, relieve the back of the claw a bit as shown. What you need to visualize is the two sides of the claw, the tips, folding over and meeting in the middle, but only just. The back of the claw should come down to the point of the stone so that there will be no pressure on that most important of areas. The stone should sit down in the bearing without any rocking. If it rocks from side to side, that usually means that it's resting on the point. This is not good. Make it perfect and the rest of the operation will go well for you, trust me.

The tips are then folded over the stone and, yes, it's time to use the pliers again. The claws are moved over a bit at a time ensuring that the stone is not moved off-level. Stop before the pliers start to slip, that is, when the tips are about half-way down to the crown of the stone. I suppose I could draw about a hundred pictures to make this clear, but it is so much a matter of feel that such an exercise would be pointless. As will your stone, if you're not careful.

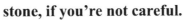

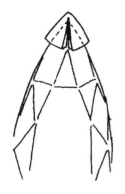

A pusher is used in a judicious manner to lay the tips down the rest of the way, burnishing them against the crown. If you find that the tips are meeting in the middle, it may be necessary to relieve them a bit where they are touching. For this, I generally use my triangular graver. This has the added advantage of creating an angle that will allow the tips to lie down flat without too much pressure. Now it's simply a matter of trimming the tips so they're pretty. You may have gotten the tips to flop down perfectly, with no gap between them, good for you. While this looks cool and is strong as all get out, in my opinion it lacks grace. What we do instead is cut away the inner area, leaving just the "V". There's no real need for a tremendous tonnage of material over the crown. What you need is for the sides of your stone to be held by the "V" almost to the end. Once again, in my experience, a properly set marquise will not fall out of the setting, even if the tip of the claw is worn down smooth with the crown of the stone. The stone should be held tightly by the pressure of the claw at the girdle.

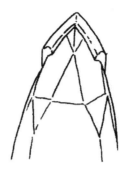

This style of claw is, as I said, also the basis for the other pointy stones, with a bit of variation, naturally. The thing to remember is that you must clear the corner with the triangular graver often, as this is where the trouble is sure to be found.

Collet Setting

A collet is like a bezel, only different.

By my definition, a bezel is a strip of metal bent to the shape of a stone (generally a cabochon) so as to surround it tightly. Then a bearing is provided, either by soldering a ring of wire around the inside of the bezel, or soldering the bezel to a flat sheet. In the

former,

you are providing support for an open-backed bezel to allow light to shine through a transparent or translucent stone. In the latter, you are trying to enhance the stone, either by providing a reflective surface (foiling), or a black surface to change a washed-out jelly opal to a striking fake black opal. It works.

A collet, contrariwise, is generally used for facetted gems and is a tube with an inside diameter just barely smaller than the diameter of the stone. The outer diameter is a matter of taste and practicality; how much metal can you, or do you want to, force over the stone.

Having decided on that and made a tube of the requisite dimensions the operation starts out more or less like any stone-setting. Cut a bearing.

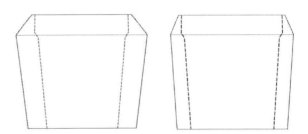

This can be cut with a setting bur and cleaned up with an offset graver, or you can just tear in there with the graver, but be warned, it's real tough to cut the bearing perfectly level. It's good practice, though, so go for it.

You want the stone to be tight in the collet, so it's best to work your way up to the correct size. If the stone is the least bit out of round, and they all are, it's handy to mark it temporarily so that you are fitting it in the same way each time. A little spot of India ink on a star facet works.

Put the stone in the collet and attempt to push it down into firm contact with the bearing. Don't force it, of course. If it doesn't go, pop it out and look at the inside of the collet. You will see little bright lines where the stone rubbed the metal. This is where you cut. Just remove the shiny bit and the metal below it because we already know that the stone goes down to that point.

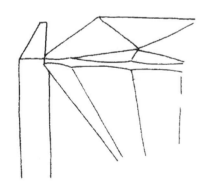

Refit the stone, making sure the marked portion is in the right direction (north, say) and give it another push. Take your time and the stone will just slide in with no sweat and no shake.

Oh, yeah. How deep do we set it? Well, deep enough, but not too deep. Or should I just fuck off now?

Since the collet is in contact with the stone all the way around, not a lot of metal needs to be over the stone at any given point. This allows the stone to be shown off to great advantage while still being double-plus secure. Ideally, if you were to file off the metal over the crown of a properly secured stone, it would remain held in by the pressure of the outer rim of the collet. I have unset stones that were set properly, and it's not easy on account of this.

That being said, you still need to have enough metal in the vicinity to preclude wear, and enhance the appearance of the stone. Basically, most of the metal should be above the girdle and outside the girdle rather than over the crown. Look at the picture.

In order to cause the metal to move in a controlled manner, we have to file a bit of an angle on the top edge. The exact angle depends on a lot of different variables. You know.

The thickness of the material, crown height/angle, and the desired effect all come into it. Sometimes you want the setting to all but disappear to give the effect of a stone suspended in space. At other times the collet really becomes part of the design and you want it to stand out like a big shiny doughnut.

As in claw setting, we're not so much concerned with folding metal over the crown as compressing it; almost forging it into place so that it's uniform and easy to trim properly.

What happens if you try to "fold" a bunch of metal over is that it is stretched over the girdle and sort of bunches up as the top is moved inward. Then, as you trim back the metal, you realize that the metal is not actually in contact near the girdle where it really matters. At this point the metal is so stressed that it is too hard to be burnished down properly. Better we should plan ahead.

So you file a bit of an angle and, at the same time, determine whether the height of the collet (depth of the stone) is correct.

I generally use a round-ended pusher to do the initial work on collets as it moves a substantial quantity of metal in a controlled manner with little risk of creasing the metal or crushing the stone.

The face of the pusher should be ground on a coarse wheel so's to give it a bit of "tooth" which keeps it from slipping. This is important since we are using it in such a way that we can easily control its lateral motion, but are forcing it in a direction that would cause it to crush the stone should it slip. And we can't have that, now, can we?

Move some metal over the stone with a bit of a rocking motion. Don't try to move it all the way right now. We're just trying to lock the stone in. Check that the stone hasn't shifted, then move to the opposite side and repeat. Then do the quarters, then the eighthses, then the sixteenthseses, 'til you're basically just going around removing lumps. Increase the angle of attack and start to force the metal down onto the crown using the same kind of motion, smoothing out lumps as you go.

By this time, you're confident that the stone is well locked in and the metal is firmly compressed against the girdle of the stone, so you go around again and make sure the former top edge of the collet is making contact with the crown all the way around.

(Sometimes I start the trimming process a little early and make a cut around the inner edge. This allows for a better view of the proceedings as the inner edge has been quite distorted through compression. Then you can go back to the pusher.)

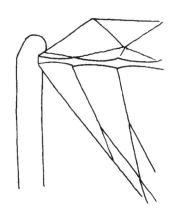

The last thing you do with this pusher is to do some smoothing and finishing at this point of contact. What you'll be doing is actually pushing almost parallel to the crown and outwards so as to compress the metal even more. In the ideal collet setting, very little trimming is actually necessary as the metal is being burnished smooth as we go, any excess metal having been filed away before. Very efficient.

Now, with a flat pusher, we go around the outside of the collet and smooth out any lumpy bits. This is actually a form of planishing, smoothing the surface with pressure. Ideally, you should be able to finish the outer surface with fine sandpaper, no filing necessary.

Remember what I said earlier about compressing metal, as opposed to stretching it? Well, what we're doing here is compressing the metal, forging it into place over the stone so that all the metal available is used with a minimum of waste. By waste, I mean time, effort, and peace of mind. You're moving the metal, shaping it like clay into a perfect ring so that you've got a smooth surface when it comes time to trim.

The inner, concave surface is trimmed with a very sharp flat graver. Don't try to remove all the rough bits at one go, just even things out, get the edge up to a point about half-way up the girdle facets. This distance will vary according to the crown angle. High crowns require that the collet extend a little bit farther up the girdle facet. Right is right.

Now that it's nice and smooth, you can show off by bright-cutting it. Sharpen up your graver so perfectly that you just can't stand it, we're talking desperately sharp, and go around one more time. You're not trying to take off a whole bunch of metal, just the barest of shavings, leaving a gorgeous mirror-bright surface. It's a happy thing.

Flush Setting

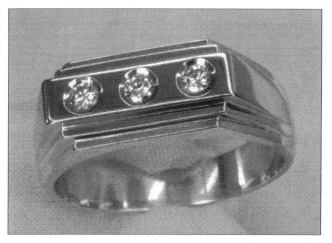

When working with collets, we looked at various thicknesses of material to achieve different effects.

The thinner the material, the closer we were to the concept of the bezel; actually folding material over the stone. With thick metal, we're using compression to move the metal down and out (away from the centre of the stone) into contact with the crown.

Now, imagine an infinitely thick collet. This is flush setting. You can't expect to move metal in the same way as with a bezel, so you have to rely on careful fitting and oh so careful trimming to ensure that the stone stays in place.

As with thick collets, all of the metal must come from above the girdle. Therefore, we must make absolutely certain that the edge is sharp and the hole perfectly vertical. What? Look at the picture, grasshopper, and all will become clear.

Once we've used all the standard tricks to determine that the stone is perfectly fitted (level, tight, firmly supported all around...), it's easy to see that the metal to hold the stone can only come from one place.

It's almost a riveting process, only inside-out.

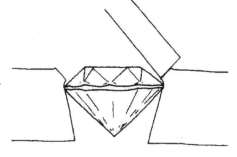

Use a sharp, round ended pusher and push down and out at one point on the edge. The radius ground into the end of the pusher will vary as the diameter of the stone, as well as the height of the crown. That is to say that, once again, experience will determine the appropriate shape. Sorry, but there's no magic formula. That's one of the reasons that we use worn-out square needle-files to make these particular pushers. They get used up, don'tcha know. I usually use a cutoff disc to finish the end after rough grinding as it's important to have a sharp, crisp edge on the end of the pusher. This will allow you to get the metal right down to the crown of the stone without putting unnecessary pressure on the stone itself.

What you want is an end that will move metal without creasing the edges of the hole and creating trimming problems later. Pushing out and down at about a 45° angle should get you where you're going. Don't try to mash down too much right now. Just get the metal moving and check that you're not knocking the stone off-kilter.

You should see that the edge of the hole has moved down and over just a bit. Do the other side and check it again. It's kind of important because this process is all but irreversible. If you blow this, it's fucked and you're back to square one. A new ring, maybe.

Scared yet?

Well, don't sweat it too much. If the stone has been forced off level, then the bearing wasn't perfect. For shame. What you need to do is poke the stone out from underneath and oh so carefully, using a tapered punch or worn beader of the correct size, open the hole back up so that the stone drops in properly. You do not, I repeat, you do not want to cut away any material from the sides of the hole. There is precious little metal to work with as it is, and we need it all. Worst case scenario, you may have to replace the stone with one just slightly larger. With little stones this is no sweat if you have a good selection of smalls, but larger stones get a little expensive to go replacing all the time. It's a balancing act to decide if you want to replace a stone or the whole ring. Best you should be careful so the decision doesn't come up.

So, once the stone is locked in, it's a simple matter to move around the stone, in effect burnishing the edges of the hole down over the girdle facets. Don't try to mash too much down at once, and try to maintain a consistent angle relative to the crown. You want that compressed portion to be as smooth and consistent as possible so that almost no metal needs to be removed in trimming.

Trimming is done with a desperately sharp flat graver. It has to be honed flat and true as you only really get one shot at this.

Once again, maintain a constant angle and slice metal away so as to leave a smooth bright finish all the way around. I usually cut around once clockwise, then sharpen and recut back the other way for the final finishing bright-cut.

An alternative to the bright-cut is to use your skinny little burnisher to put the final polish on the setting. Be careful that no pressure is applied to the crown of the stone if it's not a diamond. Actually, using the burnisher *after* the graver is ideal, because what we are looking for is a very crisp, sharp effect.

Like so many aspects of life, this style of setting is so simple as to be nearly impossible to perfect. It'll humble you, but it's rewarding.

Wax Carving

Tapered Band

This part of the book is somewhat concerned with the making of some simple waxes, but is also a place for me to espouse some of my basic ideas about the ideal proportions of a well-made ring. My opinion, of course, but hey, it's my book.

For example, when I emphasize accuracy in cutting and finishing a blank to perfect right angles in the section soon to come, I am well aware that there are mitre-block gizmos that allow a blank to be cut off at a perfect right angle quickly and, more or less, accurately. This is all well and good once you know how to cut straight, but keeping up the skills is also important. Like, for example, sawing and filing quickly and accurately. I want the flat parts absolutely flat, and the rounded sections rounded smoothly and the sooner in the operation that this can be accomplished, the more likely a satisfying finished product will result. I'm fussy that way.

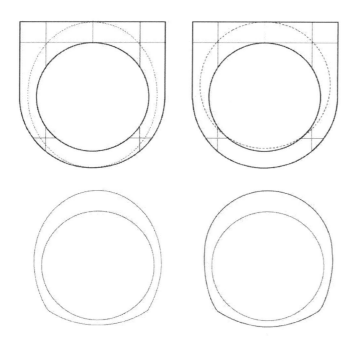

The first concept that I will deal with is enhancing the flow of a design using ellipses versus circles. The ring itself is based on a circle, of course, because fingers are mostly round. Since only plain bands are also circular on the outside, we have to come to grips with the shapes that will allow us to have raised areas on the ring, either to allow depth for stones, or simply for style points. This illustration demonstrates the subtle difference between a layout based on a circular arc versus an ellipse. Notice that the shoulder area of the shape at bottom right seems chunkier and not as elegant. This game is about the fine points, after all. You'll also notice the little bumps at the back of the shank. We call those "little bumps", and will continue to do so until something better comes along. More on these, later.

The other factor that makes for a comfortable and elegant design is the avoidance of acute angles. In my opinion, an angle less than ninety degrees is a cutting edge, and not something you want to wear on your person.

In this illustration, you can see the difference between bringing a flat side all the way to the top of the band. The one on the right looks top-heavy, ungainly, and uncomfortable.

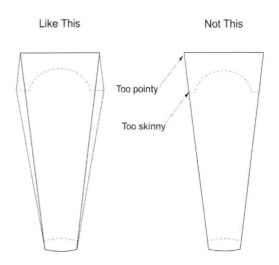

Back in the manufacturing section, we saw how easy it is to whack out a nice, simple tapered band. Okay, not that easy, perhaps, but if you want a band in a hurry, it's a very necessary skill.

Making up a heavier sort of band is possible using such techniques, but not so much practical. Mostly, it's a matter of planning and visualizing the final product and determining the best way to get there. In this case, a wax is the way to go.

There are, of course, some design features I like to include in all my pieces to ensure strength and comfort. And beauty: Mustn't forget to make it pretty. These will come up as we go. You have to have the picture clear in your head so that when it starts to go wrong, you'll be the first to know.

Signet Ring

There are six million ways to make a ring. This is just one of them.

We're going to make a simple signet ring. A nice, simple, oval signet. These things are so simple that they're virtually impossible to get right.

Yeah, that's what I meant. Because of the compound curves and flat top, any mistakes, no matter how small, will stick out like Saturday night acne. Or at least they will to me, and I'll make your life hell 'til you can see them too.

Okay, what's the most important thing to know at this point?

Well, confronted as you are by a flat-topped wax tube of indeterminate length, I would guess that you're going to want to cut the ring blank to length. This is determined, naturally, by the desired width of the finished signet.

First, you must determine that the end of the tube is exactly perpendicular to the tube itself. This is IMPORTANT. I've fixed the end of a steel rule so that it's a perfect 90° angle, and use it to check

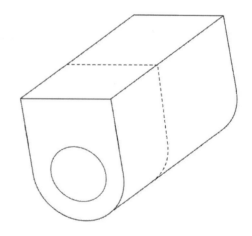

tubes. I also have a cool little machinist's square that could conceivably perform the same function, but it never seems to be handy, nor is it as adaptable. Such is the way with gizmos.

Use dividers to set off the appropriate distance for the width of the ring blank. Oh yeah, that's what we call it once we've cut it off, which we do just past the line. Then file it off flat to the line. Presto. Ring blank.

The next most important dimension is the ring size. If you skip this step, you'll hate yourself most bitterly. Make sure the file strokes are even so that the inside stays round. Count strokes, if necessary, rotate the blank often, and check, check, check.

Periodically, slide the ring up your ring mandrel and turn it a few times, under a bit of pressure. This burnishes little shiny areas inside the blank where you need to file. Flip the blank on the mandrel so it doesn't end up tapered. Once it's about a quarter of a size smaller than the final size, finish it off with sandpaper, remembering to leave a tiny allowance for the final finishing after casting. This is the *penultima pelle*, or last skin but

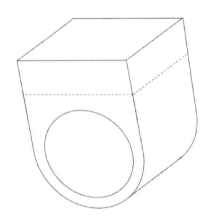

one. Cellini used the term, so it's good enough for me. (Once again, there's a gizmo that can enlarge the hole quickly and easily, but I prefer filing.)

Now, if you've been careful, you've made the hole nice and round and concentric with the outside of the blank. Measure to make certain.

If the inside and the outside are concentric and the sides are perpendicular to the top, then the blank is, as we say in the industry, straight.

Next, decide on the thickness of the head (which will be the height of the ring), and lay it out parallel to the flat top. Cut or file it down, making it nice and flat. Ensuring that the all the angles are right at this point avoids problems later. (Remember, "It's easier to keep than it is to get back.") At this point in proceedings, we can lay out some guidelines.

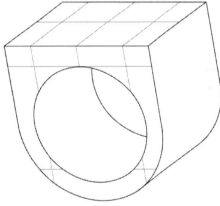

The process of laying out the blank is the same as in the previous section, the width being based on the long dimension of the oval, plus a couple millimeters to allow for the extra material that will soften the top edge.

Lay out the dimensions of the oval (LxW) on the top and while you're at it, put down some centre lines 'cause you'll want them later. It's easy to do this now, as the sides are nice and parallel, as are the ends. And if they're not, now is the time to find out.

By making your center-lines parallel to both sides and both ends, you are automatically checking their parallelism as well. If they're off by the least little bit, the two lines will not coincide.

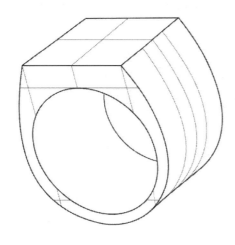

File the sides down 'til they're the appropriate thickness. This thickness will form a smooth transition from the shoulders to the shank.

This is another recurring theme that I harp on; the smooth transition thing. I'm not wild about strict geometry when it comes to my finished product, although I use it extensively in the layout and roughing out processes. You are not going to get things symmetrical if you don't pay attention to your layout lines, trust me, but once the blank is getting to be a ring-shaped object, you're going to have to finesse it into shape without giving up symmetry. By the same token (whatever the hell that means), we don't want to have a ring that looks like a flat top welded to a piece of pipe. Do we?

So, what we do is file a kind of diminishing radius curve that smoothly expands from the back of the shank to the top.

The blank is now lovely in silhouette, but is ungodly wide, namely the full length of the head. This we must fix.

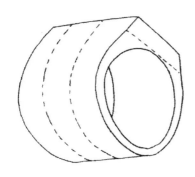

Having determined the width of the back of the shank, we must mark this on the blank. Now you file a flat on each side from your width line at the back of the shank up to the top, making sure that the angle thus formed stays parallel to the top. This is easy if you're careful, but you can lay out a line if you like. It just doesn't make any sense in print.

Hey, not bad. It's starting to look like something. Take a good look, you're about to fuck it up.

Actually, maybe you wanted a rectangular, flat-sided signet. Ta-da! You're done, you lazy bugger. Now, get out, and let the real waxsmiths get to work.

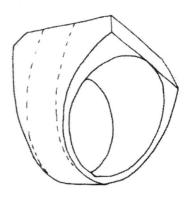

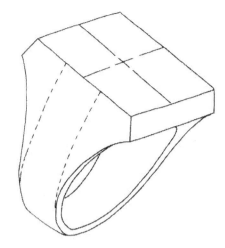

We're going to give the shank a nice, smooth curve. In order to remove material efficiently, while maintaining symmetry, we will resort to the technique of counting strokes. Yup. Counting strokes. I mentioned it earlier, in regard to the inside of the blank. It's just a method of ensuring symmetry without having to think about it too much.

This seems anal as hell, at first, but it makes tremendous sense once you've given it some thought. We want to remove wax equally from both sides consistently, reducing them gradually so that the proper shape is approached. Once again, we're looking for more of a parabolic arc than an abrupt change from straight to curve. Check, check, measure, check. Repeat as necessary.

Before we go any further, it's time again for me to mention one of my pain-in-the-ass rules; make each step perfect, then move on. The blank is now right in two directions, now we have to correct the third. Our guidelines are still in place on the surface, but now we must move on to uncharted territory. There are two or more ways to proceed. First, the bad news. We're going to count strokes again. By carefully removing corners from the top and sides, equally, a bit at a time, the head is first octagonal, then hexadecagon (sixteen sides), and gradually more oval. At the same time, the sides are

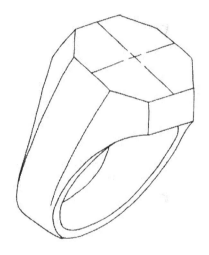

being curved. Watch each facet that is formed as you file and you can keep things even. Don't worry about filing curves at this point. They will show up as you go.

The important thing is to be aware at all times of how much material the file is removing, and from where, precisely, it is removing it. This is as much a matter of feel as it is a visual thing, and as such is something you will pick up as you become more experienced.

Go around the head gradually, maintaining a constant angle with the top. By watching the layout lines on the top, you will be able to bring the top to a perfect oval and, at the same time, curve the outer surface of the shank and, presto-change-o, 'tis now a ring.

You will notice, or more to the point, I will, that if you look very carefully at the ring from all angles, it's a bit crooked. One way or another, it will be possible to file away a small bit here and a small bit there and make it profoundly worse. As I said at the beginning, these things are so simple as to be impossible to get right.

Don't get discouraged, get advice. The longer you look at that puppy, the wronger it will appear. You have to look at it with a new eye. Either set it aside 'til later and reappraise, or ask someone else to take a good, honest look at it. Better you should fix it now than to discover later, once it's cast, that it's buggered up seven ways from Sunday.

Worst case scenario; it's fucked. You have to start over. Crush the one that's wrong and chuck it out. If it's wrong, it's wrong. In a lot of cases, you will actually save time, starting from scratch rather than piddling about trying to save a wax that was most likely screwed up several stages back. It's all experience, and as a consequence, it's never a waste. Learn a lesson, carry on.

By the way, if you have a nice x-y axis scratched into the top of the blank, there's nothing to stop you using an ellipse template to lay out an oval on top to use as you shape the top. I could have told you earlier, but why waste an opportunity to gain some experience. Always learn to do stuff the hard way before you start learning tricks. You'll be all the wiser. (That being said, the ellipse templates I've used are invariably asymmetrical, therefore useless. Best you should learn to do it the old-fashioned way.)

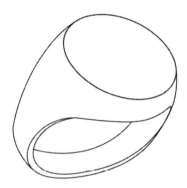

Gypsy Setting

The next most common type of ring to be carved is the gypsy mount for a single gemstone.

It's remarkable, really, how dull the initial stages of carving a wax can be, and how important attention to detail is in these early stages. What an ugly sentence.

Anyway, once the ring blank is trued up to the right length, and the size is correct, the only other immutable fact about the ring is the setting for the stone. Every other line and curve after this is up to your engineering skills and artistic vision.

I mention these two in this particular order because I believe that a well-engineered system of whatever sort is perforce a thing of beauty. Granted, a single-stone ring is a pretty simple system, but that makes attention to detail all the more important.

My primary concern, in this case, is to hold a stone on a finger. To do so simply and efficiently is the challenge. Once again, as with simple signets, the transition between the shank and the head should be smooth. No sharp changes from round to flat or vice-versa. My idea is that most happy curves are based on ellipses, parabolas, hyperbolas, and other asymptotic arcs.

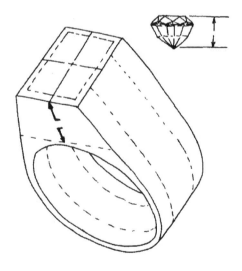

So, once again we lay out some lines on the ring blank to determine the height of the head and position of the stone. In most cases, the stone will have a finished depth such that the culet clears the victim's finger by a millimeter or so. This, of course, will vary according to a million variables, but is a good rule of thumb. Or finger, I suppose.

Okay, let's say we're setting an oval sapphire into the ring.

We've determined the height of the ring by the simple expedient of measuring the depth of the stone and adding a millimeter or more. A millimeter if it's a fairly big stone, and more if it's smaller. Right is right. It also depends if it's a lady's ring or gent's ring. There are bound to be all kinds of variables, so it's important to be clear on what we're shooting for.

Now we lay out some nice center lines and, using the dimensions of the stone as a guideline, we lay out a rectangle into which the stone will fit. 9x6mm stone into 9x6mm rectangle, you know how it works.

With a tapered bur, drill nice and straight through the center of the rectangle and gradually, oh, ever so gradually, lengthen and expand the hole towards the size of the stone.

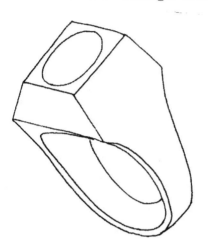

Before you go too far and cut away the sides of your rectangle, check the size and shape of the stone. You may think an oval's an oval, but you'd be wrongolini. Some are long and skinny, almost like a marquise, while some are almost cushion shaped. Best you should check. There's also the problem of asymmetrical stones. If necessary, mark one end of the stone with India ink so you know which way the stone fits best. They're all different.

As you approach the correct size, you'll be checking more often and the stone will be dropping lower into the setting. When you get to the point where the girdle starts to drop in, you'll want to give the stone a little push. I usually use the butt of my tweezers to hold the table of the stone level with the top of the ring and just wiggle it a bit. This causes the girdle to burnish a shiny spot wherever it makes contact with the hole. These little shiny spots are where you concentrate your cutting. Remove the shiny bit, refit the stone, remove, refit, and repeat until you just about can't stand it anymore. Or until the stone drops in. The stone will, at this point, be making contact all the way around, and the table will be

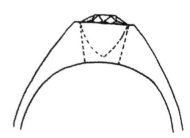

level. If it drops too much below the surface, you've fucked it up and must begin again. Tough darts, farmer.

If, however, you've been careful, then the hole will be exactly the shape of the stone and you're done this part of the operation. Let me emphasize, though, that at no point in the preceding are you cutting any sort of bearing for the stone. This will be done when the ring is cast up and ready for setting. The first thought for many is that there needs to be some sort of heavy shelf to hold the stone up. This is not the case. More on this in the setting section.

Now, all that remains is to get the ring to look like the picture. Either the picture in your head, or the one you submitted for approval to your custy. Just remember to leave the penultima pelle so you aren't in trouble once it's cast. There should be a tiny margin of the top of the original blank, complete with layout lines, sufficient to set the stone. You don't need much as this is a very secure method of securing a gem. Check out the section on collet setting in this very volume. It applies to oval stones as well as round ones.

These two examples just illustrate the importance of retaining the guidelines 'til the last possible moment and doing things in an orderly fashion so that symmetry is preserved. As well, the basic form is used in a great many rings.

Bunny Ring

A lot of rings that I find to be of pleasing proportions will fit into the basic outline of the ring blank that I have described above.

For example, here's a style that's referred to as a slave-ring (or bunny-ring, don't ask why) that I use as a jumping off point fairly often.

When I first tried to make them, I used the basic structure shown below, just whacked off the end of the wax tube, but unfortunately, what happened was that when a custie closed her hand, the point of the ring rose skyward in a most disconcerting fashion. The problem being that the center of gravity, so to speak, of the ring was way in front of the back of the shank. What had to happen to make this a wearable ring was that the basic shape, step two, as it were, needed to be balanced.

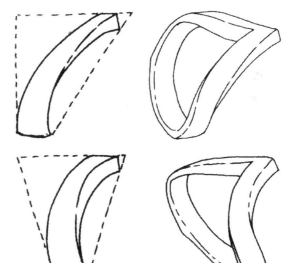

See, there's that structure, the little dotted lines are invisible, but they're always there, if you know how to look. This places the center of gravity, as it were, in the center of the ring.

What we're trying to achieve here is not some artistic triumph at the expense of practicality. Some poor bozo (bozette?) wants to wear this thing, and it's our job to make it wearable.

Four-Claw Ring

A huge preponderance of the work we do involves engagement rings, so it behooves us to lay out the process, or at least the all-important early stages of some sort of representative of the genre. The first couple steps seem to be sort of boring and anal, but it is my contention that attention paid early on will be more than repaid by making the later detail stages simpler.

First step, of course is to cut off a blank of the desired width, probably just a bit wider than the diameter of the stone. Make sure that it's perfectly parallel and flat. Ensure that all the right angles are indeed ninety degrees.

Open up the blank to the correct size because it's muy embarrassing to get too far into the process and discover that the size is wrong. Open it up evenly to keep it straight and centered on general principles, checking as you go.

Once it's the correct size and we've determined that the top is flat and square, it's time to establish some guidelines. Since we started with a squared-off blank, and were so dreadfully careful to keep things centered, we can use the existing sides to establish our guidelines. Using either dividers or your bench block and a scriber, establish some center lines, the bottom of the head, and the guidelines so important to the positioning of our little bumps. I put these little counter-balancing protuberances on virtually all the rings I make. They provide a bit of extra weight and some tactile feedback that keeps the top of the ring on top where it belongs. This is most especially important when the ring is fairly high, or when there is a stone set in it. As in a stone-set ring such as this. All will become clear as we go along.

The top of the setting will be the most important reference, so let's do that. The easiest method is to lay out a perfect square and establish some diagonal lines along which said claws will lie. For this sort of ring, the width of the ring will be just a hair wider than the diameter of the stone. This will result in a pleasing balance that displays the stone to excellent advantage, while still providing strength and protection.

Laying out the square can be a little tricky but, truth be told, it's okay if it's not perfectly square. The really important lines are the diagonals, which will provide an important reference for the shaping and positioning of the claws.

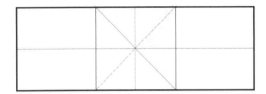

I usually lay out these diagonals with another all-purpose tool; the x-acto knife. By placing the point at one corner and carefully laying the blade down onto the top so that it crosses the center point and intersects the opposite corner, a lovely thin and accurate line is cut into the top. Make this line deep enough that it will be obvious through all the proceeding steps. Thin but deep, that's the ticket. Repeat for the other diagonal and we're good to go. I've tried using a custom-made, brass 45° triangle, which is very cute, but requires three hands to use.

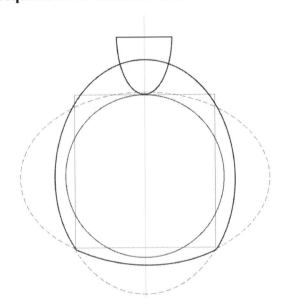

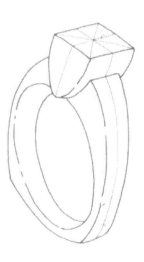

Once the top square is properly laid out, the silhouette of the ring can be established. Let's face it, the limited canvas of the standard finger ring is not conducive to a great deal of creativity, so we need to work with what we have, and for me, this is it. I like to deal with complementary and, occasionally, compound curves because it makes me happy. Since this is going to look like some kind of engagement ring, accentuating the stone would seem to be a good place to start. Once again, I'm using ellipses as my basic shapes. Getting this sort of cross-section is reasonably simple and, once done, needn't be messed with until the very end of the carving operation. Therefore we can dispense with the guidelines and move on to the process of shaping the side and top views. Before doing that, however, lay out the desired width of the shank on the side of the wax, as well as a center line for later reference.

The way the blank looks now, our options are wide open. This could be made into a channel-set ring by simply opening up the setting straight across the setting, but then I'd have to change the name of the whole section. Tapering the head would be a good idea, curving it inwards to match the curvature of the side view. Open up the setting with a suitably shaped bur. I like a parabola-shaped carbide, but a stout flame bur or ball bur will also do the trick.

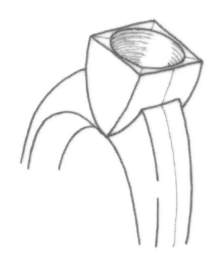

That being done, we can start forming claws. This is where our diagonal guidelines really come into their own. Start off with a fairly coarse wax file and heave away some material. Go straight across the profile, cutting out the 90° guidelines, being careful not to cut away too much of the diagonals. The number one thing to remember is to preserve those top guidelines: lose them and your life is over. Okay, maybe that's overstating it a tad, but they really do make it easier to maintain symmetry. Don't go too far down at this point as we can whittle it down as our vision of the claws' shapes become clear.

It's easiest to cut straight across between the claws in the initial stages of opening up, but the most important point to remember is that the claws must be finished up parallel to the guidelines so that the tops of the claws are more or less rectangular. Should you continue in the manner shown in the first picture, you would remove anything like a bearing for the stone. (Check out the "Bad Head" example in the Antique Head chapter of the construction section.) Better you should go at it this way. It makes it more difficult to finish up cleanly, but we're not in this bizz to take shortcuts. The transition between the parallel tops of the claws and the straight-across cuts are particularly treacherous.

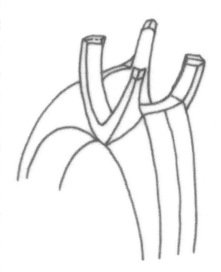

I've run out of things to say based on the pictures that I have right now, so I'll have to leave until I can draw some more. Actually, I found this cast mount that I put together on spec and it gives a pretty good look at the kind of thing we're trying to do here.

This mount has a tapered shank, but the basic technique becomes fairly obvious as long as you keep in mind that the same tools used in the final finishing of the wax should be more or less the same tools as you use when finishing the mount. In this case, a pillar file was used to establish the pointy shoulders along with a cheater file to separate the shoulders from the claws. Now, I grant you that the tops of the claws aren't the exact shape that I specified in the previous paragraph, but oh, I'll live to regret it. Had I spent the time before casting, it would be much easier to work with this mount. Perhaps that's why it never actually got made. Lost in the mists of time. Funny how much this one looks like the finished piece at the beginning of the section. Almost as though I'd planned it…

Nah.

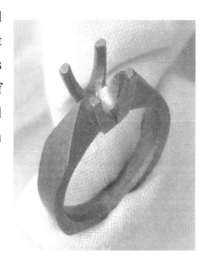

Customer #11

So, who are we doing all this for, anyway?

Face it. Very few people pay much attention to anything at all, never mind jewellery. At least that's the way it seems, considering some of the crap that I've seen coming down the pike.

Nine out of ten people barely even look at the stuff that's handed to them in a jewellery store. Part of their brain is dazzled by the sparkly little trinket blazing away under the klieg lights, while the part of their brain that is supposed to be thinking is being distracted from the issue at hand by the smarmy son-of-a-bitch whose job it is to simply get the cash and get that piece of crap out the door.

The future is the last thing on the mind of either of these numbskulls and, quite frankly, they deserve each other and the sad and empty existences to which they are condemned.

Problem is, though, this mutt may one day realize that he or she's been sold a piece of crap, and will want someone to fix it. This customer has already been burned once, and is now sensitive and wary.

This would be a great business opportunity for the conscientious and highly skilled goldsmith if he had a lick of sense, or more of the predatory instinct common in salespeople. We, the conscientious, can't understand how such a shabby example of the goldsmith's art made it past the extensive quality-control systems in place at jewellery factories.

Right?

The problem is, we end up killing ourselves trying to redeem some irretrievably botched piece when, "What this ring needs is a new ring."

We, however, are doing our level best to deliver a quality product to our people and are justifiably upset when that product isn't quite perfect. As stated above, nine out of ten people won't notice some tiny glitch that has crept into the finished article, but there is always customer number ten, who will most assuredly call you on it.

Oh, you may have excuses for the problem having slipped through, but the fact remains that it is wrong, wrong, wrongolini. And you got caught by a civilian.

What you have on your hands, now, is customer number eleven.

This particular individual is now looking very, very closely at every little detail, and is determined, by cracky, not to be fooled again. This is known as a challenge.

I don't know 'bout y'all, but I, personally, have a major problem not rising to a challenge. A failing, some might call it. My more self-aggrandizing side might be inclined to call it altruistic; the need to get the bad jewellery off the streets. I want jewelers to be trusted again.

Time was, the local goldsmith was sort of like the local notary, the man (for it was almost invariably a man) who sold you, perhaps, the only piece of jewellery you would ever own. A position of great trust. These days, however, he's just as likely to be the same schmoe who wanted to open a stereo store, but read somewhere that the margins were better in gold.

Okay, I've gone off a bit, so sue me. The fact remains that all I really want to do is make, or cause to be made, better quality jewellery. The problem is, I end up doing a great deal of so-called unscrewing work. Matter of fact, I've become quite famous for it.

This means, unfortunately, that I spend an inordinate amount of my time dealing with customer number eleven.

The most important rule to remember when dealing with such people is that, while we are more than willing to bend over backwards for our custies, we refuse to bend over frontwards, if you catch my drift.

They will *not* be satisfied, no matter how hard we try, so it behooves us not to take too much of a beating in the attempt. They are the yappy ones, however, and for good or ill, can make your reputation. As in so many other aspects of life, it's a balancing act.

Upon occasion, it may become necessary to break up with a custy. This is not an option to be considered lightly as it could, in fact, destroy you. Fact is, *not* blowing off a particularly troublesome individual can make for an untenable situation as well, so there you go. Be very discerning, but allow yourself the privilege of, say, once a year telling someone to take a walk. It'll tear you apart, or at least it should, but it's like having a heavy burden lifted from your shoulders and being kicked in the stomach at the same instant. A while later you realize that your belly doesn't hurt anymore, but you still feel the relief.

Appendices

Glossary

Alloy: Metal, or combination of metals added to gold to improve its working properties. See karat.

Beader: Basically a steel rod, tapered at the end, with a cup-shaped depression in the end. Used for forming beads. Hence the name.

Beige gold: A bastard alloy created by manufacturers seeking a workable 18k white. Due to its distinctly ghastly color, it must be rhodium-plated in order to be acceptable to the consumer. This creates an entirely new category of unscrewing work when customers decide that getting their rings replated at regular intervals is unacceptable. Big surprise. See: *Unscrewing Work*

Bezel: A setting made up of a ribbon of material to hold a stone in and a rim of metal to hold a stone up. This is as opposed to a collet, which is something else, entirely. See: *Collet.*

Borax: This is soldering flux, an anti-oxidant that promotes the flow of solder by, in effect, removing fireskin within the joint before it can cause problems. Often confused with Boric Acid. Borax is a flux, boric acid most emphatically is not.

Boric Acid: Dissolved in isopropyl alcohol, this substance, when applied to gold and heated, fuses to form a glassy barrier to prevent the formation of fireskin. It also promotes the flow of solder within a joint, while preventing its spread beyond the confines of the joint. It does this by magic.

Channel Setting: An odd sort of setting wherein the stone is held between two bars. Another variation is a modified flush setting, where the channel is cut into a flat surface and the metal convinced to hold the stone by mooshing it over like flush setting. The name channel-set comes from a Greek term meaning "comes loose all the time".

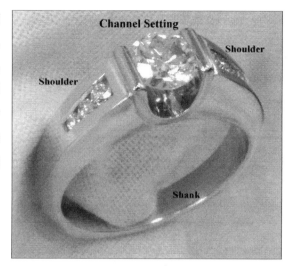

Claw: This is the support for the stone, the setting proper. Into this is cut the bearing before forcing the tips over the stone. I mention this because there is a lot of confusion between tips and claws. When doing repairs, claws cost way more than tips.

Collet: A tube-style setting, usually for a diamond, as differentiated from a bezel. The two terms are often used interchangeably, but not by me. See: *Bezel*

Culet: An extra facet often found on older cut stones that has no purpose that I can fathom. It's also the pointy bit of a modern cut diamond.

Customer #11: A customer who thinks that you cannot be trusted. The stories I could tell...

Dja: An interrogatory meaning would you or do you. See: *ngna*

File Peg: The tapered wedge of wood mounted to the front of the bench and used for filing things against. Hence the name.

Graver: The tool used in engraving and diamond-setting, a length of high-quality steel installed in a handle, as opposed to the

Engraver: The tool doing the engraving or diamond-setting. You.

Guideline: An Italian word meaning "guideline," but pronounced gwee-de-lee-nee.

Head: The topmost portion of the ring. This can be the top of a signet ring, the four claw setting holding a solitaire diamond, or a cluster head holding a bunch of little pain-in-the-ass single cuts. Also denotes a commercial, mass-produced setting to be attached to an existing piece.

Hitlering: The process of trimming away alternate sides of an object, in search of symmetry, until it is ruined. Can be avoided by making one part perfect, then making the other match. Then stopping.

Karat: The ratio of gold to alloy, always expressed as a factor of twenty-four. For example, fourteen karat (14kt. or 14k) is always fourteen parts gold and ten parts alloy, regardless of what the alloy may be.

Latagne: The proper shape for a bead in pavé setting. It should look as if a little bead has magically appeared on top of the junction between the stone and the setting. We're trying to give people a bit of magic here, hide the process.

Mechanic: It's not a term of derision, but rather a person adept at building jewellery, or repairing it for that matter, using well-fitted pieces of gold.

MicroMesh: An important alternative to sandpaper, this is a cloth-backed abrasive which is available in grits as fine as 12,000. Excellent for platinum.

Mushroom Effect: The tendency of metal to splay out under hammer blows or other compressive methods. It's a problem when forging, but is the basis of riveting and flush-setting.

Mutts: Bad jewelers. Whether they are goldsmiths or salespeople, through ignorance, greed or laziness, they are everything that is wrong with the industry. See: *SBJOS*

Ngna: A Swahili word meaning "I intend to," as in, "ngna go to the store, dja want anything?" See: *dja.*

Panic Bead: When, in the course of bead-setting a stone, you inadvertently knock off a bead and, more through good luck than good management, you haven't smashed the stone to smithereens, then you may occasionally pull a second, inferior bead from an adjacent area. It ain't pretty, but sometimes it just has to be done.

Planishing: Finishing a hammered surface by going over it with a polished-face hammer. Sort of like burnishing, but with a hammer.

Reflow: A magical method of correcting errant solder flow by thorough cleaning, covering in boric acid, and reheating to soldering temperature.

Relieve: To remove a bit of metal so as to control where it bends. Usually mentioned in regards to setting.

Ring blank: Contradictory term meaning rough wax, only vaguely ring-shaped, or length of gold bar soon to be made into a ring.

Roll-filing: A cheap and quick method of imitating a lathe. The work, a wire or small bar, is chucked into a pin vise. By twirling the piece back toward yourself while filing forward, inconsistencies are eliminated and a perfect cylinder may be created.

Saw Peg: A chunk of quarter-inch plywood, usually about 10x30cm, clamped to the top of the bench. It provides a flat, stable surface for saw-work, piercing and the like. As differentiated from the File Peg.

Sawyering: Convincing someone to do something that you don't particularly want to do by fooling them. Tom Sawyer did it with the whole fence-painting deal by making them think it was fun.

SBJOS: A small cadre of like-minded and competent goldsmiths who are intent on ridding the world of mutts. Acronym for Shoot Bad Jewellers On Sight. Current President: Me, 'Cause I have a gun. See: *Mutts.*

Seven ways from Sunday: How many ways you need to check stuff to ensure to that it's straight, level, round, flat, and like that. The other three ways are Grumpy, Dopey, and Doc.

Shank: That part of the ring below the shoulders. The bit that holds it onto your finger.

Shit Sandwich Rule: "Should you be forced to eat a shit sandwich, eat the bread last." That is, do the hardest part of the job first and the rest will be your reward.

Shoulder: Lookit the picture... There should be a picture here.

Single-cuts: Whereas most diamonds these days are cut with 56 facets, a whole lot of candy-ass jewellery is set with these things. They are cut with eight facets on the bottom, and eight on the top (excluding the table). They are referred to as miscellaneous diamonds, and are worth approximately nothing. By the way, the culet of the stone is often counted as a facet, even though it doesn't exist. Go figure.

Smithereens: I think it's a place in Ireland, but it's hard to be sure, what with the way my brain works.

Spinbarkite: "The spit that sticks 'twixt cup and lip." This is a word that I picked up from my former dentist, and I like it. In effect, it is that long suspension bridge of spit that hangs tenaciously between your mouth and the spit-sink. Perhaps it doesn't exactly belong in a goldsmithing book, but if not here, then where? (Actually, it comes into play in the use of Setter's Friend.)

Thick & Thin: I only add these to point out the difference between them, and wide and narrow. It's a tough little detail, but it comes up often enough that it bears mention. Problem is, there's no easy way to define them. Thickness, for example, is the dimension of a ring measured as the difference between the inside radius and the outside radius, whereas width is, well the width of the ring.

Tip: The end of the claw that holds the stone down. This is the bit that wears down and needs replacing most often.

Tripoli: Coarse polishing compound for removing sandpaper marks and fine scratches from a piece prior to rouging, the final finish. I only mention this because it has come to my attention that, early in the game, some of us may mishear this as "Triple-E", some kind of fancy trade name. It's not.

Unscrewing Work: Repairing or rebuilding badly made jewellery. See: *Mutts*.

Wing ring: For some reason, this is the name for a ring with raised shoulders. A very adaptable style, it is virtually impossible to ignore. See: *Ubiquitous*.

Woofer: A coarse file, usually 0 or 00 cut, which removes a lot of material in a hurry with a consequent woofing noise. Hence the name.

Tool List

As Mentioned in the intro to all this, my intent is to give the aspiring goldsmith a guide to starting up in the business based on my experience. Having presented a business plan to the Canadian Imperial Bank of Mom, I was very aware of my budget and had to consider each purchase carefully. That being said, I tried whenever possible to obtain the best quality tools available. It's been nearly thirty years and all the original major equipment is still in place, so I guess I did okay. The occasional flames that shoot out of the polishing machine motor on startup are simply crankiness and not to be considered signs of infirmity.

Bench Tools

Looking at my bench, here's a list of the tools I use regularly, in order of appearance. Over the years I have accumulated a lot of more specialized items, but this is a selection of tools that would allow you to sit down and make some jewellery without too much delay.

Gravers

Flat: #6, #10, and #14. Plus a jeezly big chisel-like jobby used occasionally.

Round: Ditto

Offset: Left- and right-hand, usually made from #10 flats.

Square: Either made from a file or commercial stock, this doesn't have a belly.

Triangular: Ditto.

Knife: I'm not sure, but I think it's a #10. Hard to keep sharp, but handy.

Onglette: Not one I use a lot, but some swear by them.

Parallel: Made from old pillar needle files, these can be indispensable.

Saw frame

The standard 2 ½ inch deep model is all you really need.

2/0 and 8/0 blades. Antilope are best.

Pliers and nippers

Chain nose: Big and little.

Round nose: Ditto.

Ring bending: Two pairs come in awful handy, but one pair minimum.

Nippers: Heavy-duty end- or diagonal-cutters and brutally expensive flush-cut ones.

Tweezers

General duty: Dumont A pattern are best for small stones and solder placement.*

Solder tweezers: Cross-locking in a couple different sizes.

Gemstone: Good quality with delicate serrated jaws for larger stones.

*If you use them for actual soldering, I'll kill you.

Mandrels

Ring mandrel: Certainly, and perhaps a slotted one if you do repairs on crap.

Bezel mandrels: I only use round ones, as a rule.

Rule

A six-inch metric rule with the square end a perfect right-angle.

Pushers

Flat: Square, about 3mm, and a small rectangular about 1x2mm.

Round: Several, of various sizes and textures. Start with big, 5mm, and small, 1x3mm.

Drills

Daily use: .75, 1.0, and 1.5mm. Keep them handy.

Calibrated: A full set from #80-#30, or .33mm to 3.0mm.

Scraper

I got mine from the Jack White stash. You'll have to make one.

Burnishers

A big one made from a big half-round file and a small one from a needle file.

Needle Files

Triangular: Usually 6-cut, one with three safe corners and one pristine.

Square: 2-, 4-, and 6-cut.

Barrette: Ditto.

Half-round: Ditto.

Pillar: 4-, and 6-cut

Crossing: Usually just a 4-cut, but a 6 would be nice.

Oval: Ditto

Round: Ditto

Cheater files: 4-, and 6-cut.

Ring files

Half-round: 00- (woofer), 2-, and 6-cut. The 6-cut is usually a wider half-round.

Barrette: 00- and 2-cut.

Pillar: 2-, or 4-cut.

Round: 4-cut.

Hammers

Ball-peen: A little two-ouncer does the job, but a bigger one is nice for whanging away.

Riveting hammer: A tiny watchmaker's hammer. Not necessary, but nice.

Sandpaper sticks

Usually one each of 320 and 600 grit, but a 1200 is lovely for fine finishing.

Sharpening Stones

India stone: For general sharpening the white is nice.

Arkansas stone: I have a black one, which is lovely. Indispensable for bright-cut work.

Diamond plates: A coarse one for heavy grinding and refinishing the India stones.

Pocket stone: For finishing tweezers.

Torch

The Hoke will work, but I prefer the Meco Midget. More expensive, but rock-solid.

Burrs, or Burs, if you prefer

Get 'em all. All.

If I was really stuck, I'd say tapered a couple of tapered reamers and a few ball burs.

Miscellaneous essentials

X-acto: The #11 is my all-purpose go-to winner.

Pin vises: The double-ended one is my favourite.

Dividers: The Starrett brand is lovely, but perhaps a bit delicate.

Carbide scriber: Doesn't have to be carbide, but it's nice.

Wax files: A large, double-ended one and a set of needle files.

Bench blocks: 3x3 inch flat steel, and a little hexagonal one with holes in it.

Bending block: A cube with shaping grooves on all sides.

The Bench

Something to keep it all in.

And a fluorescent lamp so you can see.

And a nice chair upon which to sit upon. Which.

Shop Tools

This is where the big bucks get spent. Despite this, always buy the best quality you can get your hands on. It'll pay off in the long run.

Tanks: I use a small, five pound propane and a Q oxygen.

Casting stuff: Ingot mold and a couple of crucibles.

Pickle pot: A small slow-cooker will work, but an official pot is best.

Rolling mill: As long as it's got flat and square, it's cool.

Ring bender: For heavy-duty bar-bending duty.

Polishing unit: Double-spindle with brushes and buffs and all like that.

Ultrasonic cleaner: Half- or one-gallon.

Steamer: While not an absolute essential, you're going to want one badly.

Well, kids. I'm sick of editing this for now, so we'll see you in the next iteration. And I'm always iterating away for myself. Stay tuned.

KP171111

Made in the USA
Lexington, KY
07 June 2019